Bloom's Modern Critical Views

Bloom's Modern Critical Views

J.D. SALINGER
New Edition

Edited and with an introduction by
Harold Bloom
Sterling Professor of the Humanities
Yale University

BLOOM'S
LITERARY CRITICISM
An imprint of Infobase Publishing

Bloom's Modern Critical Views: J.D. Salinger, New Edition

Copyright © 2008 by Infobase Publishing

Introduction © 2008 by Harold Bloom

Bloom's Literary Criticism
An imprint of Infobase Publishing
132 West 31st Street
New York, NY 10001

Library of Congress Cataloging-in-Publication Data
J.D. Salinger / [edited with an introduction by] Harold Bloom. — New ed.
    p. cm.   (Bloom's modern critical views)
  Includes bibliographical references and index.
  ISBN 978-0-7910-9813-4
  1. Salinger, J. D. (Jerome David), 1919—Criticism and interpretation. I. Bloom, Harold. II. Title. III. Series.

    PS3537.A426Z67 2008
    813'.54—dc22

                                        2007044662

Contributing Editor: Janyce Marson
Cover designed by Jooyoung An
Cover photo AP Images
Printed in the United States of America
Bang EJB 10 9 8 7 6 5 4 3 2 1

Contents

Contents

Editor's Note

My Introduction, after more than twenty years, seems to me still useful and accurate. Salinger has not lost too much of his younger audience, but all of his work has begun to fade into the (sometimes) antique charm of Period Pieces. The critics gathered together here do not agree with me. Time alone settles our opinions and judgments. Either they are converted into knowledge or they become Period Pieces themselves, and charmless.

James Bryan and David Galloway both examine the psychology and ethics of love in Salinger, while Alan Nadel invokes the rhetoric of the Cold War as context.

What Freud called "Family Romances" is taken as background both by David Seed and Ruth Prigozy, after which Anthony Kaufman studies the limits of love in "Teddy."

Anna Freud's formidable accounts of defense and development are applied to young Caulfield by Robert Coles, while Pamela Hunt Steinle return us to the relation between Salinger and Cold War American life.

An all-but-encyclopedic survey of *Catcher* by Eberhard Alsen is followed by Carl Freedman's personal contextualization

Yasuhiro Takeuchi elaborates Zen archery in regard to Holden, while Myles Weber concludes this volume with the somewhat desperate efforts by Salinger admirers to augment his slim body of published work.

HAROLD BLOOM

Introduction

The Salinger legend, both powerful and colorless, almost more powerful for the lack of color, seems less important now, after years of silence on the writer's part. *The Catcher in the Rye* (1951); *Nine Stories* (1953); *Franny and Zooey* (1961); *Raise High the Roof Beam, Carpenters* and *Seymour: An Introduction* (1963)—these constitute Salinger's saga. Perhaps Salinger outlived his gift; perhaps something more eventually will be published. There is a curious completeness in his four short books, taken together. The first two are minor masterpieces or minor classics and remind us that "minor" can be a descriptive as well as an evaluative word in literary criticism.

Despite his personal relationship with Hemingway, Salinger derives from Scott Fitzgerald. Holden Caulfield and Seymour Glass are clearly in the visionary mode of Jay Gatsby, and Holden's first-person narrative owes more to Nick Carraway than to Huck Finn. A comparison to Fitzgerald is dangerous for Salinger. *The Catcher in the Rye* is hardly of *The Great Gatsby*'s aesthetic dignity, nor will "A Perfect Day for Bananafish" quite survive side-by-side reading with "Babylon Revisited." This is not to deprecate Salinger but to indicate his limits; his narrative art is shadowed by Fitzgerald's.

A lack of originality is not likely to dim Salinger's permanent appeal to perpetually fresh generations of young readers. Rereading Salinger is, however, partly spoiled by his felt lack of exuberance in characterization or spontaneity through narrative invention. What once seemed original about Salinger, his Zen spirituality, now is revealed as a mere fashion of middlebrow culture in the United States of the fifties and early sixties. Seymour Glass as Zen saint is hardly a persuasive fictive representation in the United States of the twenty-first century.

The Glass family saga is a collection of period pieces, like the *Rabbit* novels of John Updike, or Walker Percy's neo-Catholic, polemical fictions that have followed *The Moviegoer*. *The Catcher in the Rye* seems much more than that, as are a few of the *Nine Stories*. Period pieces, when well wrought, eventually can acquire an antique charm, but first they go through an ambiguous phase where they are merely quaint. Salinger's skills as a writer are admirable, perhaps too overtly admirable, in the manner of *The New Yorker*, with its period styles. Scott Fitzgerald touched his own kind of American Sublime by bringing together a Conradian moral intensity with a legitimate prose version of a Keatsian lyricism. We derive an easier pleasure through reading Salinger, who cannot persuade us that he can substitute the experience of reading him for more difficult and demanding literary pleasures.

Rereading Salinger's thirteen principal stories, after almost a half-century, is a mixed experience, at least for me. All of them have their period piece aspect, portraits of a lost New York City, or of New Yorkers elsewhere, in the post–World War II America that vanished forever in the "cultural revolution" (to call it that) of the late 1960s. Holden Caulfield and the Glass siblings charm me now—though sometimes they make me wince—because they are so archaic. Their humane spirituality, free of dogma and of spite, has to be refreshing as we drift toward the millennium.

Of the stories, "Raise High the Roof Beam, Carpenters" now reads best, not for its "religious pluralism" (as one critic characterized it) but simply for high good humor. Its representation of being stuck in a Manhattan traffic jam has an exuberance that Salinger rarely manifests either in his persons or his plots. Zaniness rather than Zen-Taoist pluralism saves the story from Salinger's inverted sentimentalities and from Glass sibling affections, too frequently emotions in excess of their objects. Salinger's ear for dialogue, inherited from Hemingway and Fitzgerald, is acutely manifested throughout a bizarre narrative in which little happens, which is to be preferred to Seymour's suicide in "A Perfect Day for Bananafish," or Franny's fainting fit in the story that bears her name.

Salinger's stylistic skills are beyond question; his stories perform precisely as he intends. And they hold up as storytelling, even if their social attitudes and spiritual stances frequently now seem archaic or quaint. Their problem is that the Glass siblings are not exactly memorable as individuals. Even poor Seymour is more a type than a vivid consciousness in himself.

"Seymour: An Introduction" I find impossible to reread, partly because his brother Buddy, the narrator, never knows when to stop, and again who can tolerate this kind of smug spirituality?

Seymour once said that all we do our whole lives is go from one little piece of Holy Ground to the next. Is he *never* wrong? A reader might well retort: when is Seymour right? The accuracy of Seymour's mystic insight is not the issue. Stories must have narrative values, or they cease to be stories, and "Seymour: An Introduction" fails to be a story. That may be why Salinger's fiction stopped. Contemplation can be a very valuable mode of being and existence, but it has no stories to tell.

The pleasures of *The Catcher in the Rye* adequately are revealed by its famous first paragraph:

If you really want to hear about it, the first thing you'll probably want to know is where I was born, and what my lousy childhood was like, and how my parents were occupied and all before they had me, and all that David Copperfield kind of crap, but I don't feel like going into it, if you want to know the truth. In the first place, that stuff bores me, and in the second place, my parents would have about two hemorrhages apiece if I told anything pretty personal about them. They're quite touchy about anything like that, especially my father. They're *nice* and all—I'm not saying that—but they're also touchy as hell. Besides, I'm not going to tell you my whole goddam autobiography or anything. I'll just tell you about this madman stuff that happened to me around last Christmas just before I got pretty run-down and had to come out here and take it easy. I mean that's all I told D.B. about, and he's my *brother* and all. He's in Hollywood. That isn't too far from this crumby place, and he comes over and visits me practically every week end. He's going to drive me home when I go home next month maybe. He just got a Jaguar. One of those little English jobs that can do around two hundred miles an hour. It cost him damn near four thousand bucks. He's got a lot of dough, now. He didn't *use* to. He used to be just a regular writer, when he was home. He wrote this terrific book of short stories, *The Secret Goldfish*, in case you never heard of him. The best one in it was "The Secret Goldfish." It was about this little kid that wouldn't let anybody look at his goldfish because he'd bought it with his own money. It killed me. Now he's out in Hollywood, D.B., being a prostitute. If there's one thing I hate, it's the movies. Don't even mention them to me.

The ear, inner and outer, is certainly evident, and the tone is alive and consistent. What we miss, as we age into rereaders, is surprise, even when Holden signs off with some grace:

> D.B. asked me what I thought about all this stuff I just finished telling you about. I didn't know what the hell to say. If you want to know the truth, I don't *know* what I think about it. I'm sorry I told so many people about it. About all I know is, I sort of *miss* everybody I told about. Even old Stradlater and Ackley, for instance. I think I even miss that goddam Maurice. It's funny. Don't ever tell anybody anything. If you do, you start missing everybody.

One thinks of Huck Finn's evenhanded mode of narration, with its constant undersong of fellow-feeling and compassion, and of Nick Carraway's fair-mindedness, and even of Jake Barnes's rueful affection for almost anyone whose story he has told. Holden Caulfield has added a certain zany zest, but little else. Yet that is to grant Salinger's best book rather less than it merits, since no book can touch the universal, even for a time, without a gift of its own for the receptive reader.

Holden is derivative, but still highly likeable, and for all his vulnerability he remains an attractive survivor who has returned from illness as his narrative ends. Survival is his entire enterprise, even as freedom was Huck Finn's enterprise. This regression from freedom to survival is what gives Salinger's one novel its curious pathos, which is also its principal aesthetic virtue. Endlessly honest with the reader, Holden wistfully keeps revealing that his outcast condition is only partly a voluntary one. He is potentially self-destructive, very nearly masochistic in his psychosexuality, and religiously obsessed, to the extent that he admires poor Legion, the madman and tomb-haunter, trapped by many demons. The most unpleasant sentence in the novel is surely Holden's declaration: "If you want to know the truth, the guy I like best in the Bible, next to Jesus, was that lunatic and all, that lived in the tombs."

Any aesthetic judgment of *The Catcher in the Rye* turns finally upon its most famous passage, which is what might be called its title-passage:

> I'm not too sure old Phoebe knew what the hell I was talking about.
> I mean she's only a little child and all. But she was listening, at least. If somebody at least listens, it's not too bad.
> "Daddy's going to kill you. He's going to *kill* you," she said.

I wasn't listening, though. I was thinking about something else—something crazy. "You know what I'd like to be?" I said. "You know what I'd like to be? I mean if I had my goddam choice?"

"What? Stop *swearing*."

"You know that song 'If a body catch a body comin' through the rye'? I'd like—" "It's 'If a body *meet* a body coming through the rye'!" old Phoebe said. "It's a poem. By Robert *Burns*."

"I *know* it's a poem by Robert Burns."

She was right, though. It *is* "If a body meet a body coming through the rye." I didn't know it then, though.

"I thought it was 'If a body catch a body,'" I said. "Anyway, I keep picturing all these little kids playing some game in this big field of rye and all. Thousands of little kids, and nobody's around—nobody big, I mean—except me. And I'm standing on the edge of some crazy cliff. What I have to do, I have to catch everybody if they start to go over the cliff—I mean if they're running and they don't look where they're going I have to come out from somewhere and *catch* them. That's all I'd do all day. I'd just be the catcher in the rye and all. I know it's crazy, but that's the only thing I'd really like to be. I know it's crazy."

Old Phoebe didn't say anything for a long time. Then, when she said something, all she said was, "Daddy's going to kill you."

From "meet" to "catch" is Holden's revision, and Salinger's vital epiphany, as it were. Huck Finn's story, on this basis, might have been called *The Meeter in the Rye*. To meet is to be free; to catch is to aid survival, and somehow to survive.

JAMES BRYAN

The Psychological Structure of
The Catcher in the Rye

Standing by the "crazy cannon" on Thomsen Hill one sunless afternoon, listening to the cheers from a football game below, "the two teams bashing each other all over the place," Holden Caulfield tries to "feel some kind of a good-by" to the prep school he has just flunked out of:

> I was lucky. All of a sudden I thought of something that helped make me know I was getting the hell out. I suddenly remembered this time, in around October, that I and Robert Tichener and Paul Campbell were chucking a football around, in front of the academic building. They were nice guys, especially Tichener. It was just before dinner and it was getting pretty dark out, but we kept chucking the ball around anyway. It kept getting darker and darker, and we could hardly *see* the ball any more, but we didn't want to stop doing what we were doing. Finally we had to. This teacher that taught biology, Mr. Zambesi, stuck his head out of this window in the academic building and told us to go back to the dorm and get ready for dinner. If I get a chance to remember that kind of stuff, I can get a good-by when I need one.[1]

From *PMLA* 89, no. 5 (October 1974): pp. 1065–74. © 1974 by The Modern Language Association of America.

A careful look at this first scene in the novel provides clues for interpretation, by no means crucial in themselves, but illustrative of a pattern of scene construction and suggestive imagery which does yield meaning. Appropriate is this adolescent's sense of his "darkling plain" where, if an extravagant metaphor be allowed, "ignorant football teams clash by afternoon." In a pattern repeated throughout the novel, he thinks back to a time when he and two "nice guys" passed a football around, shared rather than fought over it, though even then the idyllic state seemed doomed. Holden is poised between two worlds, one he cannot return to and the other he fears to enter, while the image of a football conflict is probably an ironic commentary on Holden's adolescence, football's being a civilized ritualization of human aggression.

What is forcing Holden's crisis? Everything in the idyllic scene points to the encroachment of time—the season, the time of day, even such verbal echoes from his friends' names as "ticking," "bell," and "pall." Accrual of this sort of evidence will justify what may seem overinterpretation here, especially of the significance of a biology teacher's ending the boys' innocent pleasures—their idyll already sentenced by time, darkness. More than anything else Holden fears the biological imperatives of adulthood—sex, senescence, and death—which are delicately foreshadowed in the innocent October scene by the unwelcome call to dinner.

Much of the *Catcher* criticism has testified to Holden's acute moral and esthetic perceptions—his eye for beauty as well as "phoniness"—but the significance of his immaturity in intensifying these perceptions has not been sufficiently stressed nor explained. Precisely because this sixteen-year-old acts "like I'm about thirteen" and even "like I was only about twelve," he is hypersensitive to the exploitations and insensitivity of the postpubescent world and to the fragile innocence of children. A central rhythm of the narrative has Holden confronting adult callousness and retreating reflexively into thoughts and fantasies about children, childlike Jane Gallaghers, and especially his ten-year-old sister, Phoebe. These juxtapositions render both worlds more intensely and at the same time qualify Holden's judgments by showing that they are emotionally—or, as we shall see, neurotically—induced.

While a fair number of critics have referred to Holden's "neurosis," none has accepted Salinger's invitation—proffered in the form of several key references to psychoanalysis—to participate in a full-fledged psychoanalytical reading. The narrative, after all, was written in a mental hospital with Holden under the care of a "psychoanalyst guy." One problem is that Holden tells us very little about "what my lousy childhood was like" or the event that may have brought on the trauma behind all of his problems: the death of a younger brother when Holden was thirteen. We know little more than that the family has been generally disrupted since and that Holden has not come to grips with life as he should have. Allie's death takes place outside the province of the narrative, but a valuable psychological study might still be made of the progression of Holden's breakdown—how he provokes fights in which he will be beaten, makes sexual advances he cannot carry through, and unconsciously alienates himself from many of the people he encounters. As a step toward psychological understanding, I shall consider certain manifestations of Holden's disturbances. An examination of the structure, scene construction, and suggestive imagery reveals a pattern of aggression and regression, largely sexual, which is suggested in the Pencey Prep section, acted out in the central part of the novel, and brought to a curious climax in the Phoebe chapters.

I

One implication of the novel's main motif, that which polarizes childlike and adult responses, concerns the dilemma of impossible alternatives. Here characters suggest human conditions that Holden either cannot or must not make his own. In the novel's first paragraph Holden tells us that his brother D. B. has "prostituted" his writing talents by going to Hollywood—a failure implicitly contrasted throughout with the purity of Allie, the brother who died before the temptations of adulthood. Holden's first encounter is with Spencer, the old teacher who fills his mind with thoughts of age and death, while his last is with Phoebe, his emblem of unattainable childhood beauty. Stradlater and Ackley are antithetically placed to represent what Holden fears he may become if he is either sexually appropriative or repressed. Because the novel is built around these impossible alternatives, because Holden's world provides no one he can truly emulate, the many critics who read *Catcher* as a sweeping indictment of society have virtually drowned out those who attack Holden's immaturity. One feels the justice of this, yet the novel's resolution, like all of Salinger's mature fiction, transcends sociological indictment in affirming individual responsibility. When Holden answers for his own life as he verges toward some rather dreadful appropriation of his own, he begins to come to terms at once with himself and society.

At the outset of traditional quest narratives, the hero often receives sage advice from a wise old man or crone. The best old Spencer can do is to wish Holden a depressing "good luck," just as another agent of education, a woman "around a hundred years old," will do in the penultimate chapter. Spencer's plaintive "I'm trying to *help* you, if I can" and the old woman's irrelevant chatter near the end bracket the bulk of the narrative in which Holden seeks answers from without. And in both scenes the human resources that do see him through are dramatized in his compassion for the two old people.

Though the Spencer chapter serves notice that Holden has flunked the administrative requirements of education, we learn immediately that he draws sustenance from art. He returns to his room to reread in Isak Dinesen's *Out of Africa* that chronicle of sensitivity surrounded by primitive id forces. At this point he is interrupted by eighteen-year-old Robert Ackley, a grotesque possibility of what Holden may become if his manhood is similarly thwarted. Unleavened sensitivity will not be enough as we see Holden vacillating through five chapters between Ackley and Ward Stradlater, the equally unacceptable model of male aggressiveness. Stradlater's vitality is dramatized in his "Year Book" handsomeness, "damn good build," and superior strength, while Ackley's impotence is reflected in acned, unsightly looks, general enervation, and repulsive habits. Stradlater is slovenly too—Holden calls him a "secret slob"—but he elicits some admiration where Ackley is only pathetic.

Stradlater's date for the evening is Jane Gallagher, a girl with whom Holden has had a summer romance. That relationship was characterized by Jane's habit of keeping her kings in the back row when they played checkers—later on, Holden says specifically that their lovemaking never went beyond the handholding stage. In Holden's request that Stradlater ask Jane if she still keeps her kings in the back row, one critic sees Holden signaling warnings about her "sexy" date.[2] Holden tells us in another chapter that Jane was the kind of girl you never wanted to "kid too much." "I think I really like it best," he goes on to say,

> when you can kid the pants off a girl when the opportunity arises, but it's a funny thing. The girls I like best are the ones I never feel much like kidding. Sometimes I think they'd *like* it if you kidded them—in fact, *I know* they would—but it's hard to get started, once you've known them a pretty long time and never kidded them. (p. 101)

On an action level, of course, Jane did keep her checker kings in the back row and Holden is indeed talking about kidding. But such double entendres as "kidding the pants off a girl" reveal not only Holden's sexual preoccupations but the elaborate coding his mind has set up against recognizing such preoccupations for what they are. In the early parts of the novel, Salinger may be training the reader to see through Holden's words in these rather apparent ways, thus to prepare for the most subtle and crucial coding of all in the Phoebe section.

Stradlater's strength and sexuality cause Holden to discountenance his own. This night, for example, Stradlater uses Holden's "Vitalis" hair tonic and borrows his "hound's-tooth" jacket, leaving Holden "so nervous I nearly went crazy" as he thinks of this "sexy bastard" with Jane. Conversely, Holden this same night endures Ackley's droning narrative of his sexual exploits with a final comment, "He was a virgin if I ever saw one. I doubt if he ever even gave anybody a feel." Not until Holden faces the Ackley and Stradlater in himself will he be able to do the purgative writing that is of course the form of the novel itself. They are almost like doppelgangers; one will interrupt him when he reads to escape while the other rejects the composition he ghostwrites because it is escapist. Even when he attacks the cocksure Stradlater after the latter's date with Jane, Holden's brief blood initiation is, as we shall see, a needful battle against himself. Right after the fight, getting no consolation from that other polar figure, Ackley, Holden leaves Pencey Prep.

The five Stradlater and Ackley chapters make for closely woven, dramatized exposition of Holden's psychological quandary which prepares for the loose, episodic middle section of the novel where Holden goes questing after experience and wisdom. Rejecting the alternatives implicit in Stradlater and Ackley, Holden wants his life to be vital without appropriation, innocent without retrogression. In the Phoebe section where the novel tightens up again, we shall see that Holden nearly becomes *both* appropriative and retrogressive and that it is precisely Holden's awareness of this that points the way to maturity.

Immediately after arriving in New York and checking into a hotel room, Holden is treated to a fresh installment of the Ackley–Stradlater antithesis. Through one window across an airshaft he sees a transvestite dress himself and mince before a mirror, while in the window above a couple squirt water "out of their mouths at each other." Holden confesses at this point that "In my *mind*, I'm probably the biggest sex maniac you ever saw" and that he might enjoy such "crumby stuff" as squirting water in a girl's face. Characteristically, he decides to call his chaste Jane, thinks better of it, and phones Faith Cavendish, a stripper recommended to Holden as one who "didn't mind doing it once in a while." Her ritual objections to the late-hour call dispensed with, she suggests a meeting the next day. Holden declines, however, and "damn near" gives his "kid sister Phoebe a buzz," justifying the switch by describing Phoebe's charms at length. Later in a bar he is flanked on his left by "this funny-looking guy" nervously reciting to his date "every single goddam play" of a football game he had seen, and on the other side by a suave young man giving a beautiful girl "a feel under the table," over her embarrassed objections, "at the same time telling her all about some guy in his dorm that had . . . nearly committed suicide." All around him Holden sees distorted reflections of his own spasmodic aggression and withdrawal. And in the last instance cited we get an early hint of one of the most dangerous manifestations of his neurosis: his association of sex with death.

When he retreats in a panic to Grand Central Station, for example, he begins to read a discarded magazine to "make me stop thinking" about

Antolini's apparent homosexual advances. One article convinces him that his hormones are "lousy" and another that he would "be dead in a couple of months" from cancer. What seems burlesque here ("That magazine was some little cheerer upper") becomes urgent in Holden's response to an obscene legend he sees shortly after in Phoebe's school:

> Somebody'd written "Fuck you" on the wall. It drove me damn near crazy. I thought how Phoebe and all the other little kids would see it, and how they'd wonder what the hell it meant, and then finally some dirty kid would tell them—all cockeyed, naturally—what it meant.... I figured it was some perverty bum that'd sneaked in the school late at night to take a leak or something and then wrote it on the wall. I kept picturing myself catching him at it, and how I'd smash his head on the stone steps till he was good and goddam dead and bloody. But I knew, too, I wouldn't have the guts to do it. I knew that. That made me even more depressed. I hardly even had the guts to rub it off the wall with my *hand*, if you want to know the truth. I was afraid some teacher would catch me rubbing it off and would think *I'd* written it. But I rubbed it out anyway, finally. (pp. 260–61)

As we shall see, Holden is more repelled by the "obscenity" of the sexual act itself than by the obscene word. And his fear of being identified with the sort of "pervert" who planted it in Phoebe's school is reiterated when, in one more withdrawal, he goes to the mummy tomb in the museum and again finds the legend. At this point he decides,

> You can't ever find a place that's nice and peaceful, because there isn't any. You may *think* there is, but once you get there, when you're not looking, somebody'll sneak up and write "Fuck you" right under your nose. Try it sometime. I think, even, if I ever die, and they stick me in a cemetery, and I have a tombstone and all, it'll say "Holden Caulfield" on it, and then what year I was born and what year I died, and right under that it'll say "Fuck you." I'm positive, in fact. (p. 264)

It is not enough to leave it that Holden's sickness has brought about this odd commingling of lovemaking and dying in his mind. Looking back at Holden's ostensibly random comments on various fascinations and aversions, one sees a subtle but coherent psychological pattern taking shape. Early in the novel we learn of his interest in Egyptian mummification and his particular fascination—mentioned again in the tomb scene—that the process ensured that "their faces wouldn't rot or anything." After watching the "perverts" squirt water in each other's faces, Holden reflects that

> if you don't really like a girl, you shouldn't horse around with her at all, and if you *do* like her, then you're supposed to like her face, and if you like her face, you ought to be careful about doing crumby stuff to it, like squirting water all over it. (p. 81)

If there are sexual inhibitions reflected in Holden's curious concern with the "preservation of faces," they must also be implicit in his general and constant longing for a state of changelessness. He laments, for instance, that though his beloved museum never changed, he did:

> The best thing, though, in that museum was that everything always stayed right where it was. Nobody'd move. You could go there a hundred thousand times, and that Eskimo would still be just finished catching those two fish, the birds would still be on their way south.... Nobody'd be different. The only thing that would be different would be *you*. Not that you'd be so much older or anything. It wouldn't be that, exactly. You'd just be different, that's all. You'd have an overcoat on this time.... Or you'd heard your mother and father having a terrific fight in the bathroom.... I can't explain what I mean. And even if I could, I'm not sure I'd feel like it. (pp. 157–58)

Readers experienced in the strategies of unreliable narration will suspect that Holden probably does somehow "explain" and that there must be a reason why he's not sure he'd "feel like it" if he could. One notices, as a possible clue, that the museum is associated here and elsewhere with Phoebe.

> I kept thinking about old Phoebe going to that museum on Saturdays the way I used to. I thought how she'd see the same stuff I used to see, and how *she'd* be different every time she saw it. It didn't exactly depress me to think about it, but it didn't make me feel gay as hell, either. Certain things they should stay the way they are.... I know that's impossible, but it's too bad anyway. (p. 158)

Indeed, Holden's feelings about Phoebe may explain much that is puzzling in his narrative.

II

The expository sections of the novel dramatize Holden's problems as essentially sexual and moral. Yet most critical readings of the novel's ending either ignore these things or imply their absence by declaring that the resolution is "blunted" or else "humanly satisfying" while "artistically weak." Those critics who attest to a harmonious resolution generally do so on philosophical grounds, the effect being a divorce of theme from Holden's human situation. To deny a fused sexual and moral resolution of some sort in the closing emotional crescendo of the Phoebe section would, it seems to me, impugn the integrity of the novel.

I am suggesting that the urgency of Holden's compulsions, his messianic desire to guard innocence against adult corruption, for example, comes of a frantic need to save his sister from himself. It may be Phoebe's face that Holden unconsciously fears may be desecrated; hence the desire to protect Phoebe's face that compels his fascination with mummification. And it may be Phoebe who provokes his longing for stasis because he fears that she may be changed—perhaps at his own hand. Holden's association of sex with death surely points to some sexual guilt—possibly the fear that he or Phoebe or both may "die" if repressed desires are acted out.

I do not mean to imply that Holden's desires, if they are what I suggest, drive him inexorably to Phoebe's bed. The psychoanalytical axiom may here apply that a sister is often the first replacement of the mother as love object, and that normal maturation guides the boy from sister to other women. At this point in his life, Holden's sexuality is swaying precariously between reversion and maturation—a condition structurally dramatized throughout and alluded to in this early description:

> I was sixteen then, and I'm seventeen now, and sometimes I act like I'm about thirteen. It's really ironical, because I'm six foot two and a half and I have gray hair. I really do. The one side of my head—the right side—is full of millions of gray hairs. I've had them ever since I was a kid. And yet I still act sometimes like I was only about twelve. Everybody says that, especially my father. It's partly true, too, but it isn't *all* true. . . . Sometimes I act a lot older than I am—I really do—but people never notice it. (p. 13)

The narrator's overall perspective is thus mapped out: his present age representing some measure of maturity, and thirteen and twelve the vacillation that normally comes at puberty and that is so much more painful when it occurs as late as sixteen. This vacillation is somehow resolved in a climax beginning in Phoebe's bedroom (or rather the bedroom of D. B., the corrupt brother, where she sleeps) and ending at the carousel after Holden has refused to let her run away with him. However one interprets the ending, it comes as a surprise which is dramatically appropriate precisely because it shocks Holden. Hence, also, the aptness of providing only scattered hints of things to come through the quest section, hints which, in my presentation, will necessarily seem tentative.

One notes in passing, for example, Holden's sudden infatuation with Bernice, one of the prosaic Seattle girls, while they are dancing. "You really can dance," he tells her. "I have a kid sister that's only in the goddam fourth grade. You're about as good as she is, and she can dance better than anybody living or dead." A possible association might be made of the name of the young prostitute, "Sunny," with "Phoebe."[3] Certainly Sunny's childlike aspects are emphasized throughout the episode:

> She was a pretty spooky kid. Even with that little bitty voice she had, she could sort of scare you a little bit. If she'd been a big old prostitute, with a lot of makeup on her face and all, she wouldn't have been half as spooky. (p. 127)

Holden has to beg off with the excuse that "I was a little premature in my calculations." His beating at the hands of Maurice, her pimp, suggests psychic punishment as well, particularly when Holden imagines that he's dying and pretends "I had a bullet in my gut."

More can be made of an assertion Holden is constrained to repeat that Phoebe is "too affectionate." After retreating from making the date with Faith, he describes Phoebe at length and tells the reader,

> She's all right. You'd like her. The only trouble is, she's a little too affectionate sometimes. She's very emotional, for a child. She really is. (p. 89)

Later, when Holden awakens Phoebe and "She put her arms around my neck and all," he blurts out:

> She's very affectionate. I mean she's quite affectionate, for a child. Sometimes she's even *too* affectionate. I sort of gave her a kiss. (p. 209)

One begins to recognize the brilliant stratagem of imprecise adolescent qualifiers such as "sort of," "I mean," "and all," and the nervous repetition of "affectionate" which dramatize Holden's confusion of restraint and desire. This confusion develops in the first passage as language moves from firm declaration to qualification; in the second, Phoebe's presence provokes even more qualified language.

Then, there is the curious matter of "Little Shirley Beans," the record Holden buys for Phoebe:

> It was about a little kid that wouldn't go out of the house because two of her front teeth were out and she was ashamed to.... I knew it would knock old Phoebe out.... It was a very old, terrific record that this colored girl singer, Estelle Fletcher, made about twenty years ago. She sings it very Dixieland and whorehouse, and it doesn't sound at all mushy. If a white girl was singing it, she'd make it sound *cute* as hell, but old Estelle Fletcher knew what the hell she was doing, and it was one of the best records I ever heard. (p. 149)

The significance of the record is underscored by Holden's anxiousness to give it to Phoebe and his inordinate dismay when he breaks it:

> Then something terrible happened just as I got in the park. I dropped old Phoebe's record. It broke into about fifty pieces.... I damn near cried, it made me feel so terrible, but all I did was, I took the pieces out of the envelope and put them in my coat pocket. (p. 199)

One wonders if the accident wasn't psychically determined. If the Shirley Beans affair were a subject of dream analysis, the missing teeth, the shame, and the translation through "whorehouse" jazz by a singer who "knew what the hell she was doing" would conventionally suggest the loss of virginity. Hence, Holden's unconscious forces would dictate the destruction of this "record" as well as its purchase. In the same vein is the information Holden passes on, as he sneaks into the apartment to see Phoebe, that the maid wouldn't hear "because she had only one eardrum. She had this brother that stuck a straw down her ear when she was a kid, she once told me."

At one point Holden hears a child singing the song that becomes the anthem of his savior fantasies: "If a body catch a body coming through the rye." Yet in the next paragraph he buys the "Little Shirley Beans" record—the pairing symbolically dramatizes his conflict of protecting and of violating. His thoughts turn to the Olivier *Hamlet* he and Phoebe had watched and he singles out this highly suggestive scene:

> The best part in the whole picture was when old Ophelia's brother—the one that gets in the duel with Hamlet at the very end—was going away and his father was giving him a lot of

advice. While the father kept giving him a lot of advice, old Ophelia was sort of horsing around with her brother, taking his dagger out of the holster, and teasing him and all while he was trying to look interested in the bull his father was shooting. That was nice. I got a big bang out of that. But you don't see that kind of stuff much. The only thing old Phoebe liked was when Hamlet patted this dog on the head. (pp. 152–53)

In all of these early clues, one notices that the nearer Holden's desires come to surfacing, the more hesitant his language and behavior become. When the dreadful suggestions have the protective coloration of, say, the art of "Little Shirley Beans" or *Hamlet*, he is not so uneasy: "That was nice. I got a big bang out of that."

After a series of abortive adventures with women, Holden rather desperately seeks the counsel of a former classmate who was regarded as the dormitory's resident expert on sexual matters. Luce is too pompous to help, but his cutting assessments are probably accurate. He tells Holden that his "mind is immature" and recommends psychoanalysis, as he had done the last time they had talked. Holden's self-diagnosis at this point—that his "trouble" is an inability to get "sexy—I mean really sexy—with a girl I don't like a lot"—raises questions when one recalls his fraternal affection for Jane Gallagher and the relatively sexy episodes with the likes of Sally Hayes and "a terrible phony named Anne Louise Sherman." A probable answer, as we shall see, lies in his confused feelings about Phoebe.

All chances for normal sexual expression or even sexual understanding now depleted, Holden gets drunk and goes to Central Park to find "where the ducks go in winter." One critic reads this episode, filled as it is with thoughts of death, as Holden's "dark night of the soul," after which the boy begins to gain in psychic strength (Strauch, p. 109). It ought to be pointed out that Holden's breakdown occurs after the events of the narrative. His desperation in the park is certainly one extreme of his vacillation, the withdrawing extreme which is imaged by coldness and thoughts of death. Finally, he decides to see Phoebe, "in case I died and all," more explicitly associating Phoebe with death.

Holden makes his way into the apartment furtively—ostensibly to keep his parents from learning that he had flunked out of school. Yet his guilt seems obsessive. "I really should've been a crook," he says after telling the elevator operator that he was visiting the "Dicksteins" who live next door, that he has to wait for them in their hallway because he has a "bad leg," causing him to limp "like a bastard." Though his mother "has ears like a goddam bloodhound," his parents are out and he enters Phoebe's room undetected.

Phoebe is asleep:

> She had her mouth way open. It's funny. You take adults, they
> look lousy when they're asleep and they have their mouths way
> open, but kids don't. Kids look all right. They can even have spit
> all over the pillow and they still look all right. (p. 207)

Suddenly Holden feels "swell" as he notices such things as Phoebe's discarded clothing arranged neatly on a chair. Throughout the Phoebe section, double entendres and sexually suggestive images and gestures multiply, most flowing naturally from Holden's mind while others, once the coding is perceived, become mechanical pointers to the psychological plot.

When Holden awakens Phoebe and is embarrassed by her overaffection, she eagerly tells him about the play in which she is "Benedict Arnold":

> "It starts out when I'm dying. This ghost comes in on Christmas
> Eve and asks me if I'm ashamed and everything.... Are you
> coming to it?" (p. 210)

When the Benedict Arnold image recurs at the end, we shall see that the role of "traitor" is precisely the one she must play if her brother is to weather his crisis. Phoebe then tells him about *The Doctor*, a movie she has seen "at the Lister Foundation" about

> "this doctor ... that sticks a blanket over this child's face that's
> a cripple and can't walk ... and makes her suffocate. Then they
> make him go to jail for life imprisonment, but this child that he
> stuck the blanket over its head comes to visit him all the time and
> thanks him for what he did. He was a mercy killer." (p. 211)

This suggestive plot points to a horrible psychological possibility for Holden. He may "kill" Phoebe, pay his penalty agreeably, and even receive the gratitude of his victim. If interpretation here seems hard to justify, especially the implications of *Phoebe's* having suggested all this to Holden, consider the climax of the chapter in which Phoebe puts "the goddam pillow over her head" and refuses to come out. "She does that quite frequently," Holden reassures us—and then takes it all back: "She's a true madman sometimes." However innocent, Phoebe's responses to Holden's secret needs become the catalyst for both his breakdown and recovery.

Through the next chapter Phoebe hears Holden out on his "categorical aversions," in Salinger's phrase, to all the "phoniness" that has soured his world. The conversation begins in a curious manner:

> Then, just for the hell of it, I gave her a pinch on the behind. It was sticking way out in the breeze, the way she was laying on her side. She has hardly any behind. I didn't do it hard, but she tried to hit my hand anyway, but she missed.
>
> Then all of a sudden, she said, "Oh, why did you *do* it?" She meant why did I get the ax again. It made me sort of sad, the way she said it. (p. 217)

Holden spells out his dissatisfactions at length—and indeed he cites valid and depressing instances of human failings—until Phoebe challenges him several times, "You don't like *any*thing that's happening." "Name one thing," she demands. "One thing? One thing I like?" Holden replies. "Okay." At this point he finds he can't "concentrate too hot."

> She was in a cockeyed position way the hell over the other side of the bed. She was about a thousand miles away. (p. 220)

He can't concentrate, I suggest, because the truth is too close.

> About all I could think of were those two nuns that went around collecting dough in those beat-up old straw baskets. Especially the one with the glasses with those iron rims. And this boy I knew at Elkton Hills. (p. 220)

Repression has transferred the true thing he "likes a lot" to a nun, an inviolable "sister," who, we remember, had embarrassed Holden by talking about *Romeo and Juliet*, "that play [that] gets pretty sexy in parts." It may also be significant that *Romeo and Juliet* involves forbidden love that ends tragically—especially significant in connection with the other "thing" Holden thinks about, James Castle, the boy who had killed himself wearing Holden's turtleneck sweater. None of this will do for Phoebe and she repeats the challenge:

> "I like Allie," I said. "And I like doing what I'm doing right now. Sitting here with you, and talking, and thinking about stuff, and—" (p. 222)

When she objects that "Allie's dead," Holden tries to explain but gives up:

> "Anyway, I like it now," I said. "I mean right now. Sitting here with you and just chewing the fat and horsing—" (p. 223)

Her insistence drives him to the loveliest—and most sinister—fantasy in the novel:

> "You know that song 'If a body catch a body comin' through the rye'? I'd like—"
> "It's 'If a body *meet* a body coming through the rye!'" old Phoebe said. (p. 224)

Holden proceeds to conjure up the daydream of himself as catcher in the rye, the protector of childhood innocence. As Phoebe implies, however, the song is about romance, not romanticism. Because he has to, Holden has substituted a messianic motive for the true, erotic one.

In the next chapter Holden and Phoebe seem to be acting out a mock romance, much the way Seymour Glass does with the little girl in "A Perfect Day for Bananafish." The episode is at once movingly tender and ominous. Holden finds Phoebe "sitting smack in the middle of the bed, outside the covers, with her legs folded like one of those Yogi guys"—an image one critic interprets as making her an emblem of "the still, contemplative center of life" (Strauch, p. 43). This may be valid for one level of Holden's mind. When he immediately asks her to dance, however, and "She practically jumped off the bed, and then waited while I took my shoes off," his excessive justifications point to guilt:

> I don't like people that dance with little kids. . . . Usually they keep yanking the kid's dress up in the back by mistake, and the kid can't dance worth a damn *any*way, and it looks terrible, but I don't do it out in public with Phoebe or anything. We just horse around in the house. It's different with her anyway, because she can *dance*. She can follow anything you do. I mean if you hold her in close as hell so that it doesn't matter that your legs are so much longer. She stays right with you. (p. 227)

After the dance, Phoebe "jumped back in bed and got under the covers" and Holden "sat down next to her on the bed again . . . sort of out of breath." "'Feel my forehead,' she said all of a sudden." Phoebe claims she has learned to induce fever psychosomatically so that

> "your whole forehead gets so hot you can burn somebody's hand."
> That killed me. I pulled my hand away from her forehead, like I was in terrific danger. "Thanks for *tell*ing me," I said.

"Oh, I wouldn't've burned *your* hand. I'd've stopped before it got too—*Shhh!*" Then, quick as hell, she sat way the hell up in bed. (p. 229)

The parents have returned and the scene that follows—Holden gathering up his shoes and hiding in the closet as the mother interrogates Phoebe about the (cigarette) "smoke" in the bedroom and asks "were you warm enough?"—is reminiscent of nothing so much as that mainstay of French farce, the lover hiding in the closet or under the bed as the girl ironically "explains" to husband or parent. More important are the implications of Phoebe's "heat." Though she cannot really induce it, her innocent compliance in the whole sexual charade does place Holden "in terrific danger."

When the mother leaves, Holden emerges from his hiding place and borrows money from Phoebe. Phoebe insists that he take all of her money and Holden "all of a sudden" begins to cry:

I couldn't help it. I did it so nobody could hear me, but I did it. It scared hell out of old Phoebe when I started doing it, and she came over and tried to make me stop, but once you get started, you can't just stop on a goddam *dime*. I was still sitting on the edge of the bed when I did it, and she put her old arm around my neck, and I put my arm around her, too, but I still couldn't stop for a long time. I thought I was going to choke to death or something. Boy, I scared hell out of poor old Phoebe. The damn window was open and everything, and I could feel her shivering and all, because all she had on was her pajamas. I tried to make her get back in bed, but she wouldn't go. (p. 233)

Holden's breakdown, his visiting of his own suffering on the child, the chill air, and the innocence of their intimacy in this moving scene signal his growing, frightening awareness of the other sort of intimacy. From now until he sees Phoebe again, Holden is in full flight. Nonetheless, their parting is filled with suggestions of a sort one might expect after a casual, normal sexual encounter. (The emphases in the following passage are my own.)

Then I *finished buttoning* my coat and all. I told her I'd *keep in touch with her.* She told me *I could sleep with her* if I wanted to, but I said no, that I'd better beat it. . . . Then I took my hunting hat out of my coat pocket and *gave it to her.* She likes those kind of crazy hats. She didn't want to take it, but *I made her.* I'll bet she *slept with it* on. She really likes those kinds of hats. Then I told her again I'd *give her a buzz* if I got a chance, and then I left. (p. 233)

It is almost as if Holden is acknowledging the real content of the sexual charade and escaping while he can. It would also seem that realization, however vague, is equated with deed as Holden immediately indicates that he wanted to be punished:

> It was a helluva lot easier getting out of the house than it was getting in, for some reason. For one thing, I didn't give much of a damn any more if they caught me. I really didn't. I figured if they caught me, they caught me. I almost wished they did, in a way. (pp. 233–34)

Holden leaves Phoebe to spend the night with Mr. Antolini, a former teacher who during the course of the evening offers sound if stilted assessments of Holden's future which become particularly relevant in the epilogue. Antolini has been drinking, however, and disrupts the peace he has provided (Holden feels sleepy for the first time) by awakening the boy with tentative homosexual advances. Certainly Holden is victimized ("I was shaking like a madman. . . . I think I was more depressed than I ever was in my life"), but the encounter may torment him most for its parallels to his own unconscious designs on a child. Now one begins to see the significance of Holden's unfounded suspicions about Jane Gallagher's stepfather and his murderous rage at the "perverty bum" who wrote the obscenity on Phoebe's school wall—inordinate reactions pointing to fears about himself.

At this point Holden's neurosis verges on madness. Each time he crosses a street, he imagines he will "disappear" and "never get to the other side of the street." I do not take this so much as a symbolic manifestation of "identity crisis" and of his fear that he "may never reach maturity"—although both are implicit—but rather as a literal, psychologically valid description of the boy's breakdown. He retreats into wild fantasies of running away forever, living in a cabin near, but not in, the woods ("I'd want it to be sunny as hell all the time"), and feigning deaf-muteness, all to escape the confusion about to engulf him. Phoebe betrays these plans—the first ironic level of the Benedict Arnold motif—by joining in his escape. When she appears, bag in hand and the hunting cap on her head, Holden reacts wildly:

> "I'm going with you. Can I? Okay?"
> "What?" I said. I almost fell over when she said that. I swear to God I did. I got sort of dizzy and I thought I was going to pass out or something again.
>
> . . . .

> I thought I was going to pass out cold. I mean I didn't mean to tell her to shut up and all, but I thought I was going to pass out again.
>
> . . . .
>
> I was almost all set to hit her. I thought I was going to smack her for a second. I really did. . . .
>
> "I thought you were supposed to be Benedict Arnold in that play and all," I said. I said it very nasty. "Wuddaya want to do? Not be in the play, for God's sake?" That made her cry even harder. I was glad. All of a sudden I wanted her to cry till her eyes practically dropped out. I almost hated her. I think I hated her most because she wouldn't be in that play any more if she went away with me. (pp. 267–68)

These near-hysterical responses can be understood, it seems to me, only in the context that Phoebe is the very thing he is fleeing. He somehow realizes that she *must* be his "Benedict Arnold."

Holden's fury at Phoebe having set the climax in motion, Salinger now employs a delicate spatial strategy. Phoebe returns the hat, turns her back on Holden, announces that she has no intention of running away with him, and runs "right the hell across the street, without even looking to see if any cars were coming." Positioning here signifies the end of their relation as possible lovers, but love remains. Holden does not go after her, knowing she'll follow him "on the *other* goddam side of the street. She wouldn't look over at me at all, but I could tell she was probably watching me out of the corner of her crazy eye to see where I was going and all. Anyway, we kept walking that way all the way to the zoo." They are still apart as they watch the sea lions being fed, Holden standing "right behind her."

> I didn't put my hands on her shoulders again or anything because if I had she *really* would've beat it on me. Kids are funny. You have to watch what you're doing.
>
> She wouldn't walk right next to me when we left the sea lions, but she didn't walk too far away. She sort of walked on one side of the sidewalk and I walked on the other side.
>
> . . . .
>
> Old Phoebe still wouldn't talk to me or anything, but she was sort of walking next to me now. I took a hold of the belt at the back of her coat, just for the hell of it, but she wouldn't let me. She said, "Keep your hands to yourself, if you don't mind." (pp. 271–72)

Holden promises not to run away and they rejoin as brother and sister in the presence of the carousel—miraculously open in winter. Phoebe wants to ride and Holden finds a mature, new perspective:

> All the kids kept trying to grab for the gold ring, and so was old Phoebe, and I was sort of afraid she'd fall off the goddam horse, but I didn't say anything or do anything. The thing with kids is, if they want to grab for the gold ring, you have to let them do it, and not say anything. If they fall off, they fall off, but it's bad if you say anything to them. (pp. 273–74)

The substitution of a gold ring for the traditional brass one may point to Phoebe's future as a woman. In any event, Holden has renounced his designs on Phoebe and thus abrogated his messianic role. Another Salinger story has young de Daumier-Smith relinquish his sexual designs on a nun with the announcement, "I am giving Sister Irma her freedom to follow her destiny. Everyone is a nun." One need not search for literary sources to recognize that the carousel finally represents everyone's sacred, inviolable human destiny.

III

Readers now dubious about this paper's clinical approach ("aesthetic pathology," Salinger has called it) may wonder why I have thus far neglected to make a masculine symbol of Holden's long-peaked hunting cap—which he purchased, one recalls, after losing the fencing team's foils in a subway. This rather mechanical symbol does partake of the boy's masculinity or sexuality. But more than that, it becomes the most reliable symbolic designation of Holden's psychic condition through the novel. Ackley points out that it is a deer hunter's hat while Holden maintains that "This is a people shooting hat. . . . I shoot people in this hat." When one remembers that hunters wear red hats to keep from being shot and that Holden usually wears his backwards in the manner of a baseball catcher, the symbol embraces Holden's aggressive and withdrawing tendencies as well as the outlandish daydreams of becoming the messiah in the rye.

Holden's masculinity is plainly involved in such instances as when he has to retrieve the hat from under a bed after the fight with Stradlater and when it is entrusted to Phoebe's bed, but the symbol becomes more encompassing when she "restores" the hat in the climactic carousel scene.

> Then all of a sudden she gave me a kiss. Then she held her hand out, and said, "It's raining. It's starting to rain."

"I know."

Then what she did—it damn near killed me—she reached in my coat pocket and took out my red hunting hat and put it on my head.

. . . .

My hunting hat really gave me quite a lot of protection, in a way, but I got soaked anyway. I didn't care, though. I felt so damn happy all of a sudden, the way old Phoebe kept going around and around. I was damn near bawling, I felt so damn happy, if you want to know the truth. I don't know why. It was just that she looked so damn *nice*, the way she kept going around and around, in her blue coat and all. God, I wish you could have been there. (pp. 274–75)

At its deepest level, the hat symbolizes something like Holden's basic human resources—his birthright, that lucky caul of protective courage, humor, compassion, honesty, and love—all of which are the real subject matter of the novel.

As the symbolic hat gives Holden "quite a lot of protection, in a way" and he gets "soaked anyway," those human resources do not prevent emotional collapse. In the epilogue we learn that Holden went West "after I went home, and . . . got sick and all"—not for the traditional opportunity there but for psychotherapy. This would be a bleak ending were it not for the fact that Holden has authored this structured narrative, just as Antolini predicted he might:

"you'll find that you're not the first person who was ever confused and frightened and even sickened by human behavior. You're by no means alone on that score, you'll be excited and *stimulated* to know. Many, many men have been just as troubled morally and spiritually as you are right now. Happily, some of them kept records of their troubles. You'll learn from them—if you want to. Just as someday, if you have something to offer, someone will learn something from you. It's a beautiful reciprocal arrangement. And it isn't education. It's history. It's poetry." (p. 246)

The richness of spirit in this novel, especially of the vision, the compassion, and the humor of the narrator reveal a psyche far healthier than that of the boy who endured the events of the narrative. Through the telling of his story, Holden has given shape to, and thus achieved control of, his troubled past.

Notes

1. J. D. Salinger, *The Catcher in the Rye* (Boston: Little, 1951), pp. 7–8. Page numbers from this edition will be cited in the text.

2. Carl F. Strauch, "Kings in the Back Row: Meaning through Structure—A Reading of Salinger's *The Catcher in the Rye*," in *Wisconsin Studies in Contemporary Literature*, 2 (Winter 1961), 5–30; rpt. in *If You Really Want to Know: A Catcher Casebook* (Belmont, Calif.: Wadsworth, 1962), p. 104.

3. Salinger may be echoing Phoebus rather than Phoebe, the personification of the moon; but he also may have in mind an antithesis between "Sunny" and Phoebe, the cool and chaste.

DAVID GALLOWAY

The Love Ethic

Few heroes of contemporary literature have aroused so much devotion, imitation, or controversy as J. D. Salinger's Holden Caulfield, the disaffiliated adolescent whose lost weekend in New York is chronicled in *The Catcher in the Rye*. As an impressionable adolescent making his first tentative movements into an adult world, Holden becomes a sensitive register by which the values of that world can be judged. From the opening pages of this novel the world is seen to be fragmentary, distorted, and absurd—in Holden's own special vernacular, "phony." It is an environment in which real communication on a sensitive level is impossible, and when Holden unsuccessfully tries to explain his spiritual pain to Sally Hayes, there is certainly more than a coincidental suggestion of Eliot's "J. Alfred Prufrock" in the frustrated cry, "'You don't see what I meant at all'" (*CR*, 173).

Holden does not refuse to grow up so much as he agonizes over the state of being grown up. The innocent world of childhood is amply represented in *The Catcher in the Rye*, but Holden, as a frustrated, disillusioned, anxious hero, stands for modern man rather than merely for the modern adolescent. He is self-conscious and often ridiculous, but he is also an anguished human being of special sensitivity. Even though he is often childishly ingenuous, and his language is frequently comic, Holden must be seen as both a representative and a critic of the modern environment, as the highly subjective tone of the novel suggests.

From *The Absurd Hero in American Fiction: Updike, Styron, Bellow, Salinger*. Austin: University of Texas Press (1981): pp. 204–27. © 1966, 1981 by David D. Galloway.

As a misfit Holden has literary predecessors in such early Salinger stories as "The Hang of It," "The Varioni Brothers," "Soft-Boiled Sergeant," "This Sandwich Has No Mayonnaise," and "The Stranger." Holden is not unlike Rabbit Angstrom or Augie March in seeking the environment in which he can perform at his best, and the result is a painful contemporary odyssey. As the novel opens, Holden is in the process of rejecting yet another uncongenial environment, Pencey Prep. There he feels surrounded by phonies, just as he had felt surrounded by them at Elkton Hills, his previous school: "One of the biggest reasons I left Elkton Hills was because I was surrounded by phonies. That's all. They were coming in the goddam window" (19). That "Goddam Elkton Hills" is far more than an example of the social snobbery of an Eastern prep school. It comes to stand for a world in which values and perspectives have become so distorted that there seems little if any room for the sensitive individual who attempts to order the flux of human existence or to bring it into the light of a consistent aesthetic perspective. To this significant degree, the milieu in which Salinger heroes function is "absurd." Like Camus's absurd man, the Salinger hero tries to live by ethical standards in an indifferent, often nihilistic universe. An important distinction, however, must be drawn between Camus's absurd man and the absurd man in Salinger's fiction. This distinction is primarily one of consciousness, for Camus's heroes consciously acknowledge the absurdity of their struggle against reality. While the reader is in a position to see the absurdity of Holden's quixotic gestures and of Zooey's ultimate, transcendent "love" stance, he is never entirely certain that the characters themselves see their own struggles as absurd, though Zooey at least approaches this essential awareness. These characters, however, do demonstrate "disproportions" on the level of values which make the myth of the absurd applicable to their struggles. The context of the absurd does not perhaps explain as much about Salinger as it did about Updike, Styron, or Bellow, but it does help us to see what Salinger has tried to accomplish in his writing and to understand his relationship to other contemporary novelists.

Few areas of modern life escape Holden Caulfield's indictment. Among those most severely challenged are the movies (to which his brother D. B., a writer, has prostituted himself) and religious enthusiasm. Holden explains that the children in his family are all "atheists" because his parents are of different religious persuasions (foreshadowing the Irish-Jewish Glass family). Thus Holden's biting but revealing point of view is not clouded by specific religious commitments, and he can love the nuns whom he meets in Grand Central Station even though he feels that Catholicism usually throws up insurmountable barriers to communication. Just as he loves the nuns for their simplicity and honesty, he sees through the selfish religious pose of "this guy Ossenburger," an undertaker who contributes a dormitory wing to Pencey.

The phoniness of Hollywood and of religion as it is often practiced in the contemporary world come together to form a dramatic whole in the Christmas pageant which Holden attends at Radio City. Following the Rockettes and a man who roller-skated under tables, "they had this Christmas thing they have at Radio City every year": "All these angels start coming out of the boxes and everywhere, guys carrying crucifixes and stuff all over the place, and the whole bunch of them—*thousands* of them—singing 'Come All Ye Faithful!' like mad. Big deal. It's supposed to be religious as hell, I know, and very pretty and all, but I can't see anything religious or pretty, for God's sake, about a bunch of actors carrying crucifixes all over the stage" (178). The blatant, graceless *kitsch* of the movie which follows the stage show (and which has been identified as James Hilton's *Random Harvest*) is an equally commercial deception, an artificial substitute for the love and generosity which Americans have forgotten how to express. After his experience with a Radio City Christmas, Holden feels yet more agonizingly frustrated and alone. "I'm sort of glad they've got the atomic bomb invented," he comments. "If there's ever another war, I'm going to sit right the hell on top of it. I'll volunteer for it, I swear to God I will" (183).

Wherever Holden turns, his craving for truth seems to be frustrated by the phoniness of the world. From his hotel window he looks out upon scenes of perversion and distortion; in bars and night clubs he hears only the laconic accents of shallow supersophisticates or self-satisfied intellectuals. When he finds innocence or purity it is always jeopardized by evil or apathy, and he searches desperately for something to sustain him. An answer seems to come from Mr. Antolini, a former English teacher who explains to Holden that the fall he is riding for is "'a special kind of fall, a horrible kind. The man falling isn't permitted to feel or hear himself hit bottom. He just keeps falling and falling. The whole arrangement's designed for men who, at some time or other in their lives, were looking for something their own environment couldn't supply them with. Or they thought their own environment couldn't supply them with. So they gave up looking'" (243–244). Mr. Antolini urges Holden to continue to search in humility for a cause worth living for. Such a search, he assures Holden, has been chronicled by educated and scholarly men, and he promises to guide the boy into an intellectual channel that will both stimulate and comfort him. Whatever consolation there may have been in this message is destroyed when Holden awakens to find Mr. Antolini petting him—and he flees from yet another example of the world's perversion.

What prompts Holden's quest is his desire for unity, a desire that is expressed in the comfort and safety which he always felt in the Museum of Natural History:

> The best thing, though, in that museum was that everything
> always stayed right where it was. Nobody'd move. You could go
> there a hundred thousand times, and that Eskimo would still
> be just finished catching those two fish, the birds would still be
> on their way south, the deers would still be drinking out of that
> water hole, with their pretty antlers and their pretty, skinny legs,
> and that squaw with the naked bosom would still be weaving that
> same blanket. Nobody'd be different. (157–158)

That such a reassuringly ordered universe is an impossible dream is
emphasized by the fact that, when Holden visits the Museum near the
conclusion of his New York odyssey, he sees the words "'Fuck you' . . .
written with a red crayon or something, right under the glass part of the
wall, under the stones" (264). Holden wishes to erase the interminable
"Fuck you's" on all the alley walls and school corridors and sidewalks in
the world, and this intention to cancel out vulgarity and phoniness is a
poignant if naive example of the absurd.

  The Catcher in the Rye is an important articulation of one of the possible
responses which man may make to an essentially destructive life experience.
Since, Holden reasons, there is no fulfillment in the adult world, since all it
can offer man is frustration or corruption, the only worthwhile task to which
he can devote himself is that of the protector who stops children before they
enter the world of destruction and phoniness and keeps them in a state of
arrested innocence:

> "Anyway, I keep picturing all these little kids playing some
> game in this big field of rye and all. Thousands of little kids, and
> nobody's around—nobody big, I mean—except me. And I'm
> standing on the edge of some crazy cliff. What I have to do, I
> have to catch everybody if they start to go over the cliff—I mean
> if they're running and they don't look where they're going I have
> to come out from somewhere and *catch* them. That's all I'd do all
> day. I'd just be the catcher in the rye and all. I know it's crazy,
> but that's the only thing I'd really like to be. I know it's crazy."
> (224–225)

Holden's reiteration of the word "crazy" reminds us that his ambition is also
"absurd," for his Christ-like intention (suffering the little children to come
unto him) is opposed to the reality in which children like his own sister,
Phoebe, are carted off to the Lister Foundation to see movies on euthanasia
and move along grimy school corridors which flaunt the words "Fuck you!"
at them. While Holden has a vision of his role in the world, he is unable

either to live the absurdity he has outlined or to develop an absurd faith. The reasons for this failure on his part are simple and obvious. First, even though we are clearly intended to see him as a representative of modern man, Holden is an adolescent, and both his experience and his perspectives are too limited for him to offer any kind of finalized "answer" to the phoniness of the world. Second, and perhaps most important, his vision carries within itself a destructive contradiction. While Holden's intention is absurd in its opposition to reality, the goal of his intention is to help innocent children to *avoid* reality. His conclusion negates his premise insofar as it eliminates one of the two crucial terms of the absurd confrontation and offers no formula by which man can live in and with his world. Holden's intention is moving and vaguely saintly, but it involves a nostalgia which, according to Camus, the absurd man must reject. (Indeed, Holden himself rejects it when he decides that he must not attempt to protect Phoebe during her final ride on the carousel.)

What Salinger leaves us with in this novel is an often biting image of the absurd contemporary milieu. The idea of perpetuating the innocence of childhood is a philosophically untenable position, and the only other unrejected proposals in the novel are so vague that their full importance can be seen only in Salinger's later work. The first of these proposals for a stance at once self-protective and humanistically fulfilling is made by Carl Luce, who suggests a vague mystical discipline derived from Eastern philosophy as a solution to Holden's spiritual agony, but Luce's approach to this discipline seems supersophisticated and "phony." In the epilogue to the novel Holden suggests the possibility of re-entering society when he says, "I sort of *miss* everybody I told about. Even old Stradlater and Ackley, for instance. I think I even miss that goddam Maurice" (277). Holden misses even the phonies of the world because his experience has taught him something about the necessity of loving, and here Salinger sounds what is to become his major and most complex theme.

After *The Catcher in the Rye* Salinger wrote several stories examining the mystical process, and even though his mystically inclined heroes are engaging and at times inspiring, their stance must be rejected, too, in favor of a position that leads man to the world rather than to an intense but isolating subjective experience. Like efforts to recapture the innocence of childhood, mysticism (which Salinger usually considers in terms of Zen Buddhism) is finally seen as an evasion and contradiction of Western man's spiritual quest. In Zen Buddhism, the life of the mystic is only temporarily one of isolation, for after the achievement of *satori*, the state of total enlightenment and consciousness that is the goal of Zen Buddhism, the enlightened man re-enters the world to perform good works. Thus, Salinger's rejection of the transitory, unearned mystical *experience* is understandable in terms of its failure to provide a program which the individual can follow in order to give his life meaning, but his rejection of mysticism itself is more difficult to understand—especially in light of his own involvement with Zen Buddhism. Mysticism is treated as a "fever" in Salinger's writings, an isolating and therefore unfruitful discipline that inevitably leads Western man away from the paths of significant human involvement. Furthermore, while *satori* may eventually guide the Buddhist back into his world, the good works which he is prepared to perform are not necessarily those works which a spiritually enlightened Westerner should be prepared to perform. It is not through mysticism but through love that the Salinger hero at last re-enters the world.

From 1945 until 1951, J. D. Salinger published sixteen short stories, several of the same slick, predictable character as the stories he wrote for popular magazines during the Second World War. Five of those stories, however, were concerned with Holden Caulfield and his family, and three of them represented the beginning of his largest and most serious body of work—the "saga" of the Glass family. The first of these stories centers on an elusive character named Seymour Glass, whose suicide is the subject of the first story in Salinger's second book, *Nine Stories*. Little in this brief account indicates the scope of the Glass series, but it sets the stage for the rejection of mysticism as a solution to the contemporary spiritual dilemma. In order to appreciate the strength of Salinger's rejection, one must understand his fascination with the mystical process itself. Two of Salinger's *Nine Stories*, "De Daumier-Smith's Blue Period" and "Teddy," chronicle, respectively, the mystical vision and the mystical faith.

De Daumier-Smith is the fanciful pseudonym adopted by a somewhat typical Salinger *isolatoe* who brashly attempts to create a new image of himself with which he can confront a world from which he suddenly feels disaffiliated. De Daumier-Smith's rebellion resembles Holden's in that he too is hypersensitive to the phoniness of the world, but the origin of his disaffiliation is more specifically identified as the absence of love. Jean narrates his own story, and the most pertinent fact about his childhood is that he had never truly loved anyone but his mother. Shortly after her death, he moves to New York with his stepfather. Having drawn some slight attention as an artist when his family lived in Paris, Jean embroiders his experiences, draws up an imaginary list of professional credentials and friends (including Picasso) and applies for a job as an instructor at "Les Amis Des Vieux Maîtres," a correspondence art school in Montreal. What prompts him to make this sudden "quixotic gesture" is the realization that he and his father "were both in love with the same deceased woman" (*NS*, 98). This knowledge forces him out of the innocent private world in which he had formerly lived, and the very telling of his story is an attempt to give order to the experiences which greet him in the public world—a world which at first seems no more complete or fulfilling than the Oedipally narrow world in which he had previously functioned. The isolation which De Daumier-Smith suffers is underscored by the fact that we never learn his real name; he adopts a bogus identity and a preposterously contrived set of credentials in order to teach students whom he will never see in a French art school run by two Japanese. When Jean reveals to the Yoshotos that he is a student of Buddhism, they inform him that they are Presbyterians. However ambitiously ingratiating he becomes to his employers, his loneliness only increases.

What seems to offer Jean consolation is his discovery of naive beauty in the crude but talented paintings of Sister Irma of the Order of St. Joseph. In Jean's wild daydreams about the nun, she comes to represent his last chance to communicate with another sensitive spirit, and he yearns for a moment of truth and love with her which will make him spiritually whole and effect his conversion into a great healer.

When her Superior severs Sister Irma's relationship with the art school after reading Jean's passionate letter to her, the boy is cast into a painful and almost total despair; but from that dark night of the soul he passes into a period of illumination. Like the precocious members of the Glass family, Jean has been a student of comparative religions, and his study has at least partially prepared him for the epiphany which greets him and flashes like the sun into his dark night. Les Amis Des Vieux Maîtres is located over an orthopedic appliances shop, and as Jean pauses before the window, he seems to see it as a *collage* representing all of the crippling inhumanity of the world: "The thought was forced on me that no matter how coolly or sensibly or gracefully I might one day learn to live my life, I would always at best be a visitor in a garden of enamel urinals and bedpans, with a sightless, wooden dummy-deity standing by in a marked-down rupture truss" (116). Later, however, he has what he calls an "Experience," in which everything in the window is transformed: "Suddenly (and I say this, I believe, with all due self-consciousness), the sun came up and sped toward the bridge of my nose at the rate of ninety-three million miles a second. Blinded and very frightened—I had to put my hand on the glass to keep my balance. The thing lasted for no more than a few seconds. When I got my sight back, the girl had gone from the window, leaving behind her a shimmering field of exquisite, twice-blessed, enamel flowers" (121).

"De Daumier-Smith's Blue Period" offers a strong suggestion that a mystical experience may help man to alter his vision of the world so significantly that he will be able to live in it. Jean de Daumier-Smith does return to the world after his dark night of despair to spend a "normal" summer of girl-watching on the beach. While Jean has something closely related to a mystical revelation, he is not a mystic: "I'd like, if possible, to avoid seeming to pass it off as a case, or even a borderline case, of genuine mysticism" (120). While his experience offers the promise of a degree of spiritual fulfillment he had not known before, his story suggests no code by which the individual can oppose a world made up of "enamel urinals and bedpans" and ruled over by a "wooden dummy-deity." His discovery of an order and transcendent meaning in a sterile and hostile world is rather a product of chance, than the climax of experience. This situation is typical for the modern hero, to whom revelation or epiphany comes as a sudden intuitive flash, suggesting in part that visions of order or meaning are not available through reason.

In "Teddy" Salinger concerned himself with the realized mystic Teddy McArdle, a precocious ten-year-old who has achieved the enlightened consciousness of *satori*. Teddy's mysticism frees him from the grossness of his parents, but Salinger treats his mystic lyrically and impressionistically, never attempting to describe the process by which Teddy arrives at *satori*, other than by referring to the boy's intense periods of meditation, but in "A Perfect Day for Bananafish" he allegorically demonstrates that mysticism is not a solution to man's dilemma.

As we learn from later stories about the Glass family, Seymour Glass has traveled to Florida with his wife in order to "recover" from a state of acute depression. In the first half of "A Perfect Day for Bananafish," through a telephone conversation between his wife and her mother, we are given some insight into the causes of his depression. Muriel comes from a world whose main concerns are with "normalcy" and whose emotional outlets are found in the kind of melodramatic movie which to Holden Caulfield seemed a puerile commercial sham. The hotel room in which Seymour commits suicide is characterized by the smell "of new calfskin luggage and nail-lacquer remover" (18). Without the bananafish allegory the reader might see Seymour's suicide as merely a rejection of this world of crass superficiality, but it is also—and more significantly—a rejection of the mystical life itself.

While Muriel is talking to her mother and trying to reassure her that Seymour has had no more destructive urges, Seymour is on the beach with Sybil Carpenter. He catches the young girl's attention with a variety of fantasies, the most complex of which involves the bananafish. Pushing Sybil out into the water on a rubber float, he explains to her the inherent fatalism of bananafish: "'Well, they swim into a hole where there's a lot of bananas. They're very ordinary-looking fish when they swim *in*. But once they get in, they behave like pigs. Why, I've known some bananafish to swim into a banana hole and eat as many as seventy-eight bananas.' He edged the float and its passenger a foot closer to the horizon. 'Naturally, after that they're so fat they can't get out of the hole again. Can't fit through the door'" (16).

Seymour's life has been filled with erratic spiritual experiences, and to his brothers and sisters he stands as a kind of Christ-figure. Like the bananafish, however, he has become so glutted with this experience that he can no longer participate in the real world outside himself. This inability, which accounts for what he calls the "very tragic life" which the bananafish leads, is emphasized by the fact that he cannot bear the eyes of the world. After leaving Sybil on the beach, Seymour walks into the hotel elevator along with a young woman:

> "I see you're looking at my feet," he said to her when the car was in motion.
> "I beg your pardon?" said the woman.
> "I said I see you're looking at my feet."
> "I *beg* your pardon. I happened to be looking at the floor," said the woman, and faced the doors of the car.
> "If you want to look at my feet, say so," said the young man. "But don't be a God-damned sneak about it." (17)

Following this episode, Seymour enters his hotel room, takes a pistol from his suitcase, and fires a bullet through his head.

Salinger rejects the mystic's experience as a solution to man's alienation in an absurd universe because mysticism ("banana fever") removes man from reality. While Seymour is never a fully realized mystic like Teddy, it is inconsistent to explain away his suicide as despair over the idea of achieving *satori*. Seymour has already rejected *satori* because it leads him out of the world in which he feels he must live, and his rejection is overt and conscious. His life has been filled with one transcendent experience after another, with visions and intense spiritual moments which affirm his ability to achieve *satori*. Among the reminders of such experiences, Seymour notes, "I have scars on my hands from touching certain people."

> "Once, in the park, when Franny was still in the carriage, I put my hand on the downy pate of her head and left it there too long. Another time, at Loew's Seventy-second Street, with Zooey during a spooky movie. He was about six or seven, and he went under the seat to avoid watching a scary scene. I put my hand on his head. Certain heads, certain colors and textures of human hair leave permanent marks on me. Other things, too. Charlotte once ran away from me, outside the studio, and I grabbed her dress to stop her, to keep her near me. A yellow cotton dress I loved because it was too long for her. I still have a lemon-yellow mark on the palm of my right hand. Oh, God, if I'm anything by a clinical name, I'm a kind of paranoiac in reverse. I suspect people of plotting to make me happy." (*RHRB*, 88)

As we learn in "Raise High the Roof Beam, Carpenters," Seymour was so happy over his marriage to Muriel that he was unable to attend his own wedding. Seymour's wedding-day happiness came from the thought that he might at last emerge from the spiritual "hole" into which he had begun swimming as a child. Unable to resign a quest for a miraculous spiritual perfection, and simultaneously unequipped to join the world of mere possibility, Seymour chose suicide. As Dan Wakefield has noted, suicide and miracle are the extremes between which many of Salinger's characters fluctuate, but the author's primary concern is with the alternatives which exist between those extremes. No appeal to a spiritual absolute (and no transcendent spiritual experience) is a wholly successful alternative. In his later stories Salinger turns his attention to other stances which man can make in an absurd world to give his life meaning.

Salinger would certainly agree with Dan Wakefield's observation that ours is a time in which men are "'no longer feeling within themselves the idol but still feeling the altar,' and the questions of what replaces the idol which once provided a set of answers for human conduct; the question of how men act with morality and love if there is no idol which prescribes the rules, is a central and vital question."[1] Salinger begins to define his answer in "For Esmé—with Love and Squalor." The narrator of this story—who is never more fully identified than as "Sergeant X"—writes his story as a kind of epithalamium after receiving an invitation to Esmé's wedding. He had met the girl while stationed in England for special D-Day training, and the loneliness which he experienced before their meeting is idiomatic to the Salinger hero.

On a free Saturday afternoon at the end of his training course Sergeant X walks into Devon and almost by accident enters a church in which a children's choir is rehearsing. There he becomes enchanted by Esmé, a young girl of "about thirteen, with straight ash-blond hair of earlobe length, an exquisite forehead, and blasé eyes that, I thought, might very possibly have counted the house" (*NS*, 68). Later Sergeant X meets the girl in a tea room, and Esmé tries to comfort and entertain the lonely G.I. When she leaves the tea room, it is with the request that X someday write her a story "about love and squalor."

X's experience with squalor comes in Bavaria, where he is trying unsuccessfully to recover from his encounter with undefined battlefield horrors. His recovery is not aided by the loutish insensitivity of his companion, Clay, or by his own brother's request for wartime souvenirs: "'. . . how about sending the kids a couple of bayonets or swastikas . . .'" (79). X is quartered in a house recently confiscated from a family whose daughter was an official in the Nazi party; among the books which she has left behind is Goebbel's *Die*

Zeit Ohne Beispiel, a title ironically descriptive of X's condition. He opens the book to find the words "'Dear God, life is hell'" written on the flyleaf. With a sudden energy X writes under this a passage from Dostoevski, "'Fathers and teachers, I ponder, 'What is hell?' I maintain that it is the suffering of being unable to love'" (79). It is in this inscription that the inability to love is specifically articulated as the curse that visits Salinger's pilgrims. Later X is saved by a small package lying among the clutter of his desk, for the package represents a gesture of love which directly opposes the squalor of his world. In the package is an "extremely water-proof and shock-proof watch which had belonged to Esmé's dead father, and which she now sends X as a lucky talisman. X sits for a long while with the watch in his hand, and "Then, suddenly, almost ecstatically, he felt sleepy. You take a really sleepy man, Esmé, and he *always* stands a chance of again becoming a man with all his fac— with all his f-a-c-u-l-t-i-e-s intact" (85). The story which X writes for Esmé is itself a gesture of love (similarly, Salinger wrote one of his most important stories, "Franny," as a wedding present for his wife). The love which saves Sergeant X comes from an innocent child, but the idea of love as man's salvation, unlike the suggestion of mysticism, is not rejected, and it finally becomes developed into an absurd gesture which Salinger offers as the answer to an idol-less altar.

The absurd love gesture is chronicled in the two interrelated stories, "Franny" and "Zooey," which were originally published in the *New Yorker* and later combined and published as a book. Franny and Zooey are the youngest brother and sister of Seymour Glass, and part of the urban menagerie of sensitiveness and titanesque idiosyncrasy around which Salinger is constructing his contemporary saga. To understand how Franny and Zooey offer a resolution which Seymour and other mystically inclined heroes could not accomplish, it is necessary to know something of the relationships of this sprawling family.

There are seven Glass children—in order of birth, Seymour, Buddy, Boo Boo, the twins Walt and Waker, Zachary (Zooey), and Franny. Les and Bessie Glass, the parents, were once a famous vaudeville team (billed as "Gallagher and Glass") on the old Pantages and Orpheum circuits. Les is Jewish and Bessie Irish, and they are descended "from an astonishingly long and motley double file of professional entertainers." The public life of their parents has helped to give the Glass children an especially acute sense of the public world, and this sense is accented by the fact that all seven children began life as child prodigies on a radio quiz program called "It's a Wise Child." (Salinger is almost certainly aware of Telemachus' consciously cryptic reply to Athena when she questions him about Odysseus: "It's a wise child that knows its own father." This oblique reference to *The Odyssey* emphasizes the quest for identity on which each of the Glass children has at some point embarked.)

The story of Seymour Glass (1917–1948) is told directly through "A Perfect Day for Bananafish" and indirectly through "Raise High the Roof Beam, Carpenters," "Seymour—An Introduction," and "Zooey." Buddy Glass is a shy, sardonic creative-writing teacher who occasionally takes upon himself the task of narrating his family's spiritual history. In "Seymour—An Introduction" he emerges as a *persona* for Salinger himself. In spiritual training Buddy was closer to Seymour than any other member of the family, and while he hardly seems well adjusted, he is less clearly psychotic than Seymour. Boo Boo first appears in the Glass saga as Boo Boo Tannenbaum, the mother of Lionel, the sensitive child hero of "Down at the Dinghy." In this story Salinger suggested the brutality of the world in the specific guise of anti-Semitism. Lionel has isolated himself from the world because he has overheard the family cook refer to his father as a "kike." Even though Lionel believes that a kike is "'one of those things that go up in the *air*'" (*NS*, 65), he is horrified that his father should be considered such an obscurely unnatural phenomenon. Boo Boo's involvement with Zen Buddhism does not seem significant, and she is perhaps more down-to-earth than any of the other children, preferring to be thought of as a "Tuckahoe homemaker." Our only other encounter with Boo Boo is through the Sapphic scrawl which she leaves on a bathroom mirror on the day of Seymour's wedding: "'Raise high the roof beam, carpenters. Like Ares comes the bridegroom, taller far than a tall man. Love, Irving Sappho, formerly under contract to Elysium Studios Ltd. Please be happy happy *happy* with your beautiful Muriel. This is an order. I outrank everybody on this block'" (*RHRB*, 76).

Of Waker we know no more than the fact that he has presumably found peace through becoming a Roman Catholic priest. In "Zooey," however, we learn that his answer offers no promise to the other children in the family. Walt never directly enters any of the Glass stories, although he seems to have certain qualities in common with an earlier Salinger creation, Sergeant Babe Gladwaller, the hero of "The Last Day of the Furlough" and the friend of Vincent Caulfield, Holden's older brother. We do learn, however, that Walt was killed in the Army of Occupation in Japan following the explosion of a Japanese stove which he was packing for his commanding officer. Walt is a symbol of innocence and tenderness for the heroine of "Uncle Wiggily in Connecticut." When she thinks of the innocence she has lost, Eloise has an alcoholic vision of the sophisticated squalor of her life and a moment of visionary love with her escapist daughter, Ramona. Eloise, who was once engaged to Walt, feels she has been destroyed by the exurbanite world her husband Lew represents (and when she refers to his favorite author as the unheard-of L. Manning Vines, she identifies him as the company commander who grudgingly gave Buddy leave to attend Seymour's wedding in "Raise High the Roof Beam, Carpenters"). Through the innocent love of a child Eloise achieves a moment of salvation similar to that which Sergeant X achieved, and, while like his salvation, hers is temporary and unstable, it nonetheless suggests the future development of Salinger's love theme.

When Salinger first introduces Franny Glass, she is a twenty-year-old college girl and summer-stock actress; and her older brother Zooey, who guides her through a religious crisis to the absurd love stance, is a television actor in his late twenties who suffers from an ulcer and, like Holden Caulfield, from profound disgust with the world of shams in which he lives. It is Zooey who gives the final *coup de grâce* to the idea of mysticism as an answer to the absurd universe.

"Franny" opens on a brilliantly lit Yale-game Saturday with Lane Coutell, Franny's date for the weekend (and her sometime lover, as we later learn), waiting on a railroad-station platform. He is rereading a letter from Franny which creates for the reader the impression of a typical college girl enthusiastically if somewhat vaguely in love. She hopes there will be an opportunity for dancing, that the weekend will not involve tiresome receiving lines, and that her spelling is improving. When Franny steps from the train the picture given by her letter seems to be elaborately confirmed:

> Franny was among the first of the girls to get off the train, from a car at the far, northern end of the platform. Lane spotted her immediately, and despite whatever it was he was trying to do with his face, his arm that shot up into the air was the whole truth. Franny saw it, and him, and waved extravagantly back. She was wearing a sheared raccoon coat, and Lane, walking toward her quickly but with a slow face, reasoned to himself, with suppressed excitement, that he was the only one on the platform who really *knew* Franny's coat. He remembered that once, in a borrowed car, after kissing Franny for a half hour or so, he had kissed her coat lapel, as though it were a perfectly desirable, organic extension of the person herself. (*FZ*, 7)

Lane pilots his date to a fashionable French restaurant, and it is only there that we see Franny as another of the Glass family suffering from "banana fever." She has begun to retreat into a world of mysticism, but like Seymour, she realizes the importance of an answer which will permit her to live in the real world. Her efforts at presenting a typical girl-on-a-football-weekend appearance are part of a last stand in which she tries to face the public world. Lane Coutell, the slick, falsely sophisticated representative of that world, is reminiscent of Muriel Fedders and her mother, and of Eloise's husband Lew. Franny is obviously on the verge of a nervous breakdown after a sudden depressing vision of the insignificance of the world around her that is emphasized by Lane's chatter about an "A" paper on Flaubert that he has written for a professor who lacks "'testicularity'." His chief interest in Franny rests in being seen with "an unimpeachably right-looking girl—a girl who was not only extraordinarily pretty but, so much the better, not too categorically cashmere sweater and flannel skirt" (11).

In the beginning of the story Lane's own "phoniness" only encourages Franny to try more earnestly to fulfill the role he has outlined for her, but it gradually becomes clear that Franny suffers from an acute and oversensitive weariness with all that is phony in the world. Her mind wanders, and her lack of interest in Lane's distinctly "publishable" paper angers him. When he challenges her disinterestedness, she apologizes but adds that he is "'talking just like a section man',", and in her description of this Eastern college phenomenon, Franny begins to outline her disillusionment.

When Lane interrupts her frenzied dissection of the junior faculty member Franny confesses not only that she has felt "*destructive*" all week, but that she had to strain to write the "natural" letter to him. Listening to Lane's description of the events of the weekend, Franny becomes progressively depressed and begins to ridicule Wally Campbell, the person giving the inevitable cocktail party. But Wally is only a symbol of Franny's disgust with those individuals who resign themselves to the phoniness of the world: "'I don't mean there's anything horrible about him or anything like that. It's just that for four solid years I've kept seeing Wally Campbells wherever I go. . . . It's everybody, I mean. Everything everybody does is so—I don't know— not *wrong*, or even mean, or even stupid necessarily. But just so tiny and meaningless and—sad-making. And the worst part is, if you go bohemian or something crazy like that, you're conforming just as much as everybody else, only in a different way'" (25–26).

Franny's description of her illness—or at least of one of its major manifestations—is reminiscent of Celia's description of her "perplexing" illness in T. S. Eliot's "The Cocktail Party":

> An awareness of solitude.
> But that sounds so flat. I don't mean simply
> That there's been a crash: though indeed there has been.
> It isn't simply the end of an illusion
> In the ordinary way, or being ditched.
> Of course that's something that's always happening
> To all sorts of people, and they get over it
> More or less, or at least they carry on.
> No. I mean that what has happened has made me aware
> That I've always been alone. That one always is alone.
> Not simply the ending of one relationship,

Not even simply finding that it never existed—
But a revelation about my relationship
With *everybody*. Do you know—
It no longer seems worth while to *speak* to anyone.[2]

Indeed, one of the first details we learn about Franny in "Zooey" is that, following her weekend with Lane, she no longer wants to speak to anyone.

The only thing that Franny can think of worth concerning herself over is something which interests Lane only superficially—a small, pea-green book entitled *The Way of a Pilgrim*. The book has presumably been suggested to her by a professor, and she comes increasingly to see its message as her answer. When she almost loses control in the restaurant, she goes to the ladies' room and sits down with the book on her knees. "After a moment, she picked up the book, raised it chest-high, and pressed it to her—firmly, and quite briefly" (*FZ*, 22). The book seems momentarily to restore her control. The book which Franny clutches so zealously describes the search of a Russian peasant for the meaning of the Biblical commandment to "pray incessantly." The peasant learns the solution from a "starets"—"'some sort of terribly advanced religious person'" (33), who tells him to repeat the "Jesus Prayer" ("Lord Jesus Christ, have mercy on me") so often that the prayer becomes an automatic response of his heart. When the peasant has perfected his mystical prayer he walks all over Russia teaching people how to pray "'by this incredible method'" (34). "'He says'," Franny adds, "'that any name of God—any name at all—has this peculiar, self-active power of its own, and it starts working after you've sort of started it up'" (37). As Franny's excited description of the book continues, Lane's comments become as irrelevant ("'I hate to mention it, but I'm going to reek of garlic'" [34]) as the comments with which Franny had interrupted his discussion of Flaubert. Franny makes a final effort to adjust to Lane's idea of the "unimpeachably right-looking girl," but as she rises to leave, she faints, and when she awakens she is lying in a back room of the restaurant. The final satiric touch to Lane's insensitivity is given when he wonders if Franny does not simply need to go to bed with him.

"Zooey" begins on the Monday morning following Franny's weekend date with Lane; she has taken refuge on the couch in the Glass living room, where she clutches *The Way of a Pilgrim* and strokes the family cat, Bloomberg. Only two other members of the family are in the apartment, but the spirits of all the other brilliant Glass children crowd around Franny, "like so many Banquo's ghosts," threatening first to destroy her but suddenly offering her salvation. Just as Salinger warned us in "De Daumier-Smith's Blue Period" that he was not describing genuine mysticism, so he warns us in "Zooey" that what is to follow is not a mystical story but a love story which will take the form of a home movie (which in its close-ups, its attention to quotidian detail, and its casualness, it does). Pointing out that Nick Carraway in *The Great Gatsby* recognizes his cardinal virtue as honesty, the narrator says, "*Mine*, I think, is that I know the difference between a mystical story and a love story. I say that my current offering isn't a mystical story, or a religiously mystifying story, at all. *I* say it's a compound, or multiple, love story, pure and complicated" (49).

We are introduced to Zooey Glass at ten-thirty in the morning as he sits in "a very full bath" rereading a four-year-old letter from his brother Buddy. Among other things, the letter relates Buddy's arrival in Florida on the day following Seymour's suicide, but other than its value in filling in details in the ever-growing Glass legend, the letter from Buddy is important for the emphasis which it puts on the religious training which Franny and Zooey had received from their eldest brothers. Rather than urging the classics on the youngest children in the family, as they had urged them on the twins and Boo Boo, Buddy and Seymour decided to direct Franny and Zooey toward what is known in Zen as

> no-knowledge. Dr. Suzuki says somewhere that to be in a state of pure consciousness—*satori*—is to be with God before he said, Let there be light. Seymour and I thought it might be a good thing to hold back this light from you and Franny (at least as far as we were able), and all the many lower, more fashionable lighting effects—the arts, sciences, classics, languages—till you were both able at least to conceive of a state of being where the mind knows the source of all light. We thought it would be wonderfully constructive to at least (that is, if our own "limitations" got in the way) tell you as much as we knew about the men—the saints, the arhats, the bodhisattvas, the jivanmuktas—who knew something or everything about this state of being. (65)

The description of this training for a state of pure consciousness is reinforced by a Taoist tale which Buddy (as narrator) repeats at the beginning of "Raise High the Roof Beam, Carpenters." The story had been read to Franny when she was an infant, but she always maintained that she could remember Seymour's reading it. In this brief Taoist allegory Chiu-fang Kao has recently been retained by his Duke as a horse buyer, and he returns with the news that he has found a superlative horse—a dun-colored mare. When the animal turns out to be a coal-black stallion, the Duke is displeased, but his former horse-buyer exclaims with satisfaction,

"Has he really got as far as that? ... Ah, then, he is worth ten thousand of me put together. There is no comparison between us. What Kao keeps in view is the spiritual mechanism. In making sure of the essential, he forgets the homely details; intent on the inward qualities, he loses sight of the external. He sees what he wants to see, and not what he does not want to see. He looks at the things he ought to look at, and neglects those that need not be looked at. So clever a judge of horses is Kao, that he has it in him to judge something better than horses." (*RHRB*, 5)

Chiu-fang Kao had achieved the state of pure consciousness which Buddy and Seymour envisioned for Franny and Zooey, and which Teddy McArdle possessed. Teddy's proposals represented Salinger's first consideration of Zen-oriented education. Teddy believed that the first thing to be done with children was to bring them together "'and show them how to meditate'." His primary interest was in teaching children "'who they *are*, not just what their names are and things like that . . . I'd get them to empty out everything their parents and everybody ever told them. I mean even if their parents just told them an elephant's big, I'd make them empty *that* out. An elephant's big only when it's next to something else—a dog or a lady, for example'." If the children wanted to learn other "stuff"—colors, names, categories—"'they could do it, if they felt like it, later on when they were older. But I'd want them to *begin* with all the real ways of looking at things . . .'" (*NS*, 142–143). Teddy's death prevents him from implementing his scheme of education, but Franny and Zooey are the products of controlled, intelligent experiments aimed at making them buyers who can always distinguish a "superlative horse." Franny's crisis, like Zooey's cynicism, is a result of this training, and her final victory is a throwing off of the banana fever of Buddhism, which for all its beauty and hope, is not a solution for modern Western man.

Zooey's private reverie over Buddy's letter is broken by the entrance of his mother, and there follows a forty-seven-page dialogue in which we not only glimpse Zooey's cynicism (toward television, the theatre, writers, almost anyone who asks him to lunch), but also realize that beneath his cynical surface is a strong core of love. His bantering attitude toward Bessie is largely a "routine" which they have played so often that it is completely natural to them. Buddy does not understand this attitude, and in his letter had somewhat patronizingly requested, "Be kinder to Bessie, Zooey, when you can. I don't think I mean because she's our mother, but because she's weary" (57). At times Zooey's conversation with his mother seems no better integrated than Franny's conversation with Lane, but his preoccupied manner is largely the result of his own efforts to maintain an undistorted spiritual perspective. Bessie accuses Zooey of demonstrating a family failing, an inability to be "'any help when the chips are down'" (84). He scoffs at the idea of being asked to live Franny's life for her, and especially at the inevitable chicken broth Bessie offers as a cure-all. Bessie is right when she says "'You can't live in the world with such strong likes and dislikes'" (99), but she does not realize that Zooey is coming to a realization about love which will not only teach him that chicken broth is sacred, but will permit him to help Franny. Buddy (who, symbolically, can never be reached in a crisis) offers no help with his mysticism; Waker, the Catholic priest, is out of the question because, as Zooey urges, "'This thing with Franny is strictly non-sectarian'" (94); and Boo Boo is never considered.

Zooey makes the first important step toward relieving Franny's "fever" as well as his own when he realizes that *The Way of the Pilgrim* was not, as Franny told Lane, checked out of her school library, but was taken from the desk in Seymour and Buddy's old room. When he sees the pain which the mention of Seymour's name gives his mother, Zooey apologizes. "His apology had been genuine, and Mrs. Glass knew it, but evidently she couldn't resist taking advantage of it, perhaps because of its rarity" (102), to compare him unfavorably with Buddy. It is in his violent reaction to Bessie's reprimand that we first learn that Zooey is conscious of the sickness which he and Franny have inherited:

"Buddy, Buddy, *Buddy*," he said. "Seymour, Seymour, *Seymour*." He had turned toward his mother, whom the crash of the razor had startled and alarmed but not really frightened. "I'm so sick of their names I could cut my throat." His face was pale but very nearly expressionless. "This whole goddam house stinks of ghosts. I don't mind so much being haunted by a dead ghost, but I resent like *hell* being haunted by a half-dead one. I wish to *God* Buddy'd make up his mind. He does everything else Seymour ever did—or tries to. Why the hell doesn't he kill himself and be done with it?"

Mrs. Glass blinked her eyes, just once, and Zooey instantly looked away from her face. He bent over and fished his razor out of the wastebasket. "We're *freaks*, the two of us, Franny and I," he announced, standing up. "I'm a twenty-five-year-old freak and she's a twenty-year-old freak, and both those bastards are responsible.... The symptoms are a little more delayed in Franny's case than mine, but she's a freak, too, and don't you forget it. I swear to you, I could murder them both without even batting an eyelash. The great teachers. The great emancipators. My God. I can't even sit down to lunch with a man any more and hold up my end of a decent conversation. I either get so bored or so goddam preachy that if the son of a bitch had any sense, he'd break his chair over my head." (102–103)

When Zooey cites the fact that Franny's own symptoms are more "delayed" than his, we are able to see her revulsion and its crisis as a concentrated example of Zooey's own spiritual experience. Franny herself notes, after talking with Zooey from her couch-retreat, "'. . . we're not bothered by exactly the same things, but by the same kind of things, I think, and for the same reasons'" (143). In his efforts to bring Franny back into the world Zooey achieves final definition for his own struggle. Together they are able to scuttle out of the banana hole, achieving a victory important not only for its rejection of isolation but also for its emphasis on participation in the world.

In arguing against Franny's withdrawal, Zooey emphasizes her misuse of the Jesus Prayer, for instead of resisting a world whose emphasis is on piling up "'money, property, culture, knowledge, and so on and so on'" (147), she is attempting to pile up another kind of treasure, less material, but just as negotiable: "'. . . ninety per cent of all the world-hating saints in history,'" Zooey argues, "'were just as ac*quis*itive and unattractive, basically, as the rest of us are'" (147–148). Because he was brought up on the same perfectionist principles, Zooey understands Franny's mystical retreat from the world and her hope for some kind of miracle that will provide salvation. Her insistence on a mystical salvation, however, is only another example of the way in which they have been "'sidetracked. Always, always, always referring every goddam thing that happens right back to our lousy little egos'" (151). Zooey does not oppose the Jesus Prayer itself so much as "why and how and *where*" Franny is using it. Franny is not fulfilling any duty in life through the prayer but merely substituting it for her real duty. It is this fatal tendency to leave the realities of life behind which makes Franny and Zooey "freaks." "'You don't face any facts. This same damned attitude of not facing facts is what got you into this messy state of mind in the first place, and it can't possibly get you out of it'" (168). If Christ has a real function, it is not to take man up in his arms and relieve him of all his duties and make all his "nasty *Weltschmerzen*" go away.

In her dedication to the Jesus Prayer Franny has tried to make what Albert Camus regarded as the suicidal leap into faith. Franny's real crisis is not the result of the fact that she has reached an acute depth of despair, but that she is on the brink of becoming, like Seymour, a misfit who can never accept or be accepted by society. Franny is consequently in danger of joining the other Salinger heroes who refuse to come to terms with reality, confusing the life of isolation with the life of the spirit. Despite his disgust with stereotyped scripts and the "phonies" with whom he is so often cast, Zooey has fought to maintain a contact with reality. His realization of the danger of fleeing to the deceptive private world gives him an insight which the rest of the family lacks, and hence he is the only member to have forgiven Seymour his suicide because he is the only one who fully understands it. So anxious is Zooey to maintain his contact with reality—however painful it may be—that he is hesitant about the idea of going to Paris to make a movie. Any movement away from the specific world in which he has suffered seems distinctly suspect. To Franny the idea of making a movie in Paris is exciting, but Zooey counters her, "'It is *not* exciting. That's exactly the point. I'd enjoy doing it, yes. *God*, yes. But I'd hate like hell to leave New York. . . . I was *born* here. I went to *school* here. I've been *run over* here—*twice*, and on the same damn *street*. I have no business acting in Europe, for God's sake'" (136).

After trying unsuccessfully to convince Franny that the Jesus Prayer offers her no answer, Zooey enters Seymour and Buddy's old room. Picking up the phone still listed in Seymour's name, Zooey calls his sister and, disguising his voice, pretends to be Buddy. This is not the call from Seymour which Franny had said she wanted, but Buddy is so much the dead man's spiritual counterpart that there is little difference. Although Zooey's impersonation finally rings false, he has captured Franny's attention, and she is more prepared to listen than she was when he stretched out on the living room floor and lectured her. The absurd vision which Zooey is finally able to impart to Franny is that everything in the world, no matter how base or corrupt, is sacred. Salinger has continually reiterated the fact that "reality" has presented both young people impressions of deceit, pettiness, and insensitivity. The intention to see the world as sacred is, therefore, in total opposition to reality and a profound example of metaphysical absurdity. Until she adopts this vision, Zooey argues, she will never have the religious satisfaction she craves: "'You don't even have sense enough to *drink* when somebody brings you a cup of consecrated chicken soup—which is the only kind of chicken soup Bessie ever brings to anybody around this madhouse'" (194–195). Franny begins to be persuaded when Zooey argues that

> "The only thing you can do now, the only re*lig*ious thing you can do, is *act*. Act for God, if you want to—be *God's* actress, if you want to. . . . One other thing. And that's all. I promise you. But the thing is, you raved and you bitched . . . about the stupidity of audiences. The goddam 'unskilled laughter' coming from the fifth row. And that's right, that's right—God knows it's depressing. I'm not saying it isn't. But that's none of your business, really. That's none of your business, Franny. An artist's only concern is to shoot for some kind of perfection, and *on his own terms*, not anyone else's. You have no right to think about those things, I swear to you. Not in any real sense, anyway. You know what I mean?" (197–198)

Franny's realization—and now also Zooey's own—can come through dedication to her art. Camus saw art as the most complete and successful form of rebellion, since the artist reconstructs the world according to his own plan (his concern "to shoot for some kind of perfection"). "Art is the activity that exalts and denies simultaneously," and it therefore "should give us a final perspective on the content of rebellion." While Camus agrees with Nietzsche's dictum that "'No artist tolerates reality'," he also argues that "no artist can get along without reality."[3] A lack of toleration and an escape are two different things; "art disputes reality, but does not hide from it."[4] Nietzsche had argued that all forms of transcendence were slanders against this world and against life, but Camus envisions a nonsupernatural but "living transcendence, of which beauty carries the promise which can make this mortal and limited world preferable to and more appealing than any other. Art thus leads us back to the origins of rebellion to the extent that it tries to give its form to an elusive value which the future perpetually promises, but of which the artist has a presentiment and wishes to snatch from the grasp of history."[5] Art is a paramount quixotic gesture by which man attempts to give order (at least an order in the same sense of making statements about individual experience or a state of being) to a disordered world. In support of his arguments, Camus cites Van Gogh's complaint as "the arrogant and desperate cry of all artists. 'I can very well, in life and in painting, too, do without God. But I cannot, suffering as I do, do without something that is greater than I am, that is my life—the power to create'."[6]

Zooey has shown his tormented sister the absurd gesture which she can make, and suggests that in making it she will not only affirm her intention to find order and meaning in life but also realize the goal of "The Wise Child," whose obligation it is to both know and be himself. Franny recognizes the validity of this gesture, but Zooey goes on to infuse her with the absurd belief that will give the gesture its final meaning. He recalls that when as a child he had rebelled against having to polish his shoes for the "moronic" audience and sponsors of "It's a Wise Child," Seymour had taken him aside and asked him to shine them for the Fat Lady. "'He never did tell me who the Fat Lady was, but I shined my shoes for the Fat Lady every time I ever went on the air again . . .'" (*FZ*, 199). Zooey always pictured Seymour's Fat Lady sitting on her porch listening to the radio, swatting flies, and dying of cancer. He then learns that Seymour had once told Franny to be funny for the Fat Lady, and the blaring radio and cancer were part of the fantasy Franny had created just as they were part of Zooey's. In the final moments of this "pure and complicated love story" Zooey explains the Fat Lady's identity:

"I don't care where an actor acts. It can be in summer stock, it can be over a radio, it can be over *tele*vision, it can be in a goddam

Broadway theatre, complete with the most fashionable, most well-fed, most sun-burned-looking audience you can imagine. But I'll tell you a terrible secret—Are you listening to me? *There isn't anyone out there who isn't Seymour's Fat Lady.* That includes your Professor Tupper, buddy. And all his goddam cousins by the dozens. There isn't anyone *any*where who isn't Seymour's Fat Lady. Don't you know that? Don't you know that goddam secret yet? And don't you know—*listen* to me now—*don't you know who that Fat Lady really is?* . . . Ah, buddy. Ah, buddy. It's Christ Himself. Christ Himself, buddy." (200)

For a moment all Franny can do—"for joy, apparently"—is cradle the phone in her hands, but at the conclusion of the story she falls "into a deep, dreamless sleep" (201), like the sleep of Sergeant X in "For Esmé—with Love and Squalor." While neither mysticism nor religion in its traditional sense "provides an answer to the search of any of the members of the Glass family, a concern for mystic and religious experience provides a path to Zooey's and Franny's conception of perfect love . . . That conception includes, embraces, and goes beyond the ordinary conceptions of religion and morality (and in its humanness, stops short of mysticism) and can properly be called by no other name than the simple and profound name of love."[7] To love the mercenaries, the butchers, the deceivers, the phonies of the world with the idea that each of them is Christ is to assume a preponderantly absurd stance. Zooey's message is not to love man as Christ would have loved him, but to love man *as* Christ. There is no appeal to a final supernatural authority, no desire for mystical transcendence, no hope that a better world awaits man as a reward for his struggle. Zooey is at last able to convince Franny that, as Sherwood Anderson's Dr. Parcival stated, "everyone in the world is Christ and they are all crucified."

To act with morality and love in a universe in which God is dead (or, at least, in which historical preconceptions of God frequently seem invalid) is perhaps the most acute problem of our age. Salinger's intense consideration of that problem in large part accounts for the fact that, while he is one of the least prolific authors writing today, he is the most popular. The progression from early stories in which the misfit hero can find genuine love only in children to the later stories in which mysticism is rejected in favor of an absurd love stance is a progression whose scope is perhaps not fully measured in the stories which Salinger has written, but more specifically in the personal struggle he has undergone in arriving at this philosophical position. There is no question that the author loves Seymour, and it is with an uneasy feeling that the reader is compelled to reject this Christ-like man. Salinger began the Glass saga with Seymour's suicide, and since that time has been writing his way around and back to that day in 1945 in order to show where Seymour failed. Seymour is at least partly exonerated for making "freaks" of Franny and Zooey when we note that it was his death (and its admission of failure) which saved the youngest Glass children; in a metaphorical sense in no way foreign to Salinger's intention, Seymour (who could, in fact, *see more* than his contemporaries) died that Franny and Zooey might live, and it is in this sense of his almost ritualistic death, rather than in the deluding mysticism of his life, that one seizes on the essence of this character's saintliness. Through Seymour's death, Zooey learns that the Fat Lady, the eternal vulgarian, must not be passed over for any mystical discipline. As Ihab Hassan has observed, "Zooey's message constitutes high praise of life. It is the sound of humility, calling us to *this* world. The vulgarian and the outsider are reconciled, not in the momentary flash of a quixotic gesture, nor even in the exclusive heart of a mystical revelation, but in the constancy of love."[8] And in this light it can, no doubt, be safely conjectured that "the sound of one hand clapping" is precisely, triumphantly, the commonplace sound of the Fat Lady swatting flies.

NOTES

1. Dan Wakefield, "Salinger and the Search for Love," *New World Writing* 14 (1958): 79–80.
2. T. S. Eliot, "The Cocktail Party," in *The Complete Poems and Plays of T. S. Eliot*, pp. 359–360.
3. Camus, *The Rebel*, p. 253.
4. Ibid., p. 258.
5. Ibid.
6. Ibid., p. 257.
7. Wakefield, "Salinger and the Search for Love," p. 82.
8. Ihab Hassan, *Radical Innocence: Studies in the Contemporary American Novel*, p. 283.

BIBLIOGRAPHY

Barr, Donald. "Ah, Buddy: Salinger." In *The Creative Present*, ed. Norma Balakian and Charles Simmons, pp. 27–62. New York: Doubleday, 1963.

Baumbach, Jonathan. "The Saint as a Young Man: A Reappraisal of *The Catcher in the Rye*." *Modern Language Quarterly* 25 (December 1964): 461–472. Collected in *The Landscape of Nightmare*, pp. 55–67. New York: New York University Press, 1965.

Belcher, William F., and James W. Lee, eds. *J. D. Salinger and the Critics*. Belmont, Calif.: Wadsworth, 1962.

Bode, Carl. "Mr. Salinger's *Franny and Zooey*." In *The Half-World of American Culture: A Miscellany*, pp. 212–220. Carbondale: Southern Illinois University Press, 1965.

Booth, Wayne C. "Distance and Point of View: An Essay in Classification." *Essays in Criticism* 11 (January 1961): 60–79. Partially reprinted in Wayne C. Booth, *The Rhetoric of Fiction*, pp. 66, 155, 171, 213, 287. Chicago: University of Chicago Press, 1962.

Buchloh, Paul, ed. *Amerikanische Erzählungen von Hawthorne bis Salinger: Interpretationen.* Kieler Beiträge zur Anglistik und Amerikanistik, Bd. 6. Neumünster: Karl Wachholtz, 1968.

Burrows, David J.; Lewis M. Dabney; Milne Holton; and Grosvenor E. Powell. *Private Dealings: Modern American Writers in Search of Integrity.* Maryland: New Perspectives, 1974.

Detweiler, Robert. "J. D. Salinger and the Quest for Sainthood." In *Four Spiritual Crises in Mid-Century American Fiction*, pp. 36–43. Gainesville: University of Florida Press, 1964.

Faulkner, William. "A Word to Young Writers." In *Faulkner in the University: Class Conferences at the University of Virginia, 1957–1958*, ed. Frederick L. Gwynn and Joseph L. Blotner, pp. 241–245. Charlottesville: University of Virginia Press, 1959.

Fiedler, Leslie. "Boys Will Be Boys!" *New Leader* 41 (April 1958): 23–26. Collected (abridged) in Leslie Fiedler. *Love and Death in the American Novel*, p. 271. New York: Criterion Books, 1960; and in Leslie Fiedler. *No! In Thunder*, pp. 266–274. Boston: Beacon Press, 1960. Reprinted in Grunwald, *Salinger: A Portrait*, pp. 228–233.

Finkelstein, Sidney. "Cold War, Religious Revival, and Family Alienation: William Styron, J. D. Salinger and Edward Albee." In *Existentialism and Alienation in American Literature*, pp. 211–242. New York: International Publishers, 1965.

Freese, Peter. *Die amerikanische Kurzgeschichte nach 1945. Salinger, Malamud, Baldwin, Purdy, Barth.* Schwerpunkte Anglistik, 8. Frankfurt: Athenäum, 1974.

———. *Die Initiationsreise: Studien zum jugenlichen Helden im modernen amerikanischen Roman mit einer exemplarischen Analyse von J. D. Salinger's 'Catcher in the Rye'.* Neumünster: Wachholtz, 1971.

———. "Jerome David Salinger." In *Amerikanische Literatur der Gegenwart in Einzeldarstellungen*, ed. Martin Christadler, pp. 43–68. Stuttgart: Kröner, 1973.

———. "Jerome David Salinger: *The Catcher in the Rye*." In *Der amerikanische Roman im 19. and 20. Jahrhundert: Interpretationen*, ed. E. Lohner, pp. 320–336. Berlin: E. Schmidt Verlag, 1974.

French, Warren. "The Age of Salinger." In *The Fifties: Fiction, Poetry, Drama*, pp. 1–39. DeLand, Fla.: Everett/Edwards, 1972.

———. *J. D. Salinger.* New York: Twayne Publishers, 1963. Rev. ed. *J. D. Salinger.* Twayne's United States Authors Series, 40. Boston: Twayne Publishers, 1976.

———. "Steinbeck and J. D. Salinger: Messiah-Moulders for a Sick Society." In *Steinbeck's Literary Dimension: A Guide to Comparative Studies*, ed. Tetsumaro Hayashi, pp. 105–115. Metuchen, N. J.: Scarecrow, 1973.

Gardner, John. *On Moral Fiction.* New York: Basic Books, 1978.

Geraths, Armin. "Salinger: 'The Laughing Man.'" In *Die amerikanische Kurzgeschichte*, ed. Karl Heinz Göller and Gerhard Hoffman, pp. 326–336. Düsseldorf: Bagel, 1972.

Groene, Horst. "Jerome David Salinger, 'Uncle Wiggily in Connecticut' (1948)." In *Die amerikanische Short Story der Gegenwart: Interpretationen*, ed. Peter Freese, pp. 110–118. Berlin: E. Schmidt Verlag, 1976.

Gross, Theodore L. "J. D. Salinger: Suicide and Survival in the Modern World." In *The Heroic Ideal in American Literature*, pp. 262–271. New York: Free Press, 1971.

Grunwald, Harvey A., ed. *Salinger: A Critical and Personal Portrait.* New York: Harper, 1962.

Gwynn, Frederick L., and Joseph L. Blotner. *The Fiction of J. D. Salinger.* Pittsburgh: University of Pittsburgh Press, 1958. Sections reprinted in Grunwald, *Salinger: A Portrait*, pp. 102–114, 259–266; in (abridged) Belcher and Lee, *J. D. Salinger and the*

Critics, pp. 141–145; in (abridged) Marsden, *If You Really Want to Know*, pp. 45–47; in (abridged) Simonson and Hager, *Salinger's Catcher in the Rye*, pp. 93–94; and in Laser and Fruman, *Studies in J. D. Salinger*, pp. 85–87, 251–254.

Hamilton, Kenneth. *J. D. Salinger: A Critical Essay*. Grand Rapids, Mich.: Wm. B. Eerdmans, 1967.

Harper, Howard M., Jr. "J. D. Salinger—Through the Glasses Darkly." In *Desperate Faith: A Study of Bellow, Salinger, Mailer, Baldwin and Updike*, pp. 65–95. Chapel Hill: University of North Carolina Press, 1967.

Hassan, Ihab. *Contemporary American Literature 1945–1972: An Introduction*. New York: Ungar, 1973. [Pp. 42–44, 64, 71, 88.]

———. "J. D. Salinger: The Quixotic Gesture." In *Radical Innocence: Studies in the Contemporary American Novel*, pp. 259–289. Princeton: Princeton University Press, 1961.

Hipkiss, Robert A. *Jack Kerouac, Prophet of the New Romanticism: A Critical Study of the Published Works of Kerouac and a Comparison of Them to Those of J. D. Salinger, James Purdy, John Knowles, and Ken Kesey*. Lawrence, Kan.: Regents Press, 1976.

Howe, Irving. "The Salinger Cult." In *Celebrations and Attacks: Thirty Years of Literary and Cultural Commentary*, pp. 93–96. New York: Horizon Press, 1978.

Kaplan, Robert B. *Catcher in the Rye Notes*. Lincoln, Neb.: Cliffs, 1976.

Kazin, Alfred. "The Alone Generation: A Comment on the Fiction of the 'Fifties.'" *Harper's* 209 (October 1959): 127–131. Reprinted in *Writing in America*, ed. John Fischer and Robert B. Silvers, pp. 14–26. New Brunswick, N.J.: Rutgers University Press, 1960. Collected in Alfred Kazin. *Contemporaries*, pp. 207–217. Boston: Little, Brown, 1962.

———. *Bright Book of Life: American Novelists and Storytellers from Hemingway to Mailer*. Boston: Little, Brown, 1973.

———. "J. D. Salinger: Everybody's Favorite." *Atlantic* 158 (August 1961): 27–31. Collected in Alfred Kazin, *Contemporaries*, pp. 230–240. Boston: Little, Brown, 1962. Reprinted in Grunwald, *Salinger: A Portrait*, pp. 43–52; in Belcher and Lee, *J. D. Salinger and the Critics*, pp. 158–166; and in Laser and Fruman, *Studies in J. D. Salinger*, pp. 216–226.

Kermode, Frank. "Salinger." In *Modern Essays*, pp. 226–237. London: Collins, 1971.

Landor, Mikhail. "Centaur—Novels: Landor on Bellow, Updike, Styron and Trilling." In *Soviet Criticism of American Literature in the Sixties—An Anthology*, ed. Carl R. Proffer, pp. 28–61. Ann Arbor, Mich.: Ardis, 1972.

Laser, Marvin, and Norman Fruman, eds. *Studies in J. D. Salinger: Reviews, Essays and Critiques of "The Catcher in the Rye" and Other Fiction*. New York: Odyssey, 1963.

Lerner, Laurence. "City Troubles: Pastoral and Satire." In *The Uses of Nostalgia: Studies in Pastoral Poetry*, pp. 130–148. London: Chatto & Windus, 1972.

Lettis, Richard. *"Catcher in the Rye" by J. D. Salinger*. Woodbury, N.Y.: Barron, 1964.

Lundquist, James. *J. D. Salinger*. Modern Literature Monographs. New York: Ungar, 1978.

McCarthy, Mary Therese. "Characters in Fiction." *Partisan Review* 28 (March–April 1961): 171–191. Reprinted in *On the Contrary: Articles of Belief*, pp. 271–292. New York: Farrar, Straus, Cudahy, 1961.

———. "J. D. Salinger's Closed Circuit." *The Writing on the Wall, and Other Literary Essays*, pp. 35–41. New York: Harcourt, 1970.

Malin, Irving. *New American Gothic*, Carbondale: Southern Illinois University Press, 1962. [Pp. 26–35, 59–64, 117–120, 139–143.]

Marsden, Malcolm M., ed. *If You Really Want to Know: A Catcher Casebook*. Chicago: Scott, Foresman, 1963.

Miller, James Edwin. *J. D. Salinger*. University of Minnesota Pamphlets on American Writers, no. 51. Minneapolis: University of Minnesota Press, 1965.

Mizener, Arthur. "The American Hero as Poet: Seymour Glass." In *The Sense of Life in the Modern Novel*, pp. 227–246. Boston: Houghton Mifflin, 1964.

Ortseifen, Karl. "J. D. Salinger: *De Daumier-Smith's Blue Period*." In *Amerikanische Erzählliteratur: 1950–1970*, ed. Frieder Busch und Renate Schmidt v. Bardeleben, pp. 186–196. Kritische Informationen, 28. Munich: Fink, 1975.

Panichas, George Andrew. "J. D. Salinger and the Russian Pilgrim." In *The Reverent Discipline: Essays in Literary Criticism and Culture*, with a foreword by G. Wilson Knight, pp. 293–305. Knoxville: University of Tennessee Press, 1974.

Peden, William. *The American Short Story: Continuity and Change 1940–1975*. Boston: Houghton Mifflin, 1975.

Rees, Richard. "The Salinger Situation." In *Contemporary American Novelists*, ed. Harry T. Moore, pp. 95–105. Carbondale: Southern Illinois University Press, 1964.

Rosen, Gerald. *Zen in the Art of J. D. Salinger*. Modern Authors Monograph Series, 3. Berkeley: Creative Arts Book, 1977.

Rupp, Richard H. "J. D. Salinger: A Solitary Liturgy." In *Celebration in Postwar American Fiction, 1945–1967*, pp. 113–131. Coral Gables, Fla.: University of Miami Press, 1970.

Schulz, Max F. "J. D. Salinger and the Crisis of Consciousness." In *Radical Sophistication: Studies in Contemporary Jewish/American Novelists*, pp. 198–217. Athens: Ohio University Press, 1969.

Simonson, Harold P., and E. P. Hager, eds. *Salinger's "Catcher in the Rye": Clamor vs. Criticism*. New York: D. C. Heath, 1963.

Starosciak, Kenneth. *J. D. Salinger: A Thirty Year Bibliography, 1938–1968*, Wayzata, Minn.: Ross & Haines, 1971.

Stepf, Renate. *Die Entwicklung von J. D. Salingers short stories und Novelettes*. Europäische Hochschulschriften, Reihe XIV, 23. Bern and Frankfurt: Lang, 1975

Tanner, Tony. *The Reign of Wonder: Naivety and Reality in American Literature*. New York: Cambridge University Press, 1965. [Pp. 339–349.]

Voss, Arthur. "The Short Story Since 1940." In *The American Short Story: A Critical Survey*, pp. 302–343. Norman: University of Oklahoma Press, 1973.

Walcutt, Charles Child. "Anatomy of Alienation." In *Man's Changing Mask: Modes and Methods of Characterization in Fiction*, pp. 317–326. Minneapolis: University of Minnesota Press, 1966.

Weinberg, Helen. *The New Novel in America: The Kafkan Mode in Contemporary Fiction*. Ithaca, N.Y.: Cornell University Press, 1970. [Pp. 141–165, 174.]

Wiegand, William. "J. D. Salinger: Seventy-Eight Bananas." *Chicago Review* 11 (Winter 1958): 3–19. Reprinted in *Recent American Fiction: Some Critical Views*, ed. Joseph J. Waldmeir, pp. 252–264. New York: Houghton Mifflin, 1963. Also reprinted in Grunwald, *Salinger: A Portrait*, pp. 123–136; and (abridged) in Marsden, *If You Really Want to Know*, pp. 48–52.

ALAN NADEL

Rhetoric, Sanity, and the Cold War:
The Significance of Holden Caulfield's Testimony

If, as has been widely noted, *The Catcher in the Rye* owes much to *Adventures of Huckleberry Finn*,[1] it rewrites that classic American text in a world where the ubiquity of rule-governed society leaves no river on which to flee, no western territory for which to light out. The territory is mental, not physical, and Salinger's Huck spends his whole flight searching for raft and river, that is, for the margins of his sanity. A relative term, however, "sanity" merely indicates conformity to a set of norms, and since rhetorical relationships formulate the normative world in which a speaker functions, a fictional text— whether or not it asserts an external reality—unavoidably creates and contains a reality in its rhetorical hierarchies, which are necessarily full of assumptions and negations.[2] This aspect of fiction could not be more emphasized than it is by Holden Caulfield's speech, a speech which, moreover, reflects the pressures and contradictions prevalent in the cold war society from which it was forged.

I   CAULFIELD'S SPEECH

An obsessively proscriptive speaker, Caulfield's essay-like rhetorical style— which integrates generalization, specific examples, and consequent rules— prevails throughout the book, subordinating to it most of the description,

From *The Centennial Review*, vol. XXXII, no. 4 (Fall 1988): pp. 351–71. © 1988 by The Centennial Review.

narration, and dialogue by making them examples in articulating the principles of a rule-governed society. In one paragraph, for example, Caulfield tells us that someone had stolen his coat (example), that Pencey was full of crooks (generalization), and that "the more expensive a school is, the more crooks it has" (rule) (4). In a longer excerpt, from Chapter 9, we can see how the details Caulfield sees from his hotel window—"a man and a woman squirting water out of their mouths at one another"—become examples in a series of generalizations, rules, and consequent evaluations:

> The trouble was, [principle] that kind of junk is sort of fascinating to watch, even if you don't want it to be. For instance, [example] that girl that was getting water squirted all over her face, she was pretty good-looking. I mean that's my big trouble. [generalization] In my *mind*, I'm probably the biggest sex maniac you ever saw. Sometimes [generalization] I can think of *very* crumby stuff I wouldn't mind doing if the opportunity came up. I can even see how it might be quite a lot of fun, [qualification] in a crumby way, and if you were both sort of drunk and all, [more specific example] to get a girl and squirt water or something all over each other's face. The thing is, though, [evaluation] I don't *like* the idea. It [generalization] stinks, if you analyze it. I think [principle arrived at deductively through a series of enthymemes] if you really don't like a girl, you shouldn't horse around with her at all, and if you *do* like her, then you're supposed to like her face, and if you like her face, you ought to be careful about doing crumby stuff to it, [specific application] like squirting water all over it. (62)

Caulfield not only explains his world but also justifies his explanations by locating them in the context of governing rules, rendering his speech not only compulsively explanatory but also authoritarian in that it must demonstrate an authority for *all* his statements, even if he creates that authority merely through rhetorical convention.

With ample space we could list all the rules and principles Caulfield articulates. Here are a few: it's really hard to be roommates with people if your suitcases are better than theirs; "grand" is a phony word; real ugly girls have it tough; people never believe you; seeing old guys in their pajamas and bathrobes is depressing; don't ever tell anybody anything, if you do you start missing everybody. We could easily find scores more, to prove the book a virtual anatomy of social behavior. The book, however, also anatomizes Caulfield's personal behavior: he lies; he has a great capacity for alcohol; he hates to go to bed when he's not even tired; he's very fond of dancing, sometimes; he's a pacifist; he always gets those vomity kind of cabs if he goes anywhere late at night, etc.

As the author of the two anatomies, Caulfield thus manifests two drives: to control his environment by being the one who names and thus creates its rules, and to subordinate the self by being the one whose every action is governed by rules. To put it another way, he is trying to constitute himself both as subject and as object; he is trying to read a social text and to write one. When these two drives come in conflict, there are no options left.

Although reified in the body of Holden Caulfield—a body, like the collective corpus of Huck and Jim, that longs for honesty and freedom as it moves more deeply into a world of deceit and slavery—this lack of options reveals an organization of power which deeply reflects the tensions of post-WWII America from which the novel emerged. The novel appeared in 1951, the product of ten years' work. Especially during the five years between the time Salinger withdrew from publication a 90-page version of the novel and revised it to more than double its length, the "cold war" blossomed.[3]

Richard and Carol Ohmann have related *Catcher*'s immense success to the political climate of the Cold War by trying to show that Caulfield provides a critique of the phoniness "rooted in the economic and social arrangements of capitalism and their concealment" (29). Although they tend, unfortunately, to oversimplify both the text and the relationship between literature and history,[4] *Catcher* may indeed reveal what Fredric Jameson has termed the political unconscious, a narrative in which "real social contradictions, unsurmountable in their own terms, find purely formal resolution in the aesthetic realm" (79). As we shall see, Caulfield not only speaks the speech of the rule contradictions embedded in the voice of his age but also displaces it by internalizing it. He thus converts his rhetoric into mental breakdown and becomes both the articulation of "unspeakable" hypocrisy and its critic. Finally, he becomes, as well, for his audience a sacrificial escape from the implications of such an articulation.[5]

II   THE SEARCH FOR PHONIES

Victor Navasky describes the cold war as a period having

> three simultaneous conflicts: a global confrontation between rival imperialisms and ideologies, between capitalism and Communism ... a domestic clash in the United States between hunters and hunted, investigators and investigated ... and, finally a civil war amongst the hunted, a fight within the liberal community itself, a running battle between anti-Communist liberals and those who called themselves progressives.... (3)

These conflicts took not only the form of the Korean War but also of lengthy, well-publicized trials of spies and subversives, in ubiquitous loyalty oaths, in Senate (McCarthy) and House (HUAC) hearings, in Hollywood and academic purges, and in extensive "anti-Communist" legislation. Even three years before Senator Joseph McCarthy's infamous speech alleging 57 Communists in the State Department, President Truman had created a Presidential Commission on Employee Loyalty and the Hollywood Ten had been ruined by HUAC.[6] Constantly, legislation, hearings, speeches and editorials warned Americans to be suspicious of phonies, wary of associates, circumspect about their past, and cautious about their speech. A new mode of behavior was necessary, the President's Commission noted, because America was now confronted with organizations which valorized duplicity: "[these organizations] while seeking to destroy all the traditional safe-guards erected for the protection of individual rights are determined to take unfair advantage of those selfsame safe-guards."

Since uncovering duplicity was the quest of the day, in thinking constantly about who or what was phony, Caulfield was doing no more than following the instructions of J. Edgar Hoover, the California Board of Regents, *The Nation*, the Smith Act, and the Hollywood Ten, to name a very few. The President's Loyalty Commission, for example, announced as its purpose both to protect the government from infiltration by "disloyal persons" and to protect loyal employees "from unfounded accusations." The Commission's dual role, of course, implied dual roles for all citizens: to be protected *and* exonerated. Potentially each citizen was both the threat and the threatened. Because the enemy was "subversive," furthermore, one could never know whether he or she had been misled by an enemy pretending to be a friend; without a sure test of loyalty, one could not sort the loyal from the disloyal and therefore could not know with whom to align. The problem— elevated to the level of national security and dramatized most vividly by the Hiss case—was to penetrate the duplicity of phonies.

This problem manifests itself in Caulfield's rhetoric not only in his diatribe against "phonies" but also through a chronic pattern of signifiers which indicate the truthfulness of Caulfield's testimony. He regularly marks his narration with such phrases as "it (he, she, I, they) really does (do, did, didn't, was, wasn't, is, isn't, can, had, am)," "if you want to know the truth," "I (I'll, I have to) admit (it)," "if you really want to know," "no (I'm not) kidding," "I swear (to God)," "I mean it." The word "really" additionally appears at least two dozen more times in the narration, often italicized. These signifiers, along with those which emphasize the intensity of an experience (e.g. "boy!") or the speaker's desire for clarity (e.g. "I mean. . . .") make Caulfield's speech one which asserts its own veracity more than once for every page of narration.[7]

Because it is so important to Caulfield that the reader not think he is a phony, he also constantly provides ample examples and illustrations to prove each assertion, even his claim that he is "the most terrific liar you ever saw in your life" (16). Examples of such rhetorical performances abounded in the media during the novel's five-year revision period. Like many of the ex-Communist informers of the period, Caulfield's veracity rests on the evidence of his deceitfulness. This paradox is especially foregrounded by a discussion Caulfield has on the train with Mrs. Morrow, the mother of another boy at Pencey. In that discussion, he convinces the reader of his truthfulness with the same signifier he uses to make Mrs. Morrow believe his lies. Although Caulfield feels her son, Ernie, is "doubtless one of the biggest bastards that ever went to Pencey," he tells her, "He adapts himself very well to things. He really does. I mean he really knows how to adapt himself.'" Later he adds: "'It really took everybody quite a while to get to know him.'" Having used "really" as a false signifier, Caulfield in confessing to the reader italicizes part of the word: "Then I *real*ly started chucking the old crap around." The evidence which follows should thus convince the reader that the italicized "real" can be trusted, so that the more he demonstrates he has duped his fellow traveler, the more the reader can credit the veracity of the italicized "real". The *real* crap is that Ernie was unanimous choice for class president but wouldn't let the students nominate him because he was too modest. Thus Caulfield proves his credibility to the reader: he is a good liar, but when he italicizes the "real" he can be trusted. In trying to convince Mrs. Morrow, however, he adds: "'Boy, he's *really* shy'" and thus destroys the difference between italicized and unitalicized signifier (54–57).

III   THE MEANING OF LOYALTY

Although presented as a trait of Caulfield's character formalized in his speech, these inconsistencies reflect as well the contradictions inherent in a society plagued by loyalty oaths. Swearing that something is true doesn't make it true, except at the expense of anything not-sworn-to. There exists, in other words, some privileged set of "true" events marked by swearing. The swearing, of course, marks them not as true but as important to the speaker—the things that he or she wants the audience to believe, cares about enough to mark with an oath. In this way, Caulfield creates a rhetorical contract—the appeal to ethos—which legitimizes the discourse. It does so, however, at the cost of all those items not stipulated: they reside in the margins by virtue of being so obvious that they can be taken for granted or so unimportant that they need not be substantiated. Thus grouped together as the "unsworn," the taken-for-granted and the not-*necessarily*-so become indistinguishable parts of the same unmarked set. This is exactly what, as Americans were discovering, loyalty oaths did to the concept of loyalty. For all constitutions bind those loyal to them, and the failure to take that for granted becomes the failure to grant a group constituted by a common social contract. It leaves the "we" of "We the People" without a known referent and makes it impossible to distinguish the real American from the phony—the one so disloyal that he or she will swear false allegiance, will italicize *real* commitment in order to dupe others.

Since social contracts rely upon rhetorical contracts, the problem then is one of language. But Communism according to its accusers acknowledged neither the same social nor rhetorical contracts. According to a major McCarthy witness, ex-Communist Louis Budenz, Communists often used "Aesopean" language so that, "no matter how innocent the language might seem on its face, the initiate understood the sinister underlying message" (Navasky 32). Because no court recognizes a contract binding on only one party, in dealing with those outside the social and rhetorical contracts, the traditional constitutional rules no longer applied. In his 1950 ruling upholding the Smith Act, under which eleven leaders of the American Communist Party were sentenced to prison, judge Learned Hand indicated that when challenged by an alternative system, "Our democracy . . . must meet that faith and that creed on its merits, or it will perish. *Nevertheless*, we may insist that the rules of the game be observed, and the rules confine the conflict to the weapons drawn from the universe of discourse" [emphasis added]. Because the Communists do not function in the same universe of discourse, the same rules do not apply to them. But, as the need for loyalty tests proved, it was impossible to distinguish those for whom the rules did not apply from those for whom they did.

To do so requires a position outside the system, from which to perceive an external and objective "truth." In other words, one needs a religion, which as Wayne Booth implies is the only source of a truly reliable narrator.[8] All other narration must establish its credibility rhetorically by employing conventions. One of Caulfield's conventions is to acknowledge his unreliability by marking specific sections of the narration as extra-reliable. As we have seen, however, marked thus by their own confessions of unreliability, Caulfield's oaths become one more series of questionable signs, indicating not reliability but its myth. Roland Barthes has astutely demonstrated that a myth is an empty sign, one which no longer has a referent but continues to function as though it did, thus preserving the status quo. The loyalty oath is such a myth in that it preserves the idea of a "loyalty" called into question by its own presence, and in that it is executed at the expense of the field in which it plays—the constituted state to which the mythical loyalty is owed.

Like Caulfield's oaths, loyalty oaths in the public realm also proved insufficient. In a truly Orwellian inversion, the "true" test of loyalty became betrayal. Unless someone were willing to betray friends, no oath was credible.

With the tacit and often active assistance of the entire entertainment industry, HUAC very effectively imprinted this message on the public conscience through half a decade of Hollywood purges. As has been clearly shown, investigating the entertainment industry was neither in the interest of legislation nor—as it could be argued that an investigation of the State Department was—in the interest of national security. It was to publicize the ethic of betrayal, the need to name names.[9]

IV THE IMPORTANCE OF NAMES

If the *willingness* to name names became the informer's credential, furthermore, the *ability* to do so became his or her capital. Thus the informer turned proper nouns into public credit that was used to purchase credibility. Caulfield too capitalizes names. The pervasive capitalization of proper nouns mark his speech; he compulsively names names. In the first three chapters alone, the narration (including the dialogue attributed to Caulfield) contains 218 proper nouns—an average of nine per page. They include people, places, days, months, countries, novels, cars, and cold remedies. Many of the names, moreover, are striking by virtue of their unimportance. Does it matter if "old Spencer" used "Vicks Nose Drops" or read *Atlantic Monthly?* Is it important that these items are named twice? Caulfield's speech merely mirrors the convention of the Hollywood witness by demonstrating the significance of his speech lay in alacrity, not content:

> A certain minimum number of names was necessary; those who . . . could convince HUAC counsel that they did not know the names of enough former comrades to give a persuasive performance . . . were provided with names. The key to a successful appearance . . . was the prompt recital of the names of a few dozen Hollywood Reds [emphasis added]. (Ceplair and Englund 18)

Nor was the suspicion of Hollywood one-sided. Suspected by the right of being potentially subversive, it was suspected by liberals of being inordinately self-censored. Carey McWilliams, writing in *The Nation*, in 1949, bemoans the effects of the "graylist." Intimidated out of dealing realistically with social issues, the movies, McWilliams fears, were becoming more and more phony.

Not surprisingly, Caulfield too equates Hollywood with betrayal and prostitution. The prostitute who comes to his room, furthermore, tells him she is from Hollywood, and when she sits on his lap, she tries to get him to name a Hollywood name: "You look like a guy in the movies. You know. Whosis. *You* know who I mean. What the heck's his name?'" When Caulfield refuses to name the name, she tries to encourage him by associating it with that of another actor: "Sure you know. He was in that pitcher with Mel-vine Douglas. The one that was Mel-vine Douglas's kid brother. You know who I mean" (97). In 1951, naming that name cannot be innocent, because of its associations. Douglas, a prominent Hollywood liberal (who in 1947 supported the Hollywood Ten and in 1951 distanced himself from them) was, more importantly, the husband of Helen Gahagan Douglas, the Democratic Congresswoman whom Richard Nixon defeated in the contest for the California Senate seat. Nixon's race, grounded in red-baiting, innuendos, and guilt by association, attracted national attention and showed, according to McCarthy biographer David Oshinsky, that "'McCarthyism' was not the exclusive property of Joe McCarthy" (177).

If Caulfield is guilty by virtue of his association with Melvyn Douglas, then guilty of what? Consorting with prostitutes? Naming names? Or is it of his own hypocrisy, of his recognition, also inscribed in his rhetoric, that he hasn't told the truth in that he actually loves the movies, emulates them, uses them as a constant frame of reference. The first paragraph of the book begins "if you really want to know the truth" and ends with the sentences: "If there's one thing I hate, it's the movies. Don't even mention them to me." Despite this injunction, Caulfield's speech is full of them. He acts out movie roles alone and in front of others, uses them as a pool of allusion to help articulate his own behavior, and goes to see them, even when he believes they will be unsatisfactory.[10]

This marked ambivalence returns us again to the way historical circumstances make Caulfield's speech, like all public testimony, incapable of articulating "truth" because the contradictions in the conditions of public and private utterance have become visible in such a way as to mark all truth claims "phony." In their stead come rituals of loyalty, rituals which do not manifest truth but replace it. In presenting advertised, televised confessionals, which were prepared, written, and rehearsed, and then were performed by real-life actors, the HUAC Hollywood investigations not only replicated the movies, but they also denied the movies distance and benignity, in short their claim to artificiality. The silver (and cathode-ray) screen is everywhere and nowhere, presenting an act of truth-telling hard to distinguish from its former fabrications, stories for the screen which may or may not have been encoded, subversive messages. So too in "real life"—the viewers of these confessions may have been duped, made inadvertently to play a subversive role, followed an encoded script produced by a secret conspiracy of the sort they're used to seeing in the movies. And of course the movies *can* be believed, for if they cannot what is all the worry about? Why bother investigating the harmless? This was the mixed message of the HUAC hearings: movies were dangerous

because they *could* be believed, and movies were dangerous because they *could not*. One cannot escape such a message by discovering the "truth," but only by performing the ritual that fills the space created by the impossibility of such a discovery. In this light, perhaps, Phoebe Caulfield's role in her school play should be read. When Caulfield asks her the play's name she says:

> "'A Christmas Pageant for America'. It stinks but I'm Benedict Arnold. I have practically the biggest part ... It starts out when I'm dying. This ghost comes in on Christmas Eve and asks me if I'm ashamed and everything. You know. For betraying my country and everything. ..." (162)

The passage accurately summarizes the ideal HUAC witness. The former traitor now starring in a morality play that honors the state through a form of Christian ritual, the goal of which is not the discovery of truth, but the public, "educational" demonstration of loyal behavior, in which the fiction's paragon of innocence and the nation's historical symbol of perfidy validate one another by exchanging roles.

V   Simple Truth and the Meaning of Testimony

Phoebe's play unites the two central loci for phonies in Caulfield's speech, the worlds of entertainment and of education. In questioning the phoniness of all the schools and teachers he has seen, Caulfield again articulates doubts prevalent in the public consciousness, especially as he is most critical of the Eastern Intellectual Establishment. That establishment, with Harvard as its epitome, came to represent for the readers of *Time*, for example, a form of affluence and elitism that could not be trusted. In their education section, the week of June 5, 1950, for example, *Time* quoted I. A. Richards at length on college teaching:

> "You are never quite sure if you are uttering words of inspired ... aptness, or whether you are being completely inept. Often you will find yourself incompetent enough to be fired at once if anybody was intelligent enough to see you as you are. ...
> "'Am I, or am I not, a fraud?' That is a question that is going to mean more and more to you year by year. At first it seems agonizing; after that it becomes familiar and habitual." (65–66)

Again we have the same confessional paradigm. Richards gains credibility by confessing he was a fraud. He also suggests an encoded language meant to deceive the average person—anybody not "intelligent enough to see you as you are"; by implication, those who *were* intelligent enough participate in the conspiracy to keep the fraudulence hidden.

This issue becomes particularly germane in a period when teachers and professors were being forced to sign loyalty oaths and/or were being dismissed because of present or past political beliefs. The central issue, many faculty argued, was that academic personnel were being judged by non-academic standards.[11] Yet Richards' statement could suggest that "true" academic standards were really a myth created by those intelligent enough to know better. Intelligence thus signified the capacity for fraud: only someone intelligent enough to see them as they are had something to hide. Because they knew more, intellectuals were more likely to know something they should confess, and not confessing hence signified probable disloyalty rather than innocence.

Time (1/23/50) made the same inferences about the psychiatrists who testified in Alger Hiss's defense, pointing out that Dr. Murray (like Dr. Binger and Hiss) was a Harvard graduate: "He backed up his colleague, Binger. Chambers . . . was a psychopathic personality. . . . He had never seen Chambers but this did not faze him. He had psychoanalyzed Adolph Hitler *in absentia*, correctly predicting his suicide" (14).

If, filtered through *Time*'s simplifying voice, these doctors seemed foolish accomplices, Hiss himself came to stand for everything that needed exposure and rejection. About his conviction, *Time* (1/30/50) wrote: "[Hiss] was marked as a man who, having dedicated himself to Communism under a warped sense of idealism, had not served it openly but covertly; a man who, having once served an alien master, lacked the courage to recant his past, but went on making his whole life an intricate, calculated lie" (12). Thus the past existed to be recanted, not recounted. The recounted past—the truth of one's past—became living a lie, while recanting revealed Truth, discovered not in past actions but in ideological enlightenment, enlightenment which reveals that one's life was a lie. Analysis is intellectualized lying, *Time* had suggested in its treatment of Hiss's "authorities," part of the Intellectual conspiracy that did not revere the Truth but rather suggested that facts could be contravened by an unseen, subversive presence, knowable only to a trained elite whom the general population had to trust without evidence. For *Time*, truth was less ambiguous, existing in a transparent connection between physical phenomena and accepted beliefs, and with its authority lying outside the speaking subject. Hiss had transgressed by seeking to intervene, to analyze, to apply principles not grounded in Truth but in the trained intellect of a fallen mortal, fallen because he believed in the power of human intervention, the ability of the intellect to discern and interpret.

This too is Caulfield's failing, and he must recognize the error of locating himself as the discoverer, interpreter and arbiter of truth and phoniness. In other words, if his speech constitutes him both as subject and as object, it also constitutes him as testifier and judge, accuser and accused. It has the quality of testimony—the taking of oaths and the giving of evidence to support an agenda of charges. And like much of the most publicized testimony of its day, it has no legal status. As Navasky pointed out about the Hollywood hearings:

> [T]he procedural safeguards ... were absent: there was no cross examination, no impartial judge and jury, none of the exclusionary rules about hearsay or other evidence. And, of course, the targets from the entertainment business had committed no crime. . . . (xiv)

In such a context, it was hard to regard testimony as a form of rhetoric in a forensic argument. Although sometimes masked as such, it rarely functioned in the way Aristotle defined the concept. Rather it more often resembled testimony in the religious sense of confessing publicly one's sins. Caulfield's speech thus simultaneously seeped in conventions of both forensic testimony and spiritual, reveals the incompatibility of the two, in terms of their intended audience, their intended effect, and their relationship to the speaker. Most important, forensic testimony presumes truth as something arrived at through the interaction of social and rhetorical contract, whereas spiritual testimony presumes an external authority for truth; its rhetoric *reveals* the Truth, doing so in such a way as to exempt the speech from judgment and present the speaker not as peer but as paragon.

These distinctions apply particularly to the concept of incrimination. A witness giving forensic testimony always risks self-incrimination; recognizing this, our laws allow the witness to abstain from answering questions. The paragon, who gives spiritual testimony, however, is above such self-incrimination; the paragon knows the Truth and has nothing to fear. Exercising the legal protection against self-incrimination (as many HUAC witnesses chose to do) meant the speaker was offering forensic testimony not spiritual, had thus not found the Truth, and therefore could not be trusted. Designed to protect the individual from self-incrimination, the Fifth Amendment then became the instrument of that self-incrimination. In a society that determined guilt not by evidence but by association and/or the failure to confess, people often found that the only way not to incriminate others was to claim they would be incriminating themselves. Since that claim became self-incriminating, they purchased silence by suggesting guilt. They thus internalized the dramatic conflict between social contract and personal loyalty, with the goal not of catharsis but silence. Autobiography, always potentially incriminating, had become recontextualized as testimony, but testimony itself had been freed of its evidentiary contexts and become an unbound truth-of-otherness. It potentially revealed the other—the subversive—everywhere but in the place he or she was known to be, even in the audience of investigators and/or in the speaker. The speaker, by virtue of testimony's two voices and self-incrimination's merger with its own safeguard, was as much alienated in the face of his or her own speech as in the face of his or her silence.

VI   THE CASE FOR SILENCE

The battle waged internally by so many during the Cold War, between spiritual and forensic testimony, public and personal loyalty, recounting and recanting, speech and silence, created a test of character. No matter how complex and self-contradictory the social text, the individual was supposed to read it and choose correctly. This is exactly the dilemma Caulfield's speech confronts from its first words:

> If you really want to hear about it, the first thing you'll probably want to know is where I was born, and what my lousy childhood was like, and how my parents were occupied and all before they had me, and all that David Copperfield kind of crap, but I don't feel like going into it, if you want to know the truth. In the first place, that stuff bores me, and in the second place, my parents would have about two hemorrhages apiece if I told anything pretty personal about them. (1)

Caulfield will try to tell the truth to this "hearing" without incriminating himself or his parents. But at every turn he fails, constantly reflecting rather than negotiating the contradictions of his world. Against that failure weighs the possible alternative, silence, in the extreme as suicide. The memory of James Castle's suicide haunts the book. Castle, the boy at Elkton Hills, refused to recant something he had said about a very conceited student, and instead committed suicide by jumping out a window. Caulfield too contemplated suicide in the same manner after the pimp, Maurice, had taken his money and hit him (104). This image of jumping out the window not only connects Caulfield with Castle but also epitomizes the fall from which Caulfield, as the "catcher in the rye," wants to save the innocent.

The image of jumping out the window also typified, as it had during the stock market crash of 1929, admission of personal failure in the face of unnegotiable social demands. In 1948, for example, Lawrence Duggan fell or threw himself from the window of his New York office. Immediately Congressman Karl Mundt announced the cause was Duggan's implication in a Communist spy ring; along with five other men, his name had been named at a HUAC meeting. The committee would disclose the other names, Mundt said, "as they jump out of windows."

On April 1, 1950, F. O. Matthiessen, "at the time," in the words of William O'Neill, "the most intellectually distinguished fellow traveler in America" (173), jumped to his death from a Boston hotel window. In his suicide note, he wrote: ". . . as a Christian and a socialist believing in international peace, I find myself terribly oppressed by the present tensions" (Stern 31). Although Matthiessen did not commit suicide solely for political reasons, for the general public his death symbolized the culpability and weakness of the Eastern Intellectual Establishment. His powerful intellect, his political leanings and, especially, his longstanding affiliation with Harvard identified him clearly as the kind of analytic mind that typified the intellectual conspiracy *Time*, Joseph McCarthy, et al. most feared and despised. Like Hiss, he was led astray by his idealism which, in true allegorical fashion, led to deceit and ultimately the coward's way out. *Or*: like many dedicated progressives, he was hounded by witch hunters forcing him to choose between the roles of betrayer and betrayed, and leading him ultimately to leap from melodrama into tragedy. Hero or coward, Christ or Judas—in either case, in the morality drama of his day, he graphically signified the sort of fall from innocence against which Caulfield struggles.[12]

But, in the end, Caulfield renounces this struggle, allowing that one cannot catch kids: ". . . if they want to grab for the gold ring, you have to let them do it *and not say anything*. If they fall off, they fall off, *but it's bad if you say anything to them*" [emphasis added] (211). Thus the solution to Caulfield's dilemma becomes renouncing speech itself. Returning to the condition of utterance, stipulated in his opening sentence, which frames his testimony, he says in the last chapter—"If you want to know the truth . . ." (213), this time followed not with discourse but with the recognition that he lacks adequate knowledge for discourse: ". . . I don't *know* what I think about it" (213–14). From this follows regret in the presence of the named names:

> I'm sorry I told so many people about it. About all I know is, I sort of *miss* everybody I told about. Even old Stradlater and Achley, for instance. I think I even miss goddam Maurice. It's funny. Don't ever tell anybody anything. If you do, you start missing everybody. (214)

These last sentences of the book thus replace truth with silence. The intermediary, moreover, between Caulfield's speech—deemed unreasonable—and his silence is the asylum, and we could say that the whole novel is speech framed by that asylum. It intervenes in the first chapter, immediately after

Caulfield asks "if you want to know the truth" and in the last, immediately before he says he does not know what to think. In this way, the asylum functions in the manner Foucault has noted—not to remove Caulfield's guilt but to organize it "for the madman as a consciousness of himself, and as a non reciprocal relation to the keeper; it organized it for the man of reason as an awareness of the Other, a therapeutic intervention in the madman's existence" (247).

> Incessantly cast in this empty role of unknown visitor, and challenged in everything that can be known about him, drawn to the surface of himself by a social personality silently imposed by observation, by form and mask, the madman is obliged to objectify himself in the eyes of reason as the perfect stranger, that is, as the man whose strangeness does not reveal itself. The city of reason welcomes him only with this qualification and at the price of this surrender to anonymity. (249–50)

In this light, we can see that the asylum not only frames Caulfield's speech but also intervenes throughout as an increasing awareness of his otherness, marked by such phrases as "I swear to God, I'm a madman." Given the novel's frame, it is not astonishing that Caulfield's speech manifests traits of the asylum. In that his speech also manifests the contradictions of McCarthyism and the Cold War, the novel more interestingly suggests that the era in many ways institutionalized traits of the asylum. To prove the validity of his "madman" oaths, Caulfield again must assume the dual roles of subject and object, for as Foucault demonstrates, the intervention of the asylum (and, by extension we can say the Cold War) functioned by three principal means: perpetual judgment, recognition by the mirror, and silence.[13]

Notes

1. Heiserman and Miller make this connection. Others examining the book's relationship to *Adventures of Huckleberry Finn* include: Aldridge (129–31), Branch, Fiedler, Kaplan, and Wells.

2. The relationship between reality and rhetoric has been most fully developed, of course, by Auerbach and, in some ways, modified and extended by Iser's concept of the "implied reader" who is led by an author's strategies of omission to complete the text's implied reality. It is important to note, therefore, that I am not using the word "negation" here in the sense that Iser does, but rather to suggest the "blanks" of Lacanian discourse—something akin to the "blindness" of a text which, for de Man, its rhetoric signifies. For Lacan, de Certeau notes, "'literary' is that language which makes something else heard than that which it says; conversely psychoanalysis is a literary practice of language. . . . At issue here is rhetoric, and no longer poetics" (53).

3. Grunwald (20) and French (26) mention this shorter 1946 version.

4. Miller's response demonstrates that their reading tends to be reductive and ignores much significant textual evidence.

5. For discussion of Caulfield as Christ figure, surrogate, saint or savior, see: Barr, Baumbach 55–67, French 115–17, and Rupp 114–18.

6. See Oshinsky's discussion of "The Red Bogey in America, 1917–1950" (85–102). The literature on American history and politics in the five-year period following WWII is, of course, extensive. Caute provides an excellent bibliography (621–50) for additional references beyond my necessarily selective citations.

7. Approximately one third of the novel is dialogue rather than narration.

8. As a result, the voice-of-God narrator, as typified in the Book of Job, serves as the paradigm of authority against which Booth analyzes other forms of narrative.

9. See Navasky, Ceplair and Englund 254–98, 361–97; Caute 487–538.

10. Oldsey discusses the movies in the novel.

11. See Caute 403–45.

12. Stern: "Those were years in which a person searching for a community of shared socialist and Christian concerns needed the greatest personal support and fortitude to keep from the bottle, from an ignominious abandonment of all previous social concerns, or from the window ledge. Matthiessen chose to end his life, but others of his contemporaries I have known who shared his ideas at some point gave up lifelong commitments to socialism for goals far less honorable during the period" (30).

13. See Foucault 241–78.

Works Cited

Aldridge, John W. *In Search of Heresy: American Literature in an Age of Conformity*. New York: McGraw-Hill, 1956.

"'Am I A Fraud?'" *Time* 5 June 1950: 65–66.

Auerbach, Eric. *Mimesis: The Representation of Reality in Western Literature*, Trans. Willard R. Trask. Princeton: Princeton UP, 1953.

Barthes, Roland. *Mythologies*. Trans. Annette Lavers. New York: Hill & Wang, 1978.

Baumbach, Jonathan. *The Landscape of Nightmare: Studies in the Contemporary American Novel*. New York: New York UP, 1965.

Booth, Wayne. *The Rhetoric of Fiction*. Chicago: U of Chicago P, 1961.

Branch, Edgar. "Mark Twain and J. D. Salinger: A Study in Literary Continuity." *American Quarterly* 9 (1957): 144–58.

Caute, David. *The Great Fear: The Anti-Communist Purge under Truman and Eisenhower*. New York: Simon and Schuster, 1978.

Ceplair, Larry, and Steven Englund, *The Inquisition in Hollywood: Politics in the Film Community 1930–1960*. Garden City, NY: Doubleday-Anchor, 1980.

de Certeau, Michel. *Heterologies: Discourse on the Other*. Trans. Brian Massumi. Theory and History of Literature, vol. 17. Minneapolis: U of Minnesota P, 1986.

Fiedler, Leslie. "The Eye of Innocence." *Salinger*. Ed. Henry Anatole Grunwald. New York: Harper, 1962.

Foucault, Michel. *Madness and Civilization: A History of Insanity in the Age of Reason*. Trans. Richard Howard. New York: Random-Vintage, 1973.

French, Warren. *J. D. Salinger*. New York: Twayne, 1963.

Galloway, David D. *The Absurd Hero in American Fiction*. Revised edition. Austin: U. of Texas P, 1970.

Grunwald, Henry Anatole. "The Invisible Man: A Biographical Collage." *Salinger*. Ed. Grunwald. New York: Harper, 1962.

Hassan, Ihab. *Radical Innocence: Studies in the Contemporary American Novel*. Princeton: Princeton UP, 1961.

Heiserman, Arthur, and James E. Miller. "J. D. Salinger: Some Crazy Cliff." *Western Humanities Review* 10 (1956): 129–37.

Iser, Wolfgang. *The Implied Reader: Patterns of Communication in Prose Fictions from Bunyan to Beckett*. Baltimore: Johns Hopkins UP, 1974.

Jameson, Fredric. *The Political Unconscious: Narrative as a Socially Symbolic Act*. Ithaca: Cornell UP, 1981.

Kaplan, Charles. "Holden and Huck: The Odysseys of Youth." *College English* 18 (1956): 76–80.

Lacan, Jacques. *Speech and Language in Psychoanalysis*. Trans. Anthony Wilden. Baltimore: Johns Hopkins UP, 1968.

Lundquist, James. *J. D. Salinger*. New York: Ungar, 1979.

McWilliams, Carey. "Graylist." *The Nation* 19 Oct. 1949: 491.

de Man, Paul. *Blindness and Insight: Essays in the Rhetoric of Contemporary Criticism*. New York: Oxford UP, 1971.

Navasky, Victor. *Naming Names*. New York: Viking, 1980.

Ohmann, Carol and Richard Ohmann. "Reviewers, Critics and *The Catcher in the Rye*." *Critical Inquiry* 3 (1976): 64–75.

Oldsey, Bernard S. "The Movies in the Rye." *College English* 23 (1961): 209–15.

Oshinsky, David M. *A Conspiracy So Immense: The World of Joe McCarthy*. New York: Macmillan-Free Press, 1983.

O'Neill, William L. *A Better World: Stalinism and the American Intellectuals*. New York: Simon and Schuster, 1982.

Rupp, Richard H. *Celebration in Postwar American Fiction 1945–1967*. Coral Gables, FL: U of Miami P, 1970.

Salinger, J. D. *The Catcher in the Rye*. 1951. New York: Bantam, 1964.

Stern, Frederick C. *F. O. Matthiessen: Christian Socialist as Critic*. Chapel Hill: U of North Carolina P, 1981.

"Trials—The Reckoning." *Time* 30 Jan. 1950: 11–12.

"Trials—Some People Can Taste It." *Time* 23 Jan. 1950: 14.

Wells, Arvin R. "Huck Finn and Holden Caulfield: The Situation of the Hero." *Ohio University Review* 2 (1960), 31–42.

DAVID SEED

Keeping it in the Family:
The Novellas of J.D. Salinger

In contrast with the extensive critical attention devoted to *The Catcher in the Rye* the novellas of J.D. Salinger have, with very few exceptions, either been greeted with silence or disapproval. They have been attacked for being 'hopelessly prolix' (Irving Howe), the products of 'an impersonator of adolescence' (Leslie Fiedler), the result of contradiction since 'Salinger can . . . exercise his art with reverence, while still despising the "culture" which makes it possible' (Frank Kermode), or the result of lost detachment since Salinger 'identifies himself too fussily with the spiritual aches and pains of his characters' (Alfred Kazin).[1] More recently Malcolm Bradbury has argued that Salinger's efforts in these novellas to break through the unavoidable deceits of fiction almost destroy the narrative.[2]

In these attacks there is a consensus that Salinger had lost the critical detachment necessary to view his characters—and especially Seymour Glass—objectively, but in what follows I shall be arguing that the creation of the Glass family as a whole enables Salinger to use a variety of narrative methods which he might otherwise not have had available to him. For the family structure becomes crucial in the definition of his characters and even makes it possible for Salinger to incorporate the reader's anticipated criticisms into his own narrative. Salinger himself evidently viewed his own fictional family with relish for when *Raise High the Roof Beam, Carpenters* and *Seymour—An Introduction*

From *The Modern American Novella*, edited by A. Robert Lee. London: Vision Press; New York: St. Martin's Press (1989): pp. 139–161. © 1989 by Vision Press Ltd.

were published together in book form he declared on the dust jacket that 'the joys and satisfactions of working on the Glass family peculiarly increase and deepen for me with the years.'[3] It is a relish, however, which has not kept him free of repetition or a certain tortuous self-consciousness.

Salinger's first published novellas, *The Inverted Forest* (1947) and *Franny* (1955), both deal with examples of failed self-realization, but use diametrically opposed methods. *The Inverted Forest* differs markedly from his '50s novellas in covering a considerable timespan (1917–37) through an intermittent narrative. The protagonist, Corinne von Nordhoffen, notes in her diary that she loves and intends to marry a boy called Ray Ford. The opening childhood scenes show Corinne's birthday-party (ruined by Ray's non-appearance) and the eviction of Ray and his mother from their apartment. Ray drops out of Corinne's life for twenty years, during which time she jealously guards the privacy of her memories in spite of the perception of one of her dates ('When he found out just how regularly Corinne was making private trips back to her childhood, he tried to do something about it. With the best intentions he tried to set up some kind of detour in Corinne's mind')[4]. His sudden and ludicrous death prevents the 'detour' from materializing, and Corinne makes a successful career for herself on a New York magazine. Coming across some of Ray Ford's poems one day, she arranges a meeting, starts dating him and—in spite of warnings to the contrary—marries him. There now enters the third character in this triangle, an aspiring poet called Mary Croft who brings some of her pieces to New York for Ray to read. Unbeknown to Corinne, they start an affair and run away together. The narrative closes with Corinne's unsuccessful attempt to reclaim her husband.

Salinger's use of a limited point of view, namely Corinne's, is then actually phrased in the third person which implies an alternative perspective without spelling it out. One such implication, for instance, is that Corinne builds up her romantic hopes to fill the void in her personal life whose routine is summarized as a mock-office memorandum shortly before Ray Ford reappears. In fact Salinger makes considerable play of absences, hiatuses and interruptions in this novella to reveal Corinne's sense of value (her office career pales into insignificance before her 'romance') and then to demonstrate the failure of her love. Physical absence—introduced in the early scene of flawed domesticity at Corinne's birthday party—becomes the central theme of this novella where romantic yearning degenerates finally into an undignified and fruitless pursuit. If Corinne's desires become the expression of emotional need, it is yet another irony to this bleak narrative that she should look to a neurotic for satisfaction. Salinger glances repeatedly at Ray Ford's erratic behaviour, his terrifying nightmares and increasing alcoholism, to suggest that he is not in control of his own actions and never responsive to Corinne's overtures. The stylistic expression of this emotional distance is the pointed formality which the narrator adopts in the second half of the novella. Take, for example, the final meeting between the Fords after Ray has inexplicably failed to arrive during the evening:

> At approximately four A.M., having twice walked completely around the block, Mrs. Ford encountered Mr. Ford under the canopy of their apartment house as he was getting out of a taxi. He was wearing a new hat. Mrs. Ford said hello to Mr. Ford and asked him where did he get the hat. Mr. Ford did not seem to hear the question.[5]

The use of what is described as a 'private detective's log' for enumerating actions sets up a gap between Corinne's implied feelings and what is registered in the description. Salinger offers details such as Ford's purchase of his new hat to suggest that there is another action going on elsewhere. If Ford would not take the trouble to dress well for his wife, then who is appreciating the new hat?

As its title suggests, *The Inverted Forest* turns romance and domesticity on their heads. Even Salinger's choice of a name for his protagonist plays its part here, possibly drawing on Madame de Staël's romantic novel *Corinne* (1807) where the eponymous heroine, herself a poetess, holds back from committing herself to the lord she loves and ultimately dies of grief when he marries her half-sister. By retaining this name Salinger points to the grand passions and tragic romantic destiny which are *not* available to his Corinne. In his novella romance is constantly deflated, reduced to absurdity and denied any resolving glamour. *The Inverted Forest* repeatedly reverses romance and domesticity, presenting their absence as farce or black comedy. After Ray and Mary run away together 'Miss' Croft's husband appears at Corinne's apartment, explains that his marriage has been failing, and then tries to proposition Corinne! When Corinne finally tracks down the two fugitives in a mid-Western city her visit takes on a bizarre tone from the constant observation of social courtesies. Not only has the original situation of Mary's visit reversed, but there is no recognition that Ray is Corinne's husband. She rings their bell 'casually, like a salesman or a friend', and the subsequent scene confirms the analogies. This technique of understatement effectively isolates Corinne within a series of events which resemble a comic nightmare. Mary Croft's husband actually reinforces one of the novella's most pointed implications (of Corinne's self-ignorance) when he presents to her an appallingly hearty visiting card which reads: 'I'M HOWIE CROFT. Who the Hell are you, Bud?' When Corinne leaves her husband's new apartment she runs off into night, physically enacting her search for an identity which the novella as a whole has suggested she will never find.

The Inverted Forest exemplifies a category of novella identified by Mary Doyle Springer as 'degenerative or pathetic tragedy' which 'consists in the relentless, relatively simple [in plot], and swift degeneration of a central character into unrelieved misery or death'.[6] Salinger's irony excludes tragedy but retains the degenerative pattern. This pattern emerges through narrative hints, through the use of scenic comment and parallelism (Corinne's visit to her husband's flat repeats Mary's visit to her own), and also through narrative concealment. Salinger's hints direct the reader towards what is *not* disclosed even more than to what is evident on the narrative surface, and this exploitation of a subtext becomes crucial in Salinger's next novella, *Franny*.

With *Franny* Salinger changes his conception of length entirely. *The Inverted Forest* reads at points like a compressed novel, summarizing events of secondary importance so as to narrate the whole fate of its protagonist. For his second novella Salinger contracts the span of the action into a few hours, yet extends their duration by brilliantly exploiting every physical detail and nuance of speech. The location is almost entirely one scene in a restaurant; the occasion is the beginning of a weekend date between two students (Franny and Lane). Where the narrative ironies of *The Inverted Forest* revolve partly around movement from place to place, gesture now assumes importance. Where romance is firmly inverted or blocked (there is no correlation between Ray's poetry and his rôle as lover, for instance) at the expense of any feeling other than panic, Salinger now investigates romantic disappointment with far greater psychological subtlety. Franny's feelings do not follow a trajectory of high hopes being followed by disappointment. What is much more threatening to her is routine, the slippage of her emotions and desires into clichéd patterns.

The narrative begins with a group scene, specifically a group of male students waiting for their dates to arrive by train. Lane stands to one side as if to define himself against the group, but Salinger is careful to state that 'he was and he wasn't one of them.' This apparent paradox really raises a question about the limitations of Lane's individuality. Throughout his writings Salinger shows an acute sensitivity to social cliché and stereotype, sometimes allowing characters to take on substance only after they have been registered as, for instance, 'the gray-haired man' or 'the girl' (in 'Pretty Mouth and Green My Eyes' (1951)). In the case of Lane, Salinger intermittently reminds the reader that he is either typical or likely to conform to typical rôles. Even the lunch which he eats with Franny in Sickler's restaurant is the latest in a series of dates. Unlike Lane, Franny explicitly identifies a number of social types even while she is herself conforming to a typical situation. The girls she has seen on the train and the section men (i.e. students who stand in for tutors) she has described all fit into ironically clear categories, to the annoyance of Lane since she even pluralizes his friend Wally Campbell into a type (Wally Campbells being tiresome name-droppers). Franny's attitude comes to resemble the ironic detachment of the overall narrative voice, but not without physical and emotional cost.

One urgency established in the novella is her efforts to salvage her identity, to prevent herself from becoming a cliché. Hence the recurring pattern in her utterances of critical assertions being followed by waves of revulsion against herself. When Franny tells Lane that she has abandoned a play she was acting in, the text alerts us to a possible histrionic dimension in Salinger's own characters' behaviour. The first conversation in the restaurant is presented in terms of style not content, the latter being almost completely excluded. The following passage is typical:

> Lane was speaking now as someone does who has been monopolizing conversation for a good quarter of an hour or so. . . . He was slouched rhetorically forward, toward Franny, his receptive audience, a supporting forearm on either side of his Martini.[7]

Even Lane's body is rendered theatrically as if his torso were a leading actor and his arms the supporting cast. Franny is a captive audience within a conversation where the participants wait their turn to deliver monologues. The quotation also demonstrates a crucial change in perspective between this work and Salinger's first novella. In *The Inverted Forest* Salinger implicitly demonstrates that Corinne is the foolish victim of her own romantic hopes. Here the ostensible narrative tone is once again impassive, but in fact Salinger's comparison between Lane's posture and a type ('as someone does who . . .') suggests that the narrator is endorsing Franny's own critical insights into typical patterns of behaviour. Indeed, the sense of social behaviour as theatre is everywhere present in *Franny*, emerging through the vocabulary of simulations and semblances. The repeated ways in which Franny and Lane arrange their features so as to play their parts more efficiently, and through such ironies as Franny searching for her obligatory 'lines' after she faints.

Franny has decided to abandon acting when she was backstage, and Salinger also takes us 'backstage' with his protagonist in a number of ways. Franny's revulsion from the patterns of social behaviour defamiliarizes the novella's central situation—a lunch—and transforms it into an exercise of tactics, a psychological struggle between the two participants. Her opposition to Lane emerges partly through her refusal to play out the rôle of a weekend date being wined and dined by her boyfriend, so that she orders a chicken sandwich instead of the restaurant's famous snails. Thwarted from acting out the role he has been expecting, Lane exploits his anger to try to force conformity on Franny—but with no success. Her answers to questions are less than satisfactory ('No, Yes and no. I don't know') and the distance between the two characters widens, Franny watching Lane 'as if he were a stranger, or a poster advertising a brand of linoleum, across the aisle of a subway car' (p. 19). As speech and behaviour become divorced from feeling, Franny's anxieties increase and she seeks refuge in the ladies' room. This withdrawal (she sits in a foetal position) and obliteration of visual perception into a 'voidlike black' is a moment of intense privacy, and Salinger grants us a unique access to her temporary breakdown just as we also gain significant access to her consciousness (Lane's few recorded thoughts are sometimes phrased as hypotheses). Since the use of language in society for Franny is tainted with inauthenticity, then Salinger seems to be setting up an extra-social perspective on Franny.

Unlike the vernacular of *The Catcher in the Rye* (whose careful blend of slang, borrowings from the movies, etc. implies a social group containing Holden and the implied reader), the narrator of *Franny* uses a scrupulously neutral register which contrasts ironically with Lane's idiom. Through this neutral but not unsolicitous language Salinger presents Franny's gradual collapse. The physical symptoms (trembling, nausea, etc.) are clear enough, but even chance remarks ('I look like a ghost') reinforce the sombre theme of Franny's disintegrating identity. Like Holden Caulfield she imagines her own disappearance and experiences waves of vertigo. It should by now have become clear what an enormous gap there is between the novella's ostensible and actual subjects. On the surface Salinger is presenting a weekend date, but beneath the realistic surface he is dramatizing a critical point in a character's breakdown. At this point we should turn to the novella's psychological dimension.

In a long and detailed Freudian reading of *Franny* Daniel Seitzman exposes what he calls the 'psychodynamics' of the work.[8] He locates beneath the surface of the text a struggle for sexual supremacy between Franny and Lane, so that, whatever subject they may be discussing, there is always a deeper and more intense drama going on which becomes more and more evident as the narrative progresses. In summary 'the more Lane tries to prove that he truly possesses the male organ the more Franny tries to prove that he is just as deficient as she.' Seitzman's analysis is particularly useful for drawing our attention to the implications of physical gesture and utterance, and also to the combative logic to the dialogues in the novella which carry from monologue to attack and defence. He is certainly right that Salinger uses speech as part of psychological tactics, and right too that the letter from Franny which Lane reads consists of thinly veiled sexual threats. Thus she writes: 'I hate you when you're being hopelessly super-male and reticent. Not really *hate* you but am constitutionally against strong, silent men. Not that you aren't strong . . .' (p. 10). Hatred and sexual opposition are glossed over by her as charming gaffs, but Franny gives Lane (and the reader) his lead by inviting him to analyze the letter.

Psycho-analysis is a slippery and ambiguous topic in Salinger's fiction. On the one hand (and here his fiction blends entirely into the *New Yorker* ethos of the 1940s and 1950s), it is routinely the subject of ironic jokes. On the other, Salinger clearly builds psycho-analytical subtleties into his fiction, especially the longer works of the fifties. As Seitzman notes, Lane claims not to be a 'Freudian man' in explicating literature, but he then proceeds to act as an amateur psychoanalyst. This activity is complicated by the fact that he is not a disinterested party so that his amateur psycho-analysis becomes part of the overt narrative content, masking his drive for sexual supremacy. After Franny faints she comes to on the couch of the manager's office, i.e. in the posture of a patient undergoing psychoanalysis. Lane then opportunistically uses her passivity to insist on his sexual rights to her, once again partly camouflaging this pressure as concern for her physical welfare. In a sense Lane has won at the end of the novella since Franny is now entirely at his disposal, passively submissive to his plans for the rest of the day.

The one buffer against collapse which Franny carries around with her is a slim volume entitled *The Way of a Pilgrim*. Seitzman's argument would assimilate this text into Salinger's psychological themes, relating it to Franny's repressions. Given the context of allusions to psychoanalysis, it is impossible not to see the book (and the Jesus prayer it contains) in therapeutic terms. However, to do so implicates the reader in the discredited tactics of Lane and goes against the perspective of the novella itself. If Franny defines the measure of importance, then we obviously need to pin down the book's significance for her flight from self-consciousness. *The Way of a Pilgrim* is an anonymous nineteenth-century narrative of spiritual searching by a Russian who travels around the country trying to attach clear meaning to the injunction in I. Thessalonians v, 17, 'pray without ceasing'. Formally *The Way of a Pilgrim* contrasts strikingly with *Franny* in many respects. It is a travel-narrative where Franny herself is relatively immobile; it is punctuated by moments of insight and the seeker is guided by a religious sage, whereas Franny's insights are ambivalent, incoherent and solitary; it is also a text about *using* texts since the pilgrim carries a manual of prayer with him (*The Philokalia*), and a text for use itself, although Franny retreats behind agnosticism in the face of Lane's attacks. The particular episode which Franny describes is a mealtime scene where the pilgrim is welcomed with great hospitality. There is an obvious enough contrast here between the one scene and the situation in Salinger's novella, where Lane interrupts Franny's account by commenting on the frog's legs he is eating.

These intertextual ironies underline the pathos of Franny's predicament, and the Jesus prayer surely tantalizes her by suggesting a way in which words can be once again joined to meaning. The pilgrim's guide (the *starets*) tells him:

> Carry your mind, i.e. your thoughts from your head to your heart. . . .
> As you breathe out, say 'Lord Jesus Christ, have mercy on me'. Say
> it moving your lips gently, or simply say it in your mind.[9]

The prayer is partly about reforming the connections (head to heart, words to truth) which have broken in Franny's case. What fascinates her is the possibility that certain words or even a name 'has this peculiar, self-active power of its own' (p. 34). Where she is trying to resacralize words (to use them repetitively as a kind of mantra), to Lane 'God' is only available as an exclamation. Salinger carefully refuses to be explicit over Franny's degree of success here. When she moves her lips at the end of the novella, there is a clear allusion to the Jesus prayer. But equally well Franny could have lapsed into silent withdrawal.

When *Franny* was published in book form with a companion novella, *Zooey*, John Updike shrewdly pointed out that the volume presented *two* Frannies—one without a background, and one related to the Glass family.[10] This change marks a crucial turning-point in Salinger's career. From now on the family takes on major importance in determining the kinds of narrative he constructs and the kinds of relations available to his characters. *Franny* as a separate novella gains a lot of force from the isolation of its protagonist from any kind of family context. Partly this is a question of Franny's lack of support which increases her vulnerability to Lane's psychological bullying; partly it reflects the novella's emphasis on the present, on the moment-by-moment developments within the immediate situation. When the novella is revised into a family context, Franny is given a past and our view of her changes considerably. The introduction of the Glass family was not an entirely new phenomenon in Salinger's career. As early as 1941 Salinger was considering writing stories about the members of a family—this time the Caulfields—and he subsequently published two narratives ('Last Day of the Last Furlough', (1944) and 'This Sandwich has no Mayonnaise' (1945)) dealing with Holden Caulfield's brothers. Through the 1940s Salinger considered assembling his Caulfield stories into a sequence, but chose instead to incorporate at least two previously published sketches into *The Catcher in the Rye*, which was published in 1951 but which had originally been completed in 1946 as a ninety-page novella.[11]

The first dramatization of a member of the Glass family occurs in the story 'A Perfect Day for Bananafish' (1948), in which Seymour commits suicide. This carefully constructed piece tantalizingly hints at Seymour's behaviour through comments made during a telephone conversation between his wife Muriel and her mother. The latter cryptically refers to 'funny business' or 'the business with the window', although Muriel under-reacts throughout. In her, nonchalance is taken to the point of indifference, suggesting within the first few pages of the story a possible clash of character between husband and wife. The second section, where Seymour chats to a little girl on the beach, raises a second problem in the implied disparity between childish innocence and a near-paranoid sensitivity to other adults, a disparity which informs most of Salinger's fiction.

Two points need stressing here. One is that Salinger first imagined Seymour as a suicide; in the subsequent Glass family novellas he becomes an absent character, a figure who usually precedes the specific narrative. Secondly 'A Perfect Day' conforms to a pattern of well-made short stories published in such journals as the *New Yorker* or *Esquire* in the 1940s and early 1950s which use a dispassionate narrative voice and which conclude with an ironic twist. Seymour's suicide is an understated event which startles the reader and throws him back into the text to look for symptoms. But not much will be discovered because the story's very brevity minimizes information and maximizes the suicide's final impact. Once the suicide has been assimilated into the Glass family mythology a longer narrative form is needed so that the members of that family can ruminate over this appalling event. Seymour (and specifically Seymour's death) becomes a crucial reference-point within the Glass family.

Franny demonstrates several characteristics of Salinger's early stories in spite of its length: the generalized scene-setting, playing off one character against another, the suggestion of imminent crisis and the ambivalent ending. Once seen as a companion piece to *Zooey*, however, it is given a past and sequel; in other words, it becomes relocated within a longer narrative sequence. Even Franny's psychology changes. What emerged initially as a general revulsion from social hypocrisy becomes revised into a specific consequence of Seymour's influence over Franny. The question of identity which Howard Nemerov sees as crucial to the novella form also undergoes revision. Nemerov states that

> the mutual attachment or dependency between A and B [the 'agonists' of the novella] has a mortal strength; its dissolution requires a crisis fatal to one or the other party; but this dissolution is required as salvation.[12]

The application of this generalization to the psychological struggle between Franny and Lane is clear enough.

In *Zooey* the eponymous protagonist replaces Lane as an *ant*agonist, this time with reference to a figure no longer present—to Seymour. Zooey himself makes this replacement explicit (and strengthens links with the preceding novella) by attacking Lane but also takes on Franny's earlier rôle by explaining the meaning and origin of *The Way of a Pilgrim*. His conversations with Franny take up where the first novella left off, since she is again lying on a couch in the posture of a patient. Partly for this reason Daniel Seitzman sees the conversations as 'sessions' where Zooey tries to break down the armour of Franny's identifications, using techniques which are so blatant that they are antitherapeutic.[13] Once again he demonstrates Salinger's psychological subtlety with the difference now that Zooey is well aware what he is doing. The attacks on Franny are all the more telling because they are skilfully directed at vulnerable areas of her adopted piety; Zooey charges her with escapism, sentimentality and spiritual acquisitiveness, making an oddly old-fashioned appeal to duty. He is careful to distinguish his actions from the normalizing procedures of Freudian analysis. Addressing his mother he declares:

> You just call in some analyst who's experienced in adjusting people to the joys of television, and *Life* magazine every Wednesday, and European travel, and the H-Bomb . . . and I swear to you, in not more than a year Franny'll either be in a *nut* ward or she'll be wandering off into some goddam desert with a burning cross in her hands. (p. 88)

Zooey's ironic recitation of all the 'gloriously normal' factors of American life in the mid-'50s suggests a disengagement, a standing off from stereotyped patterns of social behaviour. He is well aware that even piety can fall into these grooves, mocking his mother's dismay that religion might involve inconvenience through a side-swipe at the application of marketing techniques to personality-development by such figures as Norman Vincent Peale.[14]

Our sense of the apartment as a home is crucial here. In *The Catcher in the Rye* Holden's return to his parents' apartment is ambiguous. It cannot function as a refuge, nevertheless it tugs him back; he pays a visit, but almost like a thief since he is only seen by his younger sister Phoebe. In *Zooey* the detailed description of the contents of the family medicine cabinet, of bookshelves and furnishings, becomes an important part of the novella's rhetoric. Buddy describes the living-room as 'a kind of visual hymn to commercial American childhood and early puberty' (p. 97) and states that the furnishings were 'old, intrinsically unlovely, and clotted with memory and sentiment' (p. 98). The slow enumeration of details—purple passages because the sheer detail constantly overwhelms whatever is locally necessary—becomes a means of indicating the past. In an odd and rather cloying way the Glass apartment resembles a private museum dedicated to the vaudeville career of Les and

Bessie, and to the memory of their children's intellectual precocity. When Bessie waxes nostalgic over the years when the children were all together, she is making explicit an emotional undercurrent in Salinger's depiction of their apartment. Similarly Les Glass (one of the most shadowy members of the family), we are told, lives entirely in the past, his one function in this novella being to reminisce over the old days with Franny. The many references to theatre do not at all function like similar references in *Franny* where the reader is invited to consider patterns in behaviour, but are rather assimilated into the family's collective history. They become a means of cementing domestic solidarity because they include Les and Bessie's career, the children's performance on a radio quiz show called 'It's a Wise Child' (no doubt based on an actual show from the '30s called 'Quiz Kids'), and Zooey's present occupation as actor. In the conversations between Zooey and his mother and Zooey and Franny, there is always present an element of the histrionic and appreciation by one speaker of the other's style. While Zooey and Franny may be jockeying for the leading rôle (Zooey says at one point, 'I hate like hell to play Martha to somebody else's Mary' (p. 125)), this rôle is constantly swinging from one to the other as they engage in performances for each other's benefit.

A family is by definition a collective structure of relations, one which can be revealed in fiction by one member talking about another. It is a common tactic in Faulkner's fiction, for instance, for characters to be placed through such 'relating' terms as 'cousin' or 'uncle'. The implied approval between the narrator's intelligence and Franny's view of society in her novella changes into an altogether more explicit relation in *Zooey* where the narrator is named as Buddy Glass, her brother. Immediately our earlier impression of Franny's existential isolation is lost, especially as the sources of information multiply to include Zooey and their mother Bessie Glass. Subject-matter becomes more and more introverted as the members of the Glass family discuss themselves. Now the danger is that Salinger will not multiply points of view rendering problematic the existence of a family structure (as happens in *The Sound and the Fury*) but that he will create a mutual admiration society. Whatever incidental humour the opening conversation of *Zooey* may carry (fussy mother vs. sophisticated and long-suffering son), it also enables the reader to start building up a picture of the family. Narrative comments help this process because they interpret physical reactions on an implied basis of long familiarity ('. . . a flicker came into her eyes—no more than a flicker, but a flicker—of connoisseur like, if perverse, relish for her youngest, and only handsome, son's style of bullying' (p. 68)). The detailed description of Zooey's ablutions (he is taking a bath at the beginning of the novella) does not define him dramatically against another character (as in *Franny*), but draws out his actions as part of a gradual revelation of the Glass family. It is a family which is the real subject, the real focus of attention, and one which absorbs Franny's breakdown into a much broader context.

If the Glass family is a unit, it is a unit without some of its main members. Curiously, as with his planned Caulfield sequence, Salinger only decided to use the family after its leading member had been killed off. When Buddy begins his narrative, he admits that of the seven Glass children 'the senior five will be stalking in and out of the plot with considerable frequency, like so many Banquo's ghosts' (p. 47). In spite of their physical absence Seymour and Buddy exert an important pressure throughout the narrative, so much so that Zooey exclaims against them: 'this whole goddam house stinks of ghosts' (p. 84). If the apartment is haunted, then one way in which Franny's cure could be seen is as a coming to terms with the ghost of Seymour. So when Zooey enters Seymour's bedroom towards the end of the novella, the tone becomes appropriately reverential as if Zooey has entered a shrine. Once again the narrative is slowed down so that the angle of vision can pan round the room registering Seymour's desk and his collage of quotations from world literature. Zooey in effect steps back into the past just as Franny is transformed back into a child as she sleeps ('as though, at twenty, she had chucked back into the mute, fisty defenses of the nursery' (p. 99)), and as she enters her parents' bedroom when her dressing gown 'looked as if it had been changed into a small child's woollen bathrobe' (p. 146). Having both regressed into the past it is appropriate that Zooey's piece of therapeutic wisdom to Franny about the Fat Lady (a composite audience—and fantasy-figure) should come from the dead Seymour.[15] This novella has been attacked repeatedly for being too garrulous, Warren French complaining that 'the author *talks* too much and *shows* too little', but that is not the main problem.[16] Salinger slows down and elongates his narrative so that he can extract the maximum relish out of his cherished Glass family. The length of the novella now offers Salinger the opportunity to savour the gradual release of narrative information, not to unfold a drama, but to build up a picture of the past. The Glass family supplies narrative means (Buddy), leading characters (Zooey and Bessie), subject (Franny) and privileged reference-point (Seymour); thus the family engrosses all the formal aspects of its own narrative. Even an outsider's view of the children as intellectual freaks is assimilated into the family's collective self-consciousness, and this to a certain extent is defused as criticism.

Another critical problem in Salinger's use of the Glass family is that it blurs the boundary of each text and constantly hints at significant events having taken place before the specific narratives begin. The significance of these events has to be taken on trust because the reader is given no direct or impartial access to them. Unfortunately the development of the Glass series has gone hand in hand with the gradual inflation of Seymour into a failed god-seeker. Eberhard Alsen, the only critic to examine the notion of series in any detail, has described the narratives as a composite novel about Seymour's life and his teachings.[17] He sees the guiding principle behind the series as an inspirational theory of art and makes no bones about placing Seymour as leading character. The works are linked, he continues, partly through Buddy's narrative voice and partly through what he calls 'shared references'; i.e. certain key events in the Glass history, most notably Seymour's suicide, which become common points of reference for the Glass novellas. Significantly Seymour's suicide only takes on its portentous significance once Salinger started developing his series. It is never described in the series, only alluded to constantly. Alsen's reading of the Glass series simply accepts Seymour's piety at face value and says little about the rhetorical tactics Salinger uses to convince us of his stature. It is one thing to find a continuity from novella to novella and quite another to reduce all their issues to the single problem of Seymour's stature, which is anyway not constant.

Raise High the Roofbeams, Carpenter falls between *Franny* and *Zooey* in the sense that Seymour is taking on importance but has not yet been transformed into a sage. Like *Franny* it has a naturalistic structure—a segment of Seymour's wedding day in 1942. When he does not appear for the ceremony, the guests disperse in the hired cars. Buddy (the narrator) finds himself squeezed between a Mrs. Silsbury, a benign dwarf who turns out to be a deaf-mute, and the Matron of Honor and her husband. Held up in the New York traffic, Buddy leads them to the Glass children's apartment and supplies them with drinks. When they hear that Seymour and Muriel have eloped, the guests leave. Buddy narrates these events in an ironically distanced tone which concentrates humorously on the variety of reactions to Seymour's non-appearance. In this narrative his absence acts as a comic stimulus to the indignation of the guests, specifically that of the Matron of Honor who attacks Seymour most vociferously. Partly to delay the revelation of his own identity Buddy maintains his silence through these attacks, only 'answering back' through his narrative comments: her stare 'seemed to come from a one-woman mob'.[18] He actually argues with her once he has been fortified with alcohol.

Throughout this novella a dialogue is going on between the Matron of Honor's bullying version of normality and Buddy's general defence of his brother. In that sense *Raise High* restates in comic form the themes of *Franny* where psychological conflict is replaced by temporary disguise. Buddy uses silence to delay revealing his identity, but nothing worse than physical discomfort is at stake for him—certainly not breakdown. Where Franny would like to withdraw from all social forms, Buddy fills the gap left by Seymour to act as host to the others. *Raise High* skilfully balances internal and external views of the Glass family, which suggests that Seymour's status has not yet been fixed, but that it is still a matter of one perspective playing against its opposite. Seymour's piety in *Zooey* has yet to come.

Apart from its situational comedy *Raise High* also devotes a lot of attention to the transmission of information between the members of the Glass family. Once again the effect is to prevent Seymour's significance from being fixed. Buddy's rôle is thus both verbal (as narrator) and transmissive in the sense that he collects the various Glass communications and conveys them to the reader—from his sister Boo Boo's letter about the marriage through to the messages scrawled on the mirror in Buddy's flat to the excerpts he reads from Seymour's diary. The immediate narrative of the characters' movements through the streets of New York foreshadows the diary excerpts in several respects: they are halted by a parade while Seymour's excerpts begin with a parade; his criticism by Mrs. Fedders (his fiancée's mother) have been anticipated by the Matron of Honor, and so on. Temporarily Seymour takes over as narrator giving his version of himself, a psychoanalysis of Muriel and declarations of love which conflict implicitly with his usual criticism of her ('Her marital goals are so absurd and touching').

In spite of being a diary, i.e. a day-to-day narrative, Seymour's account is mostly phrased in the past tense and as such is retrospective. Seymour's account thus joins other accounts in this novella which is ultimately about an enigma. Buddy's narrative is carefully dated at 1955, about 1942 (and he constantly reminds the reader of his youthful naïveté at that time). Seymour's narrative is dated 1941 to 1942, i.e. the months leading up to his marriage. But between the novella's time of action (1942) and time of narration (1955) Buddy has thrown out an intervening date: 1948, the year of Seymour's suicide. In other words, the reader knows about Seymour's fate long before he hears that he has not appeared for his marriage. After Buddy closes Seymour's diary we hear that Seymour and Muriel have eloped. This reads like a romantic resolution but is complicated by Buddy's (and the reader's) knowledge of his death. At the beginning of *Raise High* Buddy recounts a Taoist tale which Seymour had read to Franny when she was very young. It is a parable on perception where a character named Kao is described as follows: 'In making sure of the essential, he forgets the homely details; intent on the inward qualities, he loses sight of the external' (p. 5). Buddy carefully refuses to disclose why he retells this tale—it is certainly not just to supply biographical data about Seymour. The tale, then, is introduced as an enigma and in that respect anticipates the enigmatic qualities of Seymour himself. The crux of the tale is to distinguish between incidental and essential qualities. By stressing how young and confused he was in 1942 Buddy surely implies that he himself was incapable of drawing such distinctions at that time.

Might he not have missed some tell-tale signs in Seymour's diary, for instance, which would explain the mystery of his suicide? *Raise High* seems to be about romantic beginnings but varies its narrative means (having a story within the story and briefly a narrator within a narrator) to raise questions about Seymour's puzzling end.

The development in narrative method from *Franny* through the four subsequent novellas also reflects a growing introversion. *Franny* is recounted by an anonymous self-effacing narrator. *Raise High* introduces Buddy as both narrator and protagonist, but with relatively few asides. In *Zooey* (1957) Buddy offers the reader what he calls a 'prose home movie', implicitly made by the family for its own consumption. He anticipates objections to his own narrative by recasting characters (Bessie, Franny, Zooey) as critics and demonstrates a far-greater self-consciousness about the processes of narration and the verbosity of his own style. In *Seymour—An Introduction* (1959) this self-consciousness reaches its maximum. Plot and narrative sequence give way to a monologue on writing. Bernice and Sanford Goldstein have described this work rightly as a 'fictional treatise on the artistic process', although 'treatise' sounds rather heavy to describe Salinger's ruminating and often playful prose style.[19]

As the title of the piece suggests, Salinger is particularly concerned with beginnings, hence his preliminary skirmishings with the 'general reader' and with the then modish image of the writer as neurotic. The preamble shows Salinger trying to avoid such images and labels, and trying too to avoid any connections with Beat Literature.[20] It becomes increasingly evident that notional distinctions between Buddy as narrator and Salinger himself must break down from the narrator's unmistakable allusions to *The Catcher in the Rye* and to himself as a famous writer. Salinger simultaneously invites the reader to view his statements as directly confessional but sets up a theatrical screen of verbiage where Fieldingesque digressions and agile shifts of narrative posture prevent any sustained self-image from taking shape. John O. Lyons has compared these tactics with the self-conscious Romantic style of Byron's *Don Juan*. He notes:

> In every case there is a difference between the writer and the narrator or hero, but the reader is constantly teased with the similarities between the historical writer and his professional mask or his hero.[21]

Seymour now becomes the personification of a fictional subject, the focus and origin of formal problems of expression. Salinger genially makes it clear why he has abandoned the tightly knit short-story form of his early career using fictive gestures reminiscent of the opening of *Lolita*:

> ... on this occasion I'm anything but a short-story writer where
> my brother is concerned. What I am, I think, is a thesaurus of
> undetached prefatory remarks about him. I believe I essentially
> remain what I've almost always been—a narrator, but one with
> extremely pressing personal needs. I want to introduce, I want
> to describe, I want to distribute mementos, amulets, I want
> to break out my wallet and pass around snapshots, I want to
> follow my nose. In this mood, I don't dare go anywhere near the
> short-story form. It eats up fat little undetached writers like me
> whole. (p. 125)

Salinger humorously identifies himself literally with his own words so that
he becomes a disembodied voice, a series of verbal constructs so expansive
that he needs the extra space of the novella form. In effect he realizes a fear
he expressed on the dust jacket of *Franny* and *Zooey*: 'there is a real-enough
danger, I suppose, that sooner or later I'll bog down, perhaps disappear
entirely, in my own methods, locutions, and mannerisms.'

In *Seymour—An Introduction* these mannerisms are foregrounded so
that their expression becomes the main narrative. Whereas in Franny gaps
in the text corresponded to passages of time where nothing important was
happening (going from the station to the restaurant, for instance), now the
text is ostentatiously interrupted so that the 'author' can get his much-needed
sleep. Ihab Hassan has generalized this verbal self-consciousness into a
characteristic of all of Salinger's novellas which 'makes use of all the resources
of language, including accident, or distortion, to convey an unmediated
vision of reality'. Hassan locates the main theme of this particular novella
as a justification of language 'which must, in the same breath, try and fail to
encompass holiness'.[22] The difficulties and ultimate failure of narrative does
indeed become the subject of *Seymour—An Introduction*.

Although Salinger lays down a credo about the value of the artist-seer
at the end of his preamble, the true progression to his 'introduction' is a
rhythm of composition-decomposition-recomposition. He admits previous
versions of himself but finds it impossible to escape from this egotism
since to do so would be to escape from language itself. So he describes, for
instance, Seymour the Oriental expert, and then dismisses his 'somewhat
pustulous disquisition' on Seymour's poetry before moving on to a new tack.
His monologue (his 'fool's soliloquy' as he calls it at one point) constantly
makes gestures towards his subject, but the biographical data about the Glass
family are repeatedly superseded by comments which remind the reader
of the immediate present, the now of narration; Seymour as subject even
becomes assimilated into the narrator's own self-consciousness as a critic of
his short stories.

In this rôle he is inseparable from the narrator's critical (and usually hostile) attitude to his own sentences, an attitude that leads him to exclaim 'let me not screen every damned sentence, for once in my life, or I'm through again' (p. 122). Just as the narrator breaks his brother down into different Seymours or into different physical details (hair, nose, etc.), so he divides himself into two rôles—the describer and the critic, constantly claiming a mock-reluctance to divulge information. Consistent with its own self-consciousness the narrative does not conclude but ends with a discussion of the impossibility of endings.

This novella is Salinger's most experimental work and one which skilfully converts his characters' anxieties about their identity into problems of fictional representation. The narrator is alert to a critical charge repeatedly brought against Salinger's Glass fiction—that he is trying to induce a mood of reverence in the reader—and this time attempts portrayals of Seymour from different partial angles. Now Seymour becomes interesting not from any insistent guru-like status, but because he eludes portrayal, because the reader cannot quite locate the referent of his name.

Seymour—An Introduction represents a fictional extreme beyond which Salinger cannot go, but it is not the last novella to deal with the Glass family. In 1965 Salinger published *Hapworth 16, 1924*, essentially an extended footnote to the series.[23] It is a fictive transcript of a letter written by Seymour in 1924 to his family from summer camp, edited and transcribed by Buddy. This novella is somewhat staid coming after *Raise High* which complicates chronology and narration to show how Seymour eludes explanation, and after *Seymour—An Introduction* where a scepticism about the efficacy of narration feeds Salinger's one work of meta-fiction. The latter narrative is worthy of Beckett in its repeated gestures towards representation which are immediately followed by destructive dismissals.

In *Hapworth 16, 1924* Salinger has returned to a more conventional literary form (the epistle) where a single document becomes the whole narrative, suggesting that, as Eberhard Alsen points out, Salinger's audience has contracted down to the Glass family itself.[24] *Seymour—An Introduction* brings into question all texts about the Glass family, so that a return to conventional coherence looks like an act of bad faith. Not only that. The very fiction of publishing a letter suggests a presumption of importance in the subject, but the letter is written in a most turgid style (grotesque for a child aged 7!) which Seymour admits but continues. The attempted evocation of precocious wisdom actually becomes a supercilious self-important account of the other children, the attendants and the camp routines. In all of Salinger's six published novellas length is used for quite different purposes—to allow an ironic narrative sequence to take its course, to develop the implications of a specific situation (*Franny*), to unfold a brief sequence of events relating to

Seymour (*Raise High*), to reveal the Glass family (*Zooey*), and to reflect on the actual processes of literary composition (*Seymour—An Introduction*). Here the main point of length seems to be self-display. Seymour disingenuously admits that he is writing a 'very long, boring letter', but presses on regardless, even finishing with a list of books he wants borrowed from the local library. *Hapworth 16, 1924* demonstrates all too clearly Salinger's difficulties with his central character. Seymour simply does not live up to his inflated presentation by the rest of his family. No character could. The use of the Glass family, which goes so far to explain the particular themes and methods of Salinger's novellas, has ended as a pretext for repetition.

NOTES

1. Irving Howe 'The Salinger Cult', *Celebration and Attacks* (London: André Deutsch, 1979), p. 95; Leslie Fiedler, 'Up from Adolescence', *Partisan Review*, 29 (Winter 1962), 128; Frank Kermode, 'One Hand Clapping', *Continuities* (London: Routledge Kegan Paul, 1968), p. 195; Alfred Kazin, 'The Along Generation', in Marcus Klein (ed.), *The American Novel Since World War II* (New York: Fawcett, 1969), pp. 120–21.

2. Malcolm Bradbury, *The Modern American Novel* (Oxford: Oxford University Press, 1983), pp. 145–46.

3. There is evidence within *Hapworth 16, 1924* (Salinger's last published novella) that he was planning to pair it with a story about a party. It is rumoured that this story was actually submitted to the *New Yorker* and then withdrawn.

4. *The Inverted Forest*, *The Complete Uncollected Stories* n.p. [1974], Vol. 2, 19. This work was first published in *Cosmopolitan* (December 1947).

5. *The Inverted Forest*, p. 40.

6. Mary Doyle Springer, *Forms of the Modern Novella* (Chicago: University of Chicago Press, 1975), p. 12. Warren French, one of the few critics to have noticed this novella, sees it as an allegory of the artist's burden (*J.D. Salinger* (Indianapolis: Bobbs-Merrill, 1976), pp. 66–76). One problem with this reading is that it would privilege Ford as protagonist.

7. *Franny and Zooey* (Harmondsworth: Penguin Books, 1964), p. 15.

8. Daniel Seitzman, 'Salinger's "Franny": Homoerotic Imagery', *American Imago*, 22 (1965), p.62.

9. *The Way of a Pilgrim*, trans. R.M. French (New York: Seabury Press [1974]), p.10.

10. John Updike, '*Franny and Zooey*', *Assorted Prose* (New York: Fawcett, 1969), p.182.

11. William Maxwell, 'J. D. Salinger', *Book-of-the-Month Club News*, 7 (1951), 6.

12. Howard Nemerov, 'Composition and Fate in the Short Novel', *Poetry and Fiction: Essays* (New Brunswick, N. J.: Rutgers University Press, 1963), p. 236.

13. Daniel Seitzman, 'Therapy and Antitherapy in Salinger's "Zooey"', *American Imago*, 25 (1968), 140–62.

14. A useful discussion of Peale's exploitation of mass-marketing techniques in the postwar period can be found in Donald Meyer's *The Positive Thinkers* (New York: Anchor, 1960), Ch. xxi.

15. Seitzman (op. cit., pp. 150–51) discusses the complex symbolism of the Fat Lady.

16. Warren French, op. cit., p. 143. His distinction between telling and showing is taken from Wayne C. Booth's *The Rhetoric of Fiction*, but hardly relevant here. A guiding principle of Salinger's Glass fiction is that particular members of the family should bear witness.

17. Eberhard Alsen, *Salinger's Glass Stories as a Composite Novel* (Troy, N.Y.: Whitstow, 1983), p. 109.

18. *Raise High the Roofbeam, Carpenters* and *Seymour: An Introduction* (Harmondsworth: Penguin Books, 1964), p. 26.

19. Bernice and Sanford Goldstein, '"Seymour: An Introduction": Writing As Discovery', *Studies in Short Fiction*, 7 (Spring 1970), p. 249.

20. Salinger's conservative and aloof attitude to the Beats is echoed without the saving grace of the former's witty style by Anthony West who reviewed *The Dharma Bums* in the *New Yorker* for 1 November, 1958: 'As a Zen Buddhist who badly wants to be a Buddha, Mr. Kerouac is even more of an aesthete, and even less of an artist, than he was a hipster—a white bourgeois bohemian pretending just as hard as he could to be a Negro rebel' (p. 164).

21. John O. Lyons, 'The Romantic Style of Salinger's "Seymour: An Introduction"', *Wisconsin Studies in Contemporary Literature*, 4 (Winter 1963), 64.

22. Ihab Hassan, 'Almost the Voice of Silence: The Later Novelettes of J. D. Salinger', *Wisconsin Studies in Contemporary Literature*, 4 (Winter 1963), 6, 14.

23. Published in the *New Yorker* (19 June 1965).

24. Alsen, op. cit., p. 94.

RUTH PRIGOZY

Nine Stories:
J.D. Salinger's Linked Mysteries

From its publication in April 1953, through the heyday of "the Salinger industry" in the 1960s, and intermittently through the 1970s and 1980s, J.D. Salinger's *Nine Stories* has proven an unusually seductive text for critical theorizing.[1] Indeed, even those most devoted to Salinger studies, after the first burst of scholarly enthusiasm, welcomed a moratorium on further efforts to interpret Salinger's *oeuvre*, including this collection for which there apparently could be no final word. What is most striking, after thirty years of critical attention, are the contradictory, even antipodal responses to each of the collected stories. At the heart of *Nine Stories* is a mystery, perhaps epitomized by the "monstrous vacuole" that the narrator sees below the nose of the Laughing Man.[2]

Further, within each story there lie other mysteries, some trivial, some profoundly complex, but all defying easy solutions. To search for a unifying principle in *Nine Stories* is to admit that the individual stories must be bent and shaped to conform to a preconceived pattern. But these stories stubbornly resist such attempts. The clue to the cryptic nature of the collection lies in the Zen koan epigraph that subtly instructs the reader to forgo the effort to devise a too logical scheme linking the individual works that follow. Whatever linkage we may find in the stories derives as much from what is *missing* as from similarities of subject, structure, voice, symbolism, character, milieu,

From *Modern American Short Story Sequences: Composite Fictions and Fictive Communities*. Edited by J. Gerald Kennedy. Cambridge and New York: Press Syndicate of the University of Cambridge (1995): pp. 114–32. © 1995 by Cambridge University Press.

and other literary elements that provoke interpretation. In story sequences, as J. Gerald Kennedy has noted, "recurrent features may disclose differences as readily as similarities."[3] But Salinger's mysteries, finally, disgorge further mysteries, so that whatever unifying pattern we may have discovered (perhaps to render the experience of reading *Nine Stories* less disturbing) simply crumbles into those cigarette ashes that the author so obsessively describes.[4] And perhaps the mysteries in *Nine Stories* account for its continuing appeal as much as does its enormous readability.

The stories are thus characterized as much by discontinuity as by those deceptive surface similarities for which Salinger initially won critical and popular attention: brilliant mimicries of postadolescent speech, accurate depictions of upper-class, sophisticated New Yorkers, memorable evocations of childhood sensitivity and adolescent pain, and repellent glimpses into the "phony" world of material plenty and spiritual waste. Yet each story suggests another dimension beyond the narrative, a realm that exists beyond the silence of the Zen koan. John Wenke sees the Zen koan epigraph as a clue to the collection as a whole, discussing Salinger's interpretive openness and the vexing holes that appear in the narratives.[5] I would like to carry Wenke's argument a step further, by demonstrating how the unifying elements combine with the fragmenting mysteries that shadow each of the stories. Despite persuasive critical interpretations, such problems as the motive for Seymour's suicide, the cause of the Coach's failed love affair, or the impulse behind Teddy's pursuit of death, resound like the hollow echoes in the Marabar caves.[6]

The arrangement of the stories in the collection coincides with the sequence of their original publication as separate works. The first six, "A Perfect Day for Bananafish," "Uncle Wiggily in Connecticut," "Just Before the War with the Eskimos," "The Laughing Man," "Down at the Dinghy," and "For Esmé—with Love and Squalor," dating from January 1948 to April 1950, precede the publication of *The Catcher in the Rye*, and the seventh, "Pretty Mouth and Green My Eyes," was published in the same week in July as the novel. The last two stories, "De Daumier-Smith's Blue Period" and "Teddy," were published, respectively, in May 1952 and January 1953. Salinger would continue writing about characters who first appeared in this collection, the Glass family, in five later stories from 1955 through 1965.[7] He did not alter the publication sequence for the collection, and it is assumed that "De Daumier-Smith's Blue Period" was the first story he wrote after publication of *Catcher*. Although he published "Teddy" after he left New York for his permanent home in Cornish, New Hampshire, in January 1953, he had already made plans for the collection before his move. The immense popularity and immediate cult status among college students of *Catcher in the Rye* insured a wide audience for *Nine Stories*, but clearly readers were intrigued with the volume beyond their fascination with the novel.[8]

Salinger's title, *Nine Stories*, presents the initial interpretive challenge of the collection. Always interested in numbers (tantalizingly so in many instances), the author directs us only to the simple fact that nine stories have been grouped together.[9] We will never know why Salinger settled on such a spare title (think of F. Scott Fitzgerald's first collection, *Flappers and Philosophers*, or Hemingway's *In Our Time*, or Flannery O'Connor's *A Good Man is Hard to Find* for titles of first volumes designed to suggest their contents or to pique the reader's interest), but it is the first of the many puzzles pervading the sequence.

Less simple, but no less inscrutable than the title, the Zen koan epigraph reads: "We know the sound of two hands clapping, / But what is the sound of one hand clapping?" A koan is a problem that defies rational, intellectual solution, the answer having no logical connection to the question. The purpose of the koan for the Zen disciple, as Alan Watts explains, is to present "the central problem of life in an intensified form." For when we accept that there is no solution available through our traditional approaches to problems, we must stop trying, we must relinquish even our right to know and accept life as "free, spontaneous and unlimited."[10] The central fact of Zen, according to D. T. Suzuki, lies "in the attainment of 'Satori' or the opening of a spiritual eye."[11] Thus, at the outset, Salinger presents the reader with a paradox that throughout the book, grows insistent: The stories delineate the path from spiritual death to spiritual enlightenment (*satori*) at the same time that they exemplify the uselessness of imposing *any* pattern, through logical analysis, on this random collection of fiction. This contradiction persists throughout *Nine Stories*, producing a multiplicity of critical responses.

Although Salinger collected the stories in their order of publication, there are connections, illuminating juxtapositions, and incremental repetitions that suggest a more subtle arrangement. The individual titles, with the exception of the last story, derive from the texts they introduce; they are puzzling, intriguing, and literarily unique, in sharp contrast to the title of the volume. These individual titles refer to stories within the stories, or italicize a crucial moment, or allude to place or time. The title "Teddy," for example, proves as cryptic as the story it precedes and the psyche of the child it names.

The arrangement of the stories also illustrates what Kennedy describes as "purposive juxtaposition," where "the differential relationship between two conjoined narratives . . . generates supplemental meanings distinguishable from those of the collection as a whole."[12] Thus, the first two stories are linked by references to place and by similarity of character. The last two are connected by repetitive language, and "For Esmé" and "Pretty Mouth" may be said to find their complementarity in the contrast between redemption and betrayal in love. The third story, "Just Before the War," offers yet a third alternative to the two that precede it in its offering the possibility of emotional openness and compassion. And the questions raised by "The Laughing Man" are linked with those raised by "Down at the Dinghy" and "For Esmé." The following analysis of structuring devices of *Nine Stories*, culminating in questions that elude conclusive interpretation, should clarify the method by which Salinger constructs the linked mysteries of these collected stories.

As in many similar collections, the subjects, characters, and milieus of *Nine Stories* bear many superficial similarities. Four reflect the war, although only in "For Esmé" is there a wartime setting; in the other three, it serves as a catalyst for emotional distress. All but one of the stories ("Pretty Mouth") focus on either very young children or adolescents. All of them concern the plight of sensitive outsiders alienated by a society unable or unwilling to recognize and value their special qualities, their unique sensibilities. Three stories dramatize the relationship between a very young child and a parent or surrogate parent, providing suggestive glimpses into the psychic needs of both. The overriding subject of each story, directly or indirectly, is death—physical, emotional, or spiritual. Clearly, some kind of death is the price Salinger's characters pay for their inability to adapt to a hostile world.

Many of the characters, then, resemble Flannery O'Connor's misfits, although Salinger's are distinguished by minor physical imperfections or quirky behavior, rather than by the cartoonish grotesqueries of O'Connor. Indeed, Salinger's characters are appealing, rather than repellent, in their uniqueness. Seymour is pale, with narrow shoulders and a sickly look, but he is also witty and perceptive; Ramona is pitiable in her homeliness and her need for love and companionship; Eloise is cold and unfeeling, yet even she, reduced to tears by missed opportunities, evokes reluctant sympathy. And a few of the characters find the strength to transcend the banalities and petty cruelties of their world (Boo Boo Tannenbaum, Esmé, Ginnie) to find meaning in a connection to another sensitive hungry soul. Beyond their special gifts, personalities, and desires, Salinger's protagonists prove exceptionally intelligent and occasionally brilliant (Seymour, Teddy, Sergeant X). The major characters show keen insight into others; what they fail to understand they nevertheless question, repeatedly and persistently ("De Daumier-Smith's," "Teddy"). Those questions become as important for the reader as for the characters and enhance the sense of mystery and openness that marks these stories. Further, Salinger's important characters are unusually verbal. Like O'Connor he captures accurately the speech patterns and cadences of his own world, here an educated, often intellectual environment, enlivened by the vitality of adolescent verbal excesses. Like Holden Caulfield in *Catcher*, the characters in *Nine Stories* assume a life of their own (partly, too, because of the stories' lack of closure). It seems entirely fitting that Salinger was moved to continue the saga of a few of them, the Glass family, in his later stories.

The local references in *Nine Stories* clearly indicate a recognizable fictive world: New York City predominates, from the opening line in "A Perfect Day," set in Miami, but alluding to "ninety-seven New York advertising men" (3). In "The Laughing Man," the precise geography of the city forms a substructure for the double-layered story as does the east side of Manhattan for the dramatized encounters of "Just Before the War." Whether the characters are on vacation, on a ship, in a foreign country, or in a Connecticut suburb of the city, the sensibility of Salinger's world is firmly established by its references to the sophistication, polish, manners, and locales associated with the New York City of Salinger's educated upper middle class. Similarly, the temporal signs point to the post–World War II era, not only in stories that refer directly to the war, but also in those stories that capture the characteristics of the period: the sense of estrangement from the past, the reflection of Reisman's "lonely crowd," the adolescent angst seemingly rekindled after the traumatic events of the previous decade, and above all the precise evocation of the era that pondered men in gray flannel suits, their pursuit of thoroughly materialistic ends belying the expressed efforts of the war years to find meaning in a democratic society. Salinger is not a sociological writer, but as surely as in those books that sought to explain what had happened to us materially and spiritually after our wartime victory, *Nine Stories* heralds that period in our nation's history that has been since characterized as frighteningly conformist, spiritually bankrupt, and intellectually adrift—the American 1950s.

In its structural patterns, self-reflexive buried stories, and insistent symbolic motifs, as well as in Salinger's use of narrative voice and evocative language, *Nine Stories* illustrates the cryptic, elusive design of its linked mysteries. Each story, moreover, presents its own challenges.

"A Perfect Day for Bananafish" is divided into two sections, with a brief concluding epilogue. The major divisions dramatize the conversations of two sets of characters, first Muriel Glass and her mother, then Seymour Glass and the child, Sybil (a brief interlude with Sybil and her mother heightens the atmosphere created by the first section and prepares the reader for the Sybil/Seymour meeting). The last section, Seymour's return to his hotel room and stunning suicide, conveys a finality that the preceding events belie. Within the story, as elsewhere in the volume, lies a riddle, or more precisely, a series of riddles, all of which suggest diverse interpretations of Seymour's action: Muriel's mother's concerns about the trees, "that business with the window," remarks to "granny," "what [Seymour] did with all those lovely pictures from Bermuda," the bananafish story, Seymour's playful yet cryptic remarks about his nonexistent tattoo, his injunction to the woman on the elevator not to stare at his toes, his teasing colloquy with Sybil about the color of her bathing suit and other matters of interest to her, and even his faintly ominous control of the child's raft. Further, Salinger's insistent use of numbers, six in particular, invites speculation while defying resolution. After the opening paragraphs that define Muriel with withering precision, the ensuing dialogues reveal the essence of his characters, yet provide possibilities for alternative readings.[13]

Salinger uses a variety of narrative voices and perspectives in the collection. In "A Perfect Day" the narrator (whom some believe is Buddy Glass) is casually omniscient, relinquishing dispassionate objectivity to remark with cruel accuracy, "She was a girl who for a ringing phone dropped exactly nothing. She looked as if her phone has been ringing continually ever since she had reached puberty" (3). The narrative voice is familiarly conversational, blending effortlessly into two lengthy dialogues. The opening story establishes immediately the tone of the volume, an inviting informality, a series of conversations between people we might ourselves know, a perfect mimicry of the cadences and inflections of contemporary speech of his upper-middle-class city dwellers. Indeed, Salinger's language is perhaps the most consistent, recognizable element in *Nine Stories*; it is a unique voice, whether conveyed by authorial omniscience, first-person narrative, or the precise transcription of telephone conversations. That language is a clue to the deeper structure of the fictions is most evident in the first story. After the Muriel/mother dialogue, the second section begins with Sybil's prescient words to *her* mother, "See more glass." With the child's mystifying request, repeated again to her mother and then to Seymour Glass, the reader is covertly instructed to look for the hidden import of the Seymour/Sybil repartee. At the same time, Salinger alerts his readers to the multiplicity of meanings contained in even the simplest assertion.

The next story, "Uncle Wiggily in Connecticut," is structured by time and place, its three sections occurring on a winter afternoon in a wealthy Connecticut suburb. That time is a major issue becomes apparent as Eloise and Mary Jane, her guest, recall their past college days, leading Eloise to recount the tragic event in her past that has corroded her present life as suburban wife and mother. As the two women drink from afternoon into evening, Eloise shows increasing nastiness, exacerbated by the tearful revelation of her lover's violent and senseless death. She expresses her unhappiness in cruel and insensitive remarks to and about her child, in a brusque drunken response to her husband's telephone call (rejecting her maid's request that her husband be allowed to spend the night because of the bad weather), and in a furious heaving of one of her daughter's galoshes over the bannister. Eloise's violent and tragic story repeats itself in her daughter Ramona's imaginative life: The child kills her imaginary companion, Jimmy Jimmereeno. The emotional ending of the story—Eloise's refusal to countenance Jimmy's replacement, Mickey Mickeranno, her tears that wet the lenses of Ramona's glasses, her kiss for the sleeping child, and her final pitiful plea for reassurance that she once was a "nice girl"—fail to alleviate the pervasive bitterness of the narrative tone.

As in "A Perfect Day," the narration is informally omniscient, with an opening description that cruelly mimics the banality of Mary Jane's speech and the bitchiness of Eloise's response to Mary Jane's verbal mistake ("Merrick"): *"Merritt* Parkway, baby" (19). Eloise is immediately identified as someone who does not allow anyone to escape her criticism. Linguistic patterns are again both subtle and obvious: Eloise never addresses Ramona by name, and she is consistently critical and irritable as when she takes the child's galoshes off: "Gimme your foot . . . Sit down, first, please. . . . Not *there—here.* God!" (34). Eloise censures and corrects; she is unresponsive, indeed blind, to her daughter's obvious loneliness and misery. Ramona's eyes, her glasses and myopia, are linked by contrast, with Sybil's unknowingly wise misuse of Seymour's name. Salinger's language again points the reader toward meanings that lie beneath a very detailed and visually explicit surface. Here again the key moments revolve around an adult and a child and stand in sharp contrast to the affectionate exchange between Seymour and Sybil. The juxtaposition of these two stories reinforces the importance Salinger attaches to relations between adults and children.

Although "Just Before the War with the Eskimos" is not linked in the way that its two predecessors are, this two-part story with a brief epilogue nevertheless offers an oblique commentary on what we have already perceived as insensitive responses to extreme suffering. Through the central consciousness of an adolescent girl, Ginnie, Salinger offers a perspective that suggests the redemptive power of compassion. The buried stories here concern her friend Selena's "goofy" brother Franklin's unrequited love for Ginnie's sister, Joan, and his ambiguous relationship with his unpleasant, certainly homosexual friend, Eric. The two major scenes, which take place within an hour in Selena's apartment, reveal Franklin's hopeless ineptitude at life along with his desperate need for human connection (expressed by the sandwich he insists on giving Ginnie) and Eric's intangible yet faintly sinister hold over his friend. The previous stories lead one to expect despair, but this story, primarily through the narrative voice that reflects Ginnie's sustained central consciousness, offers the distinctly redemptive possibility of an unexpected and generous response to a thoroughly unattractive, deeply suffering soul. As different as this story is, it connects to the other two by Salinger's suggestive use of glasses and eyestrain, implying that vision, no matter how difficult to attain, is at the heart of his characters' often ineffectual struggles. Ginnie unconsciously shares Holden Caulfield's dream of rescuing children before they fall off a cliff; Franklin may have already fallen, but like the dead Easter chick it took her three days to dispose of some years earlier, she must save his sandwich and, in so doing, perhaps save him.

Salinger's language is particularly notable in this story; Franklin and Ginnie's loose slang dominates the first section, and Eric's revelatory italicized declamations define his orientation in the second. Throughout, the reader is treated to the observations, clearly through Ginnie's eyes, of a myriad of repellent, often physical details, as when she watches Eric "scratch his ankle till it was red. When he began to scratch off a minor skin eruption on his calf with his fingernail, she stopped watching" (46). Salinger defines his misfits consistently by unattractive physical qualities or behavior, like Ramona's repeated scratching herself and picking her nose.

The fourth story, "The Laughing Man," departs from the first three in narrative structure and voice. Told in four parts from a first-person perspective with minimum dialogue by an adult looking back to a defining moment in his youth, the story also marks the most self-reflexive fiction in the collection. On several occasions, the narrator comments on the difficulty of telling a story, of remembering important details that should not be omitted from his account of the Chief and the boys, the Chief's continuing narrative about the Laughing Man, and the buried mystery of the Chief's broken love affair with Mary Hudson. The narrator thus assures the reader that "the Chief's physical appearance in 1928 is still clear in my mind" (57), and later, referring to the story of the Laughing Man, he asserts, "I'm not saying I will, but I could go on for hours escorting the reader—forcibly, if necessary—back and forth across the Paris–Chinese border" (61). Self-consciously he directs the reader to the story's lingering mystery: "I had no idea what was going on between the Chief and Mary Hudson (and still haven't, in any but a fairly low, intuitive sense)" (70). Actually, in this complex work, three levels of narrative develop: the flashback, the Chief's relationship to Mary Hudson, and the story of the Laughing Man, which the Chief tells in installments for the delectation of the boys who spend their afternoons with him either in sports or in visits to Manhattan museums. As in "Just Before the War," the narrative voice is intimate, deeply involved in the events witnessed. And in both, a revelation of adult pain intrudes piercingly upon adolescent confusion. Here, however, the narrator tells the story of the Chief and the Laughing Man to make sense of something deeply felt, but only dimly comprehended, years ago. In so doing, he recaptures the actual voice of his younger self. The story of the Laughing Man is closely allied to events in the lives of the Chief *and* of the narrator whose identification with the older man is certainly that of a son. And both stories, the Laughing Man's and (by implication) the narrator's, suggest thwarted expectations of the family.

The location of "The Laughing Man" within the collection directs the reader to the problem of storytelling. So unlike the preceding three stories, it illuminates Salinger's exploration of the craft of fiction, and at the same time offers the reader a less tense, less hyperbolic glimpse of suffering and struggle. The language is informal and indirect, with conversations recalled rather than enacted: "I asked her if she had a cold. . . . I told her I didn't have anybody in left field. I told her I had a guy playing center field *and* left field. There was no response at all to this information" (70). The end of the Chief's romance and the violence with which he concludes the story of the Laughing Man profoundly affect the narrator. The elusiveness of both tales, with their shattering finales, adds a tragic dimension to this affectionate memoir of an unforgettable episode of his youth.

The next story, "Down at the Dinghy," returns to the earlier Salinger strategy of presenting a situation through revealing dialogue. Told in four parts by a narrative voice resembling that of the first two stories, it also centers on relationships between adults and children. Yet unlike "A Perfect Day" and "Uncle Wiggily," the key relationship—between mother Boo Boo Tannenbaum and her son Lionel—reveals the affection and understanding of a parent for her child; but structurally it resembles "Just Before the War" in its relatively strong narrative closure and its unity of time and place. The informally omniscient narrator, as in "A Perfect Day," offers with relaxed objectivity a peculiar and certainly puzzling description of Boo Boo: "Her joke of a name aside, her general unprettiness aside, she was—in terms of permanently memorable, immoderately perceptive, small-area faces—a stunning and final girl" (77). Salinger's descriptive prose often contains similarly cryptic lines that reinforce the puzzles developed by the narrative pattern. Like the Chief, Boo Boo creates a fantasy world for Lionel wherein she is the admiral calling her crew with a bugle, but the buried story in this narrative is the mystery of Lionel's repeated running away from his loving, sensitive family.

Dialogue in "Down at the Dinghy" occurs first between two employees of the Tannenbaums, revealing the author's skill at mimicking lower-class inflections and idioms to illustrate their ignorance and bigotry, and then between the mother and son, which recalls Seymour's light bantering with Sybil. Here too, language assumes importance beyond its referential meaning. Just as Sybil's three words suggest deeper implications, the too-obvious meaning of Mrs. Snell's description of Daddy as "a big—sloppy—kike" (86), which Lionel hears as "kite," suggests an adult world that this intuitive child cannot forever flee.

The subsequent story, "For Esmé—With Love and Squalor," connects with "The Laughing Man" as a self-conscious act of storytelling, the first-person narrator addressing the reader with disarming directness. We learn that indeed, it has been written for a specific reader—Esmé—and that this story fulfills a promise the narrator made to her six years earlier during the war. Placed between "Down at the Dinghy" and "Pretty Mouth," "For Esmé" assumes even greater importance than its length and complex narrative structure imply. The stories that precede and follow are dramatic, unified in time and space, whereas "For Esmé" employs two narrative voices (we learn why the voice shifts to omniscient narrator in part four) and recalls several actions occurring over a two-month period six years earlier, first in England, then in an army barracks, and later in New York City where the narrator now lives and writes his story for Esmé.

The opening of this six-part story introduces the narrator, whose voice is assured, ironic, humorous, and confiding. His description of his wife as "a breathtakingly levelheaded girl" and his almost imperceptible dislike of his mother-in-law, "Mother Grencher," stir an interest in the story he tells "to edify, to instruct." Several elusive stories inform the narrative he writes for Esmé, some of which concern the narrator's psychological and emotional breakdown, Esmé's recovery from her own war wounds, and the importance of the Goebbels book to the low-level Nazi official who has left it in the house where Sergeant X (the narrator), who arrested her, finds it. Finally, there is the unspoken question of the life the narrator has been living for the past six years. All of these stories are buried within the central narrative that links his meeting with Esmé, his breakdown and inability to function after leaving the hospital, his alienation from his insensitive fellow soldiers, and finally, the gift from Esmé that restores his hope—and his ability to sleep. An additional layer of narrative complexity lies in the language, especially in Esmé's letter, which reflects with total accuracy the inimitable pattern of her conversation with the soldier in the tea shop on a memorable afternoon in Devon. Like other conversations between adults and children in the collection, theirs is marked by the child's utterly serious demeanor, yet it is unique in the expression of her obvious insecurity, her appealing misuse, yet clear love, of language (including French), and above all her brave efforts, through words, to surmount the stunning loss of her father in the war. The bond of loneliness between Esmé and the narrator is apparent, and both treat little Charles like indulgently appreciative parents. Before Esmé returns to ask him to write an "extremely squalid moving story" (103), the narrator has confessed that her leaving the tea-room "was a strangely emotional moment for [him]" (102). Esmé's parting words, "I hope you return from the war with all your faculties intact" (103), direct the narrator, as well as the reader, to the story he will now write for Esmé.

At this point, the narrator self-consciously begins his narrative, changing the voice from first person to omniscient third person, but with the admonition to the reader not to trust the narrator's objectivity. He says, "I'm still around, but from here on in, for reasons I'm not at liberty to disclose, I've disguised myself so cunningly that even the cleverest reader will fail to recognize me" (103). He is, of course, immediately recognizable as Sergeant X, and his "reasons" become one of the buried stories in the narrative. The narrator also tells his reader that *this* is the way to tell a story.

We learn that the young man has not come through the war with his faculties intact (104) and that he is now pondering the Nazi's inscription in the Goebbels book, "Dear God, life is hell" (105). His response, to inscribe Dostoevski's "'What is hell?' I maintain that it is the suffering of being unable to love," is undecipherable, so complete is the loss of his "faculties." The penultimate section, his conversation with Corporal Z, or Clay, who quotes his girlfriend's letter offering psychological banalities about X's condition, serves as a sharp contrast to the final section when he receives Esmé's gift of her father's watch and reads her formal, precise, infinitely moving letter. Salinger maintains the omniscient narrative voice until the last line of the story, when the narrator speaks directly to Esmé, and by indirection to us, revealing in Esmé's own words the effect of that moment on the broken soldier. "For Esmé" is a long, ambitious, complex narrative that picks up several structural and narrative patterns from previous stories but adds a degree of closure that, although not resolving the questions that remain, makes the experience of reading it enormously pleasurable. Paradoxically, "A Perfect Day," which raises more questions than it can handle, and "For Esmé," which at least on the surface satisfies a reader's desire for a well-made story, remain Salinger's most popular short stories.

The next story in sequence, "Pretty Mouth and Green My Eyes," seems startlingly unlike those that precede and follow it. Both "For Esmé" and "De Daumier-Smith's" are long, multilayered, primarily first-person narratives that draw the reader into the emotional and spiritual conflicts of their protagonists. "Pretty Mouth" is a richly dramatized account of an adulterous affair between a young married woman and her older lover, who are interrupted by two phone calls from the woman's husband who is trying to locate her. The narrative voice is once again cruelly objective, noting apparently trivial details of the couple's activities while the two men are talking. After the opening passage describing the couple with unsparing precision, the ringing telephone and the gray-haired man's efforts to answer it, the rest of the story portrays, through dialogue, a sordid affair, morally squalid lives, and a brief, touching memory—the buried story—of the husband's idealized love. The pathetic second telephone call that reveals the latter's efforts to salvage his pride leave the older man stunned and perhaps angry at himself, and the reader is repelled by this brutal revelation of spiritual waste. "De Daumier-Smith's Blue Period" is constructed in ten parts, with a first-person narrator whose reliability, unlike that of the narrators of "The Laughing Man" and "For Esmé," is distinctly questionable. His narrative voice is insecure and anxious, his imagination given to fevered excursions into fantasy, his responses to situations unexpected or exaggerated. He experiences the pain of facing adulthood after the painful loss of his mother, and he feels sexually jealous of his stepfather.

That he dedicates his story to his late stepfather indicates, however, that he has at last accepted his past, left behind his "blue period," and feels compelled to acknowledge his debt to the man with whom he was engaged in an inner, secret conflict years earlier when they discovered that they were "both in love with the same deceased woman" (133). Indeed, the story, like "For Esmé," is a repayment of a debt by someone who owes his current ability to function (in whatever way he does—his present condition is not made clear in either story) to the person to whom the story is dedicated. Unlike the former soldier in the earlier story, this narrator feels the urgency of correcting a wrong in telling his story: "It's a matter of life and death" to describe his late stepfather as "adventurous, extremely magnetic, and generous," having "spent so many years laboriously begrudging him those picaresque adjectives."

The opening paragraph thus suggests that the story will describe the young man's coming to maturity, which indeed it does, but in such a veiled, convoluted way that critics have differed widely in their interpretations.[14] Once again, Salinger's narrator returns to the past, to 1928 when he was eight years old, to recount the traumatic events that left him a lonely, alienated, sensitive young man. (In this story, as in "Laughing Man" and "Down at the Dinghy," the missing or elusive father figure is the source of disturbance to a child.) In the third part of the story, set in New York's Ritz Hotel in 1939, he finds the advertisement in a Quebec newspaper that will ultimately lead to his psychological and even spiritual regeneration.

The narrative momentum of the story gradually increases after the initial leisurely descriptions of Quebec and the Yoshotos, the couple who run Les Amis Des Vieux Maîtres for whom he is employed as instructor. Parts six, seven, and eight are sharply defined by the narrator's anxiety over a three-day period after he has written to one of his students, Sister Irma, whose work has strangely touched him. The intricately structured narrative reaches its climax in the narrator's real or imagined moment of spiritual illumination—the transmutation of apparatuses (irrigation basins, a truss) in an orthopedic-appliance shop into a "shimmering field of exquisite, twice-blessed, enamel flowers" (164). The unique experiences of De Daumier-Smith raise, however, a number of unanswered questions: what does he see? what prompts his conclusion that "everybody is a nun"? and (perhaps, the most important question contained in his letter to Sister Irma) why does he remember as "pregnant with meaning" the moment at seventeen, when ecstatically happy after a long illness and walking toward Avenue Victor Hugo in Paris, he "bumped into a chap without any nose" (160)? These mysteries connect with experiences within the story, yet questions linger even after the most convincing interpretation. Perhaps because of the openness of the body of the story, Salinger imparts a rare degree of closure as the narrator describes his return to normalcy signified by his reuniting with his stepfather, the apparent resolution of his sexual conflicts (he spends the summer "investigating that most interesting of all summer-active animals, the American Girl in Shorts," 164–5), and the fate of the art school and his pupils.

Salinger once again signals at the outset that language uncovers buried meanings. The narrator recalls a significant incident in New York City when he was nineteen, his "badly broken-out forehead" signifying his difficult late adolescence, when a bus driver says to him, "All right, buddy . . . let's move that ass." For the young man, it is the word "buddy" that deeply disturbs him, and that same word is the linguistic link with the last story, "Teddy," where in the first line a father cruelly mimics his son, using "buddy" as a disparaging epithet.

Despite its verbal and thematic connections to "De Daumier-Smith's Blue Period," the concluding story, "Teddy," is nevertheless the stunning complement to the first story, "A Perfect Day." They are constructed similarly (although "Teddy" is much longer and more philosophically suggestive) and both end in sudden, shocking deaths of the major characters. Indeed, it can be argued that the ending of "Teddy" is another suicide, for if the child *knows* the future and is aware that the swimming pool is empty, then his insistence on meeting his hateful little sister at the pool is certainly an act of self-destruction. Like "A Perfect Day," the opening sections describe through dialogue Teddy's materialistic, selfish, and insensitive parents, and his younger sister Booper, whose words reveal her resentment and rage. The narrative voice remains distant and objective, save for a typical Salinger interpolation when Teddy gives his father a look of inquiry, "whole and pure" (167). Language serves as a thematic link in the first two sections which take place in the family's stateroom. Mr. McArdle repeats his initial rhetorical threat with variations, addressing Teddy by the scathing and impersonal "buddy": "I'll exquisite day *you*, buddy, if you don't get down off that bag this minute" (166) and "I'll *Queen Mary you*, buddy, if you don't get off that bag this minute" (169). The husband and wife exchange remarks that are cruel, even violent: "I'd like to kick your goddam head open" (168), he tells her. His use of "god" and "Jesus" to curse his wife relates to Teddy's rejection of Christianity in favor of Eastern religion, specifically the Vedantic reincarnation and the rejection of emotion in pursuing spiritual advancement. The emotional level of the first section is thus connected to Teddy's need to be released from a world that finds spiritual sustenance in an expensive leather suitcase, a Leica camera, and the paraphernalia of everyday existence. Teddy is a prodigy, and his replies to the young teacher, Nicholson, reveal his intellectual sophistication and youthful intensity. The last sections of the story, like those in "De Daumier-Smith's," concern time: Teddy is intent on meeting Booper at the pool at precisely 10:30 a.m., and he tries to extricate himself from Nicholson's insistent curiosity. The interchange between Nicholson and Teddy provides Salinger with the opportunity to develop the Vedantic approach to spiritual purity, and at the same time to create suspense over Teddy's fate. The last lines, narrated through Nicholson's consciousness, are matter-of-fact, in stark contrast to the horror of Teddy's death and Booper's shriek after she has pushed him into the empty pool. Among the unsolved problems in "Teddy" are the haiku poems, his journal, the origin of Booper's hatred, and above all, Teddy's gift of foreknowledge. "Teddy" provides the perfect bookend to the collection, his death the mystery linked with Seymour's suicide and the many other instances of emotional and spiritual death that pervade the sequence.[15]

The preceding analysis of structural patterns, voice, language, and story arrangement suggests that the occasional links hardly unify the whole collection. Indeed, although Salinger uses repeated symbolic motifs to familiarize the reader with his fictional world and major concerns, they fail to offer a basis for a unified or conclusive interpretation. In addition to the pervasive symbolism contained in references to vision; to repellent physical characteristics and behavior; to cigarettes, ashes, and ashtrays; and to changing seasons, the collection is most suggestive in its symbolic allusions to Dantesque motifs that reinforce the primary conflict in the collection between the material world, a modern "Inferno," and a spiritual realm fitfully imagined but given a degree of shape and substance in the last two stories. An early Salinger critic noted that most of his work "is about those who think they are in hell, a place where the soul suffers according to its qualities, and without escape."[16] In Eastern thought there is no eternal hell, and Salinger's characters, looking for escape from this world, find it either in sleep ("For Esmé") or in an afterlife that offers eternal surcease from pain.

Dantesque motifs include references to the trees (Dante's Wood of the Suicides) that figure as the "whirly woods" of "A Perfect Day" and reappear in the following story set in the same Connecticut location. Seymour's pallor recalls the "death-pale" of Dante's suicides, as does the description of Sergeant X looking like "a goddam corpse." Dante's hell is reflected not only in the "life is hell" inscription on the Goebbels diary but in the popular culture Salinger evokes. As in *Catcher*, the author's favorite expletive is "hell!"

familiar enough in contemporary speech, but symbolically suggestive in the context created by the first story. Muriel reads a magazine article, "Sex is Fun—or Hell," surely a clue to the psychosexual conflicts within most of Salinger's male characters. The tigers in "A Perfect Day" suggest the *Inferno*'s female hell-hounds; and the repeated allusions to the extreme heat in that story, followed by the deathlike cold of the next, suggest Dantesque allusions to extremes of temperature. "Pretty Mouth and Green My Eyes" has also been linked to Dante's *Inferno*, not only through the repeated religious expletives and the fire and ashes, but also through the characters' resemblance to Dante's Paolo and Francesca.[17] If Salinger's Manhattan is hell, a hell of unleashed materialism, then for the tortured souls who inhabit the city, the search for a serene spiritual existence perforce becomes central to their efforts to find meaning where none apparently exists. This, then, is the spiritual level of *Nine Stories*, and it evolves naturally out of the brilliant depiction of a modern urban hell.

Does the search for a way out of hell or for meaning in a spiritual realm create, however, a firm structure linking the stories in the collection? The vexing mysteries raised by individual stories are, if anything, more insistent than any thematic link we may perceive. Indeed, the mysteries that linger after the last story are themselves the meanings that elude us throughout the collection. There have been many brilliant and intricate speculations and interpretations, but these enigmas provide the final link among the *Nine Stories*. I have previously alluded to the questions that remain after Seymour's and Teddy's deaths and the Chief's broken relationship, but they barely hint at the accumulating questions that suggest an ineffable narrative dimension that itself functions much like a Zen koan. They concern the symbolism of the bananafish story; the recurrent patterns of numbers; Eloise's careful placement of Ramona's glasses *lenses down*; her true feelings for her daughter; the source of her sorrow; the nature of Franklin's relationship with Eric; the importance of Franklin's misery to Ginnie; the allegory in the story of the Laughing Man; the meaning of Lionel's flights; the relationship between Boo Boo and her husband; the significance of the Nazi woman's inscription on the Goebbels book; the Sergeant's relationship with his wife; the effect of Esmé's invitation on his marriage; the impulse that led the husband in "Pretty Mouth" to poeticize his wife's eyes; the noises in the Yoshoto's room; the quality of Sister Irma's painting; the connection between the narrator's dentist and Father Zimmerman, who share the same name. Finally, the last story may contain a clue to the meaning of the entire work, but we can never be certain: Teddy may be the psychologically scarred child of cruelly insensitive parents, or he may be a true guru who achieves *satori* by relinquishing his material being.

I am not suggesting that these mysteries are utterly insoluble. They have, in fact, spawned the Salinger industry. But they pose questions that remain even after the most thorough explication has apparently tied up all the loose ends. They suggest the openness of life itself; they suggest the puzzles that Salinger and we well know lie at the heart of all human existence. No attempt to explain *Nine Stories* can erase its mysteries. That is why it is a classic, as fresh today as it was on publication, forty years ago.

NOTES

1. George Steiner, "The Salinger Industry" in *Salinger: A Critical and Personal Portrait*, ed. Henry Anatole Grunwald (New York: Harper & Row, 1962), 82.

2. J. D. Salinger, *Nine Stories* (1953; rpt. New York: Bantam, 1964), 59. Subsequent parenthetical references to Salinger's *Nine Stories* will correspond in pagination to this edition.

3. J. Gerald Kennedy, "Toward a Poetics of the Short Story Cycle," *Journal of the Short Story in English* 11 (Autumn 1988): 11.

4. Two of Salinger's favorite recurring motifs are cigarette ashes and the ashtray. In 1961 Alfred Kazin criticized the excesses of the Salinger industry: "Someday there will be learned theses on *The Use of the Ashtray in J. D. Salinger's Stories*; no other writer has made so much of Americans lighting up, reaching for the ashtray, setting up the ashtray with one hand while with the other they reach for a cigarette." See Kazin, "'Everybody's Favorite,'" in *Salinger: A Critical and Personal Portrait*, 45. James Finn Cotter, acknowledging Kazin's caveat, nevertheless explicates the religious import of Salinger's ashtrays in "Religious Symbols in Salinger's Shorter Fiction," *Studies in Short Fiction* 15 (Spring 1978): 129.

5. John Wenke, *J. D. Salinger: A Study of the Short Fiction* (Boston: Twayne, 1991), 32.

6. Although most commentary on *Nine Stories* has been devoted to individual stories, there have been three major discussions of the collection as a short story sequence, by Wenke (cited earlier), Paul Kirschner, and Warren French. Kirschner finds a "completed pattern" (76) emerging from the collection; French notes that "one develops a sense of an interconnectedness among [the stories], of a progression based upon the slow and painful achievement of spiritual enlightenment ... of successive stages that a soul would pass through according to Vedantic teachings in at last escaping fleshly reincarnations." See Kirschner, "Salinger and His Society," *Literary Half-Yearly* 12 (Fall 1971): 51–60; 14 (Fall 1973): 63–78; and French, *J. D. Salinger Revisited* (Boston: Twayne, 1988), 63–4.

7. All were published first in the *New Yorker*: "Franny," 29 January 1955, 24–32, 35–43; "Raise High the Roof-Beam, Carpenters," 19 November 1955, 51–8, 60–116; "Zooey," 5 May 1957, 32–42, 44–139; "Seymour, An Introduction," 6 June 1959, 42–52, 54–111; "Hapworth 16, 1924," 19 June 1965, 32–113. All but the last story have been collected.

8. *Nine Stories* rose to ninth position on the *New York Times* bestseller list, and remained among the top twenty for three months, a remarkable record for a collection of short stories. The English publisher Hamish Hamilton feared the title would prove a handicap and persuaded Salinger to permit a change. The volume appeared as *For Esmé—with Love and Squalor, and Other Stories* (1955), without the Zen epigraph, and despite the title change, did not achieve the readership of the American edition. Today, *Nine Stories*, like all of Salinger's collected stories and novel, is available in mass-market paperback and sells steadily. See Ian Hamilton, *In Search of J. D. Salinger* (New York: Random House, 1988), 135–6.

9. These stories were selected from twenty the author had already published in such mass magazines as *Saturday Evening Post, Collier's, Good Housekeeping, Esquire,* and the *New Yorker,* as well as in the prestigious small circulation journals, *Story* and *University of Kansas City Review.* The selection reflects Salinger's correct perception of his skills: These are his most polished, skillful, and sophisticated fictions. That all but two originally appeared in the *New Yorker* led many early critics to the conclusion that Salinger's work was in part shaped by the editorial demands of that magazine. That conclusion is too simple; Salinger was already a skilled magazine writer by the time the first of the nine stories had been published. The high standards, editorial receptivity, and general ambience of the *New Yorker* provided Salinger with the ideal outlet for his fiction.

10. Alan W. Watts, *The Spirit of Zen* (New York: Grove Weidenfeld, 1958), 75.

11. D. T. Suzuki, *Essays in Zen Buddhism: First Series* (New York: Grove Weidenfeld, 1961), 37.

12. Kennedy, 16–17.

13. Although early readings of the story almost uniformly saw Muriel as a cold, materialistic woman, whose insensitivity leads Seymour to suicide, recent criticism has looked more charitably upon her and has seen his action as a far more complex response to his spiritual dilemma.

14. See, for example, the discussions by French, 80–3; Wenke, 56–60, who notes the narrator's "diseased imagination" and describes the story as the "most odd and disjunctive" in the collection (59); and Frederick L. Gwynn and Joseph Blotner's fine analysis of the Oedipal conflict in the story in *The Fiction of J. D. Salinger* (Pittsburgh: University of Pittsburgh Press, 1958), 33–40.

15. The ending of "Teddy" illustrates the varying degrees of narrative closure in the volume. "A Perfect Day" and "Teddy" are the most open, perhaps because the endings do not settle any of the questions they raise. The muted endings of "The Laughing Man" and "Uncle Wiggily" also resist closure, and "Pretty Mouth" ends abruptly, but there is no resolution for any of the characters. The other four stories, "Just Before the War," "For Esmé," "Down at the Dinghy," and "De Daumier-Smith's," are the most structurally complete, with the strongest degree of narrative closure, yet the questions within these stories are no less insistent than in those that remain open-ended.

16. Donald Barr continues: "Ten people have read and enjoyed the *Inferno* for everyone who has read the *Purgatorio* or the *Paradiso.* It is fun; like looking at real estate, it gives us a sense of our own possibilities. But Salinger's hell is different. It is hell for the good, who can feel pain, who really love or hope to love." See his "Saints, Pilgrims and Artists," in *Salinger: A Critical and Personal Portrait,* 174.

17. John Hagopian, "'Pretty Mouth and Green My Eyes': Salinger's Paolo and Francesca in New York," *Modern Fiction Studies* 12 (Autumn 1966): 353.

ANTHONY KAUFMAN

"Along this road goes no one": Salinger's "Teddy" and the Failure of Love

The reputation of J. D. Salinger rests largely on two relatively short works: *The Catcher in the Rye* and *Nine Stories*. The *Nine Stories* collection is brilliant, but it is seemingly marred by the final story, "Teddy." Salinger himself seems to dismiss the story. In what can be read as his own commentary, Salinger, through his arch, uncertain disguise as Buddy Glass, in *Seymour— An Introduction*, calls "Teddy" "an ex*cep*tionally Haunting, Memorable, unpleasantly controversial, and thoroughly unsuccessful short story" (205). Critics have generally agreed, objecting particularly to the seemingly contrived character of Teddy who claims that he is a 10-year-old perfect master, equipped with clairvoyance, and to the ambiguity of the conclusion, where it is not entirely clear what happens.[1]

But despite these seemingly well-founded objections, I will argue that the story is highly successful—indeed deeply moving—when we understand that "Teddy" is the story not of a cool and detached mystical prodigy, but of an unloved, frightened 10-year-old. Teddy has reacted defensively to an exploitative adult world by intuitively developing the persona of the mystic and clairvoyant both to gain the love he desperately needs and, paradoxically, to distance himself from his uncaring family and the grown-up world. Although critics have in general taken straight the premise that Teddy is indeed a little swami and analyzed in depth the

From *Studies in Short Fiction* 35 (1998): pp. 129–140. © 1998 by Newberry College.

importance of Zen to this story and to Salinger generally, it is only when we peel away the overlay of mysticism that the story becomes coherent and moving—and only then does "Teddy" become a valid and satisfactory conclusion to the *Nine Stories* collection. We will see, however, that the mystic elements of the story are indeed crucial, although not in the way that critics have suggested.

What has happened is this: in defensive reaction to the egotism, lovelessness, and incessant hostility of his parents toward each other and toward their children, and reinforced by his sense of the vulgarity, selfishness, and materialism of grown-up life, Teddy has instinctively felt his way to creating his persona of the mystic savant. That is, based on his precocious acquaintance (perhaps through Alan Watts and Dr. Suzuki?) in Eastern philosophy, he has convinced himself (and some of the grown-up world) of his mystic powers.[2] The benefits of this disguise to Teddy are several: not only can he withdraw from his parents, and the adult world more generally, and ward off feelings of anxiety and depression that any 10 year old might experience in his difficult family situation—he can also vent his feelings of anger toward them through his pose of studied responsibility and tolerant acceptance of their faults. He can feel distanced from a frightening world, sought-after, superior. He can believe that he has control of his 10-year-old world. His disguise of perfect master (although extreme) has affinities with the defensive use of the imagination by other children in the *Nine Stories* collection: Ramona's imaginary lover and defender Jimmy in "Uncle Wiggily in Connecticut," the precocious adult-like attitude of Esmé, and the pretentious self-presentation of De Daumier-Smith.

Thus the story "Teddy" works in two ways, both to portray Salinger's characteristic child victim (and thus it forms a satiric comment on the adult world), and also to create an interesting and credible study of the way in which a 10-year-old has intuitively defended himself against the ego, anger, and indifference that his parents and the adult world have inflicted upon him. In its portrayal of the underloved child, "Teddy" embodies the Salinger masterplot as seen in *Catcher* and the other stories of *Nine Stories*.

Yet Salinger makes another, highly important use of the mysticism Teddy explains and advocates. The doctrine of love he preaches represents a valid and necessary response to the world and suggests the author's putative answer to the problems seen throughout *Nine Stories* and, indeed, all of his published fiction. In reaction to the harshness of American life, it is necessary to return acceptance, tolerance, and love. This response is clearly seen, for example, in the longer story, "Franny," in which Zooey's sermon on the fat lady suggests this selfless way of encountering the world. I think then that Warren French is only partly correct when he insists that "One misleading thing about the story is that Teddy's palaver creates the feeling

that mysticism is in some way involved in what happens" (*J. D. Salinger* 134). If we are misled into believing that Teddy himself is truly a mystic and clairvoyant, the story fails: it is incredible. But the ethic that Teddy derives from his acquaintance with Eastern religion stands in the story as a potential response to the difficulties of life in America. Teddy's doctrine of love is both defense and valid response to the crummy world. As such, it is a satisfactory conclusion to the *Nine Stories*, all of which dramatize the difficulties of "being born in an American body."

We must see, moreover, that Teddy's sense of not being loved has produced in him an anger that is both expressed through and disguised by his pose of the junior savant. His response to the adult world is carefully controlled passive aggression, seen chiefly in his polite contempt for his parents and later the intrusive Nicholson. His obliquely expressed anger may be sensed, for example, in his response to Nicholson's inquiry about the education of children. Teddy, who equates "logic and intellectual stuff" with the fatal apple of Eden, responds: "I'd just make them vomit up every bit of the apple their parents and everybody made them take a bite out of" (106). The violent image of forcing small children to vomit up a kind of poison thrust upon them by the adult world suggests Teddy's anger and his sense that he and children generally are being poisoned by being brought up "in an American body."[3]

Like his spiritual kinsman, Seymour Glass of the collection's first story, whose importance to the later story I will discuss, Teddy, I would argue, commits suicide as the ultimate gesture of hostility and withdrawal, carefully planning it in advance to inspire terror and guilt. He deliberately designs his death so that the hateful Booper should be witness and victim, and her horror will later, of course, be shared by his miserable parents.

2

It is useful to approach Teddy through the first story in the collection: "A Perfect Day for Bananafish," since, I believe, *Nine Stories* reveals a thematic unity. The centrality of the character Seymour Glass to Salinger's fiction is well understood. Teddy and Seymour are closely related characters. Salinger called attention to the parallels between Teddy and Seymour in his introduction to *Seymour—An Introduction*, where, with irritating coyness, Salinger/Buddy says that some of the Glass family members thought that his description of Teddy's eyes looked very much like those of Seymour: "at least two members of my family knew and remarked that I was trying to get at his eyes with that description, [of Teddy's eyes] and even felt that I hadn't brought it off too badly, in a *peculiar* way" (132).[4] Surely a similarity of vision is suggested in the two characters. In *Seymour* the narrator, Buddy Glass, a writer, says with wry amusement that some people tell him that all his stories are about one person only: Seymour.

"Teddy," the last story of the collection ends, as does the first story "A Perfect Day for Bananafish," with a suicide.[5] Seymour Glass kills himself sitting three feet away from the very embodiment of a world he cannot abide, his wife Muriel, and in a way that will cause the ultimate shock and horror. Teddy also kills himself in front of a female he intends to injure, that small concentration of hostility and meanness, his sister Booper, whose "all-piercing" scream can be thought of as an echo of the scream of Muriel a microsecond after the death of Seymour, and, of course, a forecast of the response of Teddy's own parents who will shortly learn of Teddy's death. The deeply disturbed Teddy throws himself into the empty pool (untouched by Booper) to protest and escape a life he cannot abide, and to inflict guilt feelings on his family and the adult world that has violated him through its ceaseless probing of his personality. Thus understood, there is no problematic ambiguity to the conclusion of "Teddy." Salinger's deliberate reduplication of the figure of Seymour from "Bananafish" in "Teddy" tells us exactly what happens at the end of Teddy's story. The motives of suicide are alike: to escape, protest, and inspire horror and guilt: in short, to punish the unloving, grown-up world in the person of a particularly dreadful female.[6]

We may say a little more about Seymour, then, and the crucial reflection of him in Teddy. We learn more of Seymour in the second of the *Nine Stories*, "Down at the Dingy," and outside the *Nine Stories* collection, most notably in *Raise High the Roof Beam, Carpenters, Seymour—An Introduction* and "Hapgood 16, 1924."[7] Like Teddy, Seymour is, we learn in *Carpenters*, careful and responsible concerning his family, suspicious of sentimentality (53), a connoisseur of *haiku*. He is a student of mysticism: like Teddy, he keeps a diary, and notes, "I've been reading a miscellany of Vedanta all day" (70). Another diary entry reflects a central fictional concern of Salinger— that of the care of children. Married couples are to "Raise their children honorably, lovingly, and with detachment. A child is a guest in the house, to be loved and respected—never possessed, since he belongs to god" (70). Thus Seymour's diary anticipates and glosses the story "Teddy."

As seen in the other stories in which he appears, Seymour Glass was, as a child prodigy, the subject of examination by a hostile probing adult world, and this intense puzzlement about Seymour, seen both within the Glass family and the world outside the family, is ongoing. In "Bananafish," Seymour, obviously disturbed by his experience in the war, is the object of examination by all those who surround him—including the professional scrutiny of two psychiatrists named in the story. He is considered special, puzzling, something of a freak. The story begins with Mrs. Fedders, Muriel's mother, questioning Muriel about Seymour. We learn that Seymour is preoccupied with death: "Those horrible things he said to Granny about her plans for passing away" (6). His conversation with Sybil defies the "Western" logic that Teddy so discommends in his story. Intending to delight the girl, he refutes logic and reason with his witty, charming disregard for reality. He comments teasingly on Sybil's "yellow" bathing suit (actually blue) and his delight in fantasy is seen throughout their conversation. His story of the bananafish, freakish and self-destructive, defines his feelings about himself.

Like Teddy, Seymour, though on the point of suicide, is careful and responsible in his actions toward Sybil. But his hostility against the grown-up world (necessarily more suppressed in the much younger, dependent Teddy), emerges clearly: his anger toward the innocent woman in the elevator, whom he accuses of staring at his feet, reveals his hostility. Seymour projects a suicidal fantasy in the famous story of the bananafish, who, when trapped, die. At the end of the story, he kills himself. His death is an accusation: against the self-absorbed, non-understanding Muriel, against the adult world represented by her mother, Mrs. Fedders, and the psychiatrists—none of whom can understand or help him. Shooting himself while sitting close to the sleeping Muriel is the supremely hostile action, and one that he has planned in advance; he brought the gun with him to Florida.

Teddy, like Seymour, is a person of great potential at the time of his death. Like other unhappy Salinger kids in the collection, Teddy is detached from his parents, and from adults in general, secretive and withdrawn— though Teddy is seemingly the opposite: open, kind, careful, responsible. Teddy, far from being the serene little savant he seems, is in fact lonely, withdrawn, secretive, and emotionally dead, the angry victim of that "phony" adult world central to Salinger's fictional imagination. This situation, though disguised by Teddy's presentation of himself as kiddy-philosopher, is revealed in several key passages in the story and concludes in his horrific suicide.

As the story begins, Teddy is returning from Edinburgh and Oxford where he has been subject once again, as he has throughout his short life, to the puzzled examination of the academics. His curious adult-like poise, his obvious intelligence, seems to validate the sense of enlightened wisdom that he seems to embody. His life has been largely this examination; he is typically surrounded by questioning, baffled, sometimes amused, sometimes hostile adults. To his examiners, he is a freak: "kidding around and asking me a bunch of questions . . . they all kept sitting around smoking cigarettes and getting very kittenish" (192). Teddy is pleased to have some measure of comic revenge on these types: "I told them a little bit" about when they were fated to die. These scientists and academics are "phonies"—as much so as the various pedagogues in *Catcher in the Rye.* "I mean I knew that even though they teach Religion and Philosophy and all, they're still pretty afraid to die" (193). His parents, as we see in the brilliant opening scene, provide no counterbalance to this intrusive, careless world: the negligence and indeed hostility of the parents are fatal.

The first scene is set in the small stateroom of Teddy's parents. Salinger dramatizes with skill and economy the inadequacy of Teddy's parents. They are at odds: tension and hostility permeate the atmosphere as the parents lie abed late, irritable and languorous, presumably hungover after a long smoky, boozy night. The father is presented as an unpleasant failure: an impostor as a man, with his "third-class leading man's speaking voice: narcissistically deep and resonant, functionally prepared at a moment's notice to out-male anyone in the same room with it, if necessary even a small boy" (167). His voice is "theatrical" and an element of competition with his own son is suggested. His irritable carping ("I'll exquisite day you, buddy"), his incessant and slovenly smoking and whining low-grade sarcasm all suggest the weak, the unmanly. This sense is heightened by the image of his "nude, inflamed-pink, right arm" (155), flicking ashes from the cigarette. The suggestion is of the anger of this narcissistic showbiz failure—anger, prompted by jealousy of his own son— and of sickness, even degeneracy. Mrs. McArdle's hostility toward her failure of a husband is not disguised; it is expressed through her saccharin, hostile wit. Teddy's farewell kiss is unwilling and perfunctory—as she "brought her left arm out from under the sheet, as if bent on encircling Teddy's waist with it" (172), he slides away. Her hostility toward her husband is expressed in her phony display of affection for Teddy, syrupy, and suggestive of the lazily sexual and perverse. The sheet drawn "tight over her very probably nude body" (168), the anger between these two unpleasant types flares out: near the end of the scene, Mr. McArdle snarls at his wife, "I'd like to kick your goddamn head open" (168), followed by his wife's sarcastically sweet hopes for his heart attack and a funeral where she would sit as a widow dressed in scarlet in the first row, attracting male attention.

Teddy's response to this is withdrawal and passive aggression. He is detached, unhearing. The phrase, "Teddy, did you hear me," is repeated; but, pointedly, he does not respond. What is ominous here is Teddy's recurring hints concerning his own death, implicit in his suggestions that once out of sight, entities (orange peels in this case) would not exist, and culminating in "After I go out this door, I may only exist in the minds of all my acquaintances (173–74). The section ends, "He closed the door behind him" (174). And thus he closes out his life with his estranged parents.

Brother–sister relations are important in Salinger and here, although it may seem that Teddy and Booper are entirely different, I suggest Booper mirrors and thus makes clear the anger and preoccupation with death that is Teddy's psychological center. Her essence is anger, hostility, and aggression, and obviously this stems from the McArdle family situation—plus of course her jealously toward her celebrity brother. She echoes her parent's anger on a smaller scale, and she shares her mother's penchant for aggressive fantasy. She vents her anger on the hapless little boy Myron; images of death run throughout her conversation, expressing hostility toward her own parents, albeit in a disguised form. If Myron's mother dies he will be an orphan; two "giants" could throw shuffleboard disks at the passengers and kill them; they could kill Myron's parents—and "if that didn't kill them, you know what you could do? You could put some poison on some marshmallows and make them eat it" (177). As she leaves for the pool for her lesson, she once again expresses her all-consuming anger: "I hate you! I hate everybody in this ocean!" (178).

Teddy, despite his seeming tranquillity, shares this anger and his death, suicide, is a last hostile gesture, directed primarily at his parents, sister, and the rest of the prying and hostile adult world in which he feels alone and isolated. His barely disguised anger emerges in his carefully polite indifference to his parents, to Nicholson, and even in the short scenes in which he dismisses the stewardess and purser. The source of this anger is revealed when he tells Nicholson of his parents: "They don't love me and Booper—that's my sister. . . . I mean they don't seem able to love us just the way we are. They don't seem able to love us unless they can keep changing us a little bit. They love their reasons for loving us almost as much as they love us, and most of the time more" (187).

Along with anger, his feeling of isolation is the another cause of his suicide, as suggested by his recitation of the *haiku*: "Along this road goes no one, this autumn eve" (185). Seymour too writes a *haiku* shortly before his death. Teddy's feelings of being alienated from his parents and the world, his superior intelligence, his fear of and his impatience with the probing examiners leave him with no one to talk to. Teddy is unwilling to speak openly or intimately to any of the adults—most especially the stranger Nicholson whose intrusive questions Teddy seeks to avoid.

Intermingled with this sense of isolation is his emotional deadness, his fear and rejection of the feelings. He insists on this strongly everywhere—associating it, contemptuously, with poetry and sentiment. To Nicholson:

> I wish I knew why people think it's so important to be emotional. . . . My mother and father don't think a person's human unless he thinks a lot of things are very sad or very annoying or very—very unjust, sort of. My father gets very emotional even when he reads the newspaper. He thinks I'm inhuman. (186)

His reaction to his egoistic and irresponsible parents has been withdrawal, a suppression of anger and the deadening of his emotions. For Teddy, emotions are disturbing; the anger he feels must not be expressed. This becomes clear in a key diary entry—a self-revealing fantasy, just as Seymour's fantasy of the Bananafish and Gedsudski's Laughing Man reveal their most significant inner feelings. After reminding himself to ask Professor Mandell not to send any more poetry books—those compilations of emotion and sentimentality—Teddy fantasizes:

> A man walks along the beach and unfortunately gets hit in the head by a coconut. His head unfortunately creaks open in two halves. Then his wife comes along the beach singing a song and sees the halves and recognizes them and picks them up. She gets very sad of course and cries heart-breakingly. That is exactly where I am tired of poetry. Supposing the lady just picks up the 2 halves and shouts into them very angrily, 'stop that!' (180)

The implications of this fantasy in regard to his own parents are suggestive: the husband is killed violently, in a farcical, cartoon fashion; the wife previously happy, becomes very sad when she recognizes what has happened, and cries heartbreakingly. The unfortunate man involved in this farcical fantasy is both Mr. McArdle, victim of his son's hostile fantasy, and Teddy himself, eliciting the grief and guilt he desires from his mother.

His last diary entry, October 28, 1952, reveals no significant plans for future action. Indeed, the nine letters written in the morning have a farewell quality, and the previous day's memo to look up the phrase "gift horse," becomes in the next and final day, the observation "Life is a gift horse in my opinion": that is, life is seemingly delightful and amazing; actually deadly. His final entry, "It will either happen today or February 14, 1958" (182), seems to suggest ongoing deliberation about suicide.

That Teddy targets Valentine's Day, with its suggestions of erotic love, as an appropriate day for his suicide suggests that another uneasiness disturbs the preadolescent Teddy and indeed helps to trigger his decision to end his life this day and not six years later. He feels anxiety concerning his new and disturbing awareness of sex. This is seen in his awareness of his mother's nude form, encircling arm, and attempted kiss, Ensign Matthewson's lipsticky mouth, the casual brush of the stewardess's hand (a huge, blond woman), against his hair. This sexual anxiety is further clarified by Teddy's fanciful notion that in a previous life his spiritual development was going very well indeed, until sexuality entered in. His spiritual advancement was abruptly halted when "I met a lady and I sort of stopped meditating" (188). Typically of such Salinger figures, he qualifies and digresses—but there was a fall: "I wouldn't have had to get incarnated in an American body if I hadn't met that lady" (188).

Teddy's unease with his incipient sexuality is also projected in his reference to the Adam and Eve story in conversation with Nicholson. The myth that the apple transferred fatal knowledge to mankind has sometimes been understood in terms of sexuality, particularly as the story contains a seduction that leads to sexual shame and exclusion from paradise. In this pointed reference to the biblical story, one recognizes a preoccupation within Salinger's fiction at work. Critics have repeatedly noted that throughout Salinger there is a distrust, an uneasiness, with sexuality. Sex sullies and spoils. A sense of covert sexuality can be seen in Seymour Glass's relationship with the girl, Sybil. Seymour, apparently uneasy with mature sexual relations, seeks out the child, Sybil, and his encounter with her is latently sexual.[8] When he returns to the hotel, to the inevitable intimacy of his relationship with Muriel, he ends his life.

It is this new, uneasy sexual awareness that advances his decision to die immediately. He says to Nicholson:

> "For example, I have a swimming lesson in about five minutes, I could go downstairs to the pool, and there might not be any water in it. . . . I might walk up to the edge of it, just to have a look at the bottom, for instance and my sister might come up and sort of push me in. I could fracture my skull and die instantaneously. . . . That could happen, all right." (193)

His death is considered, long incubating. It is triggered by the perversity and hostility of his parents, a fresh demonstration of Booper's willfulness and anger, his disturbing awareness of his new sexuality, and yet another endless interrogation by a foolish and insensitive academic phony. That Teddy somehow does not know that there is in fact no water in the pool, that this is cleaning day, is impossible: surely this careful reader of the ship's bulletins realizes this and yet he makes an appointment to meet Booper at 10:30 and reminds her repeatedly and urgently of this appointment. It is clearly his intention to deliberately kill himself by jumping into the empty pool in front of his sister, parallel to Seymour's shocking death next to that person who most directly represents what he most despises and loathes, Miss Spiritual Tramp of 1958. The scream of course is Booper's—it is the first sign of the horror and guilt that Teddy has intentionally inflicted upon his loathsome family and the adult world more generally. It is interesting that in both "Bananafish" and "Teddy" Salinger inserts a suspenseful uncertainty. In the first story, the reader does not know what is going to happen until the last three words: until then Seymour's anger may lead him to destroy himself *or* Miss Spiritual Tramp.[9] In "Teddy," the ambiguity is more radical; yet the murder of Booper (as some readers have thought it) would make no fictional sense in context, and the signals of Teddy's approaching suicide are too strong.

3

The story "Teddy" concludes *Nine Stories* by dramatizing a potential answer to the corruption, materiality, egotism, and self-seeking of American life: individual rejection of the Western culture and the attempt to gain a truer understanding and fuller humanity through renunciation of the self and unqualified love of a very imperfect human race. Between "Teddy" and "Bananafish" are contrasting stories of redemption. We recognize the sudden understanding of human difficulty experienced by Ginnie Mannox in "Just before the War with the Eskimos," and the patient, sensitive love of a parent, Boo Boo Tannenbaum, for her highly susceptible and anxious son in "Down at the Dinghy." A gesture of human affinity, the gift by Esmé of her father's watch, thus selecting Sergeant X as her surrogate—at long distance—father, is cathartic for the man in despair. In "De Daumier-Smith's Blue Period," the troubled adolescent is saved and returned to sanity by a realization of the purity of Sister Irma and a sudden comic glimpse of Eden in the midst of an image of human despair.

It is ironic and tragic that this gift of love, as mediated though a figure like Esmé, Boo Boo, or Sister Irma, is unavailable to Teddy even though he insists on the possibility of redemption through love. He can feel in himself no power of forgiveness and tolerance through redemptive love. Unlike his literary relation Franny, he has no Zooey to mediate between his feelings of anger and despair, and the love he seeks. A frightened, loveless child, Teddy attempts to maintain his defensive posture as little savant, but finally even this extraordinary persona fails him. Like Seymour, fear and anger overwhelm him.

That Salinger's advocates of this doctrine of redemptive love, Seymour and Teddy, both take their own lives in unexpected and shocking manner irrevocably compromises the positive thematic implications of the collection. Universal love may be an ideal, but very possibly it is impossible to achieve when one is imprisoned "in an American body."

The significance of "Teddy" to the rest of *Nine Stories* is clear. Teddy's doctrine offers a potential solution, if a problematic one, to the problem of being born in an American body. We see that what Teddy *claims* he has done (rejected the materialism and egotism of American life) is exactly what must be done, according to Salinger, and this possibility is seen again in certain other stories of the collection. Yet "Teddy" closes the collection on a note of failure forecast in the opening story: the possibility of redemptive love is fleeting and in most cases, ungraspable. Without the mediation of healing love, Teddy, Seymour and their kind are isolated and doomed: "Along this road goes no one, this autumn eve."

Notes

1. Frederick L. Gwynn and Joseph L. Blotner note the "growing diffuseness of the story and the ambiguity of the conclusion" (40). James Lundquist complains of inadequate characterization and the weakness of the dialogue between Teddy and Nicholson and: "... the major thing wrong with the story is that it does not move. Its static quality is the consequence of contrast without conflict" (108). Paul Kirschner concludes that the story "... seems no more than the tantalizing adumbration of a religious philosophy" (75). Laurence Perrine concludes that while Teddy is "a vivid and brilliantly written story ... its focus is uncertain and its conclusion mystifying." Perrine maintains that the ambiguity of the conclusion "suggests that the author either was unclear in his aims or lacked the courage of his conviction" (223).

2. French suggests that "Teddy's attitude ... may also be an extremely bright and hypersensitive young person's rationalization of his desire to escape from what he finds an intolerable situation" (*Revisited* 85). But I certainly disagree with French's insistence that Teddy is a cunning little hypocrite, with a shrewdly calculating nature. French finds Teddy "one of the most obnoxious puppets in the whole history of bratty children" (*Revisited* 133). I suggest that his whole presentation of himself as a mystic and clairvoyant is his intuitive, defensive response to an intolerable situation. It is significant that nobody in the story is entirely convinced of his authenticity as mystic and clairvoyant. His professional examiners in Oxford and Boston are impressed, but not entirely convinced. They are puzzled, annoyed, disturbed, and so on.

3. Teddy's dreadful little sister Booper, his mirror and foil, speaks gleefully of poisoning: "You could put some poison on some marshmallows and make them eat it" (177).

4. Teddy's eyes are "slightly crossed," surely Salinger's hint, evoking as it does the term cock-eyed, the ersatz quality of Teddy's powers as mystic and clairvoyant.

5. T. L. Gross (263) points out the centrality of suicide to Salinger's fiction. "The act of suicide—at times it seems the only act in all of Salinger's fiction—occurs ... when Salinger first begins to write with a clarity of focus and with real efficacy...."

6. Thomas Kranidas insists that Teddy's suicide is not tragic, since it is the decision of an enlightened ("immortally composed") person to leave an unsatisfactory existence. "There ought not to be worry over the death of Teddy, whose very message was transcendence" (91). I argue of course that the story is primarily a psychological study of a child who reacts to his difficult situation by claiming to possess authentic mysticism and supernatural powers. He is certainly not a conscious hypocrite. Instead he consciously believes in what he announces to the world.

7. James Bryan notes the similarity of Seymour in "Hapgood" to Teddy. Both are incredibly precocious and also disturbed by incipient sexuality (357).

8. In "Raise High the Roof Beam, Carpenters," Seymour fails to appear at his own wedding. In "Bananafish," the sexual desire he feels for the girl Sybil emerges when, to her consternation, he grasps and kisses her foot.

9. Earlier in "Bananafish" there is considerable uncertainty as to Seymour's intentions to the little girl, Sybil. He pushes her farther and farther out to sea and she grows frightened. Is he going to drown her? Seymour's obvious mental disorder leads the reader to feel anxiety

as to his intentions, especially as we recall the highly ambiguous kissing of the little girl's foot as he pushes her out to deeper waters.

WORKS CITED

Bryan, James. "A Reading of Salinger's 'Teddy.'" *American Literature* 40 (1968): 352–69.

French, Warren. *J. D. Salinger*. Rev. ed. Boston: Twayne, 1963.

———. *J. D. Salinger Revisited*. Boston: Twayne, 1988.

Galloway, David D. "The Love Ethic." *J. D. Salinger*. Ed. Harold Bloom. *Modern Critical Views*. New York: Chelsea House, 1987. 29–51.

Goldstein, Bernice, and Sanford Goldstein. "Zen and Salinger." *Modern Fiction Studies* 12 (1966): 313–324.

Gross, T. L. "J. D. Salinger: Suicide and Survival in the Modern World." *The Heroic Ideal in American Literature*. New York: Free Press, 1971. 262–71.

Gwynn, Frederick L., and Joseph L. Blotner. *The Fiction of J. D. Salinger*. Pittsburgh: U of Pittsburgh P, 1958.

Kirschner, Paul. "Salinger and his Society: The Pattern of *Nine Stories*." *Literary Half-Yearly* 14 (1969–70; rpt. 1973): 63–78.

Kranidas, Thomas. "Point of View in Salinger's 'Teddy.'" *Studies in Short Fiction* 2 (1964): 89–91.

Lundquist, James. *J. D. Salinger*. New York: Ungar, 1979.

Perrine, Laurence. "Teddy? Booper? Or Blooper?" *Studies in Short Fiction* 4 (1967): 217–24.

Salinger, J. D. *Nine Stories*. New York: Bantam, 1964.

———. *Raise High the Roof Beam* and *Seymour—An Introduction*. London: Penguin, 1963.

Stein, William Bysshe. "Salinger's 'Teddy': *Tat Tvam Asi* or That Thou Art." *Arizona Quarterly* 29 (1973): 253–56.

ROBERT COLES

Anna Freud and
J.D. Salinger's Holden Caulfield

For many years I was lucky, indeed, to get to talk with Anna Freud, who almost single-handedly founded the discipline of child psychoanalysis. She lived in London during the last decades of her life, on Marsefield Gardens, where she saw patients who knew, many of them, that her father once lived there—as W.H. Auden put it in his memorial poem to Sigmund Freud, "an important Jew who died in exile," one more beneficiary of that capital city's cosmopolitan generosity. But she often came to "the States"—so she called the country she visited, thereby speaking as the Englishwoman she'd become. While on the American side of the Atlantic, she taught college students at Yale, medical students there, also; and of course, she worked with psychiatrists and psychoanalysts, an effort she had pursued for many years in Austria, then England.

Once, in 1975, she looked back a half a century (my tape-recorder whirling), and she recalled, really, the origins of child psychoanalysis, not to mention the consequences such a development had for parents and for teachers, for film-makers and writers: "Those were exciting days, during the first quarter of this century (and now we are headed for the last quarter!). In Vienna we began to take my father's ideas so seriously [that] we tried to apply them not only with the adults who came to see us, but with children. That was the heart of what Freud [so she sometimes called him] contributed

From *The Virginia Quarterly Review*, vol. 76, no. 2 (Spring 2000): pp. 214–224. © 2000 by the Virginia Quarterly Review, the University of Virginia.

to our thinking—he looked back in a [patient's] life in order to understand where it is going, and why, and in order to help change its direction. I had worked with children as a teacher, but in the 1920s I began seeing them in an office, and training or enlisting others to do so. Today the world knows of the work done by August Aicchorn with delinquents [described in *Wayward Youth*], or Erik Erikson, through his books [*Childhood and Society, Young Man Luther*] but back then we were not as (how shall I say it?) 'reputable' as we seem to have become for so many."

She went on to give an extended account of the techniques of child psychoanalysis developed in those bold, breakthrough years—and then, abruptly, unexpectedly, made mention of a book she'd recently been reading, after hearing so much of it, over and over, from her colleagues; and very important, from her students and patients, or analysands, as she often called them: "I've been told for years about this *Catcher in the Rye*, the book, the novel with that title—I think of it, of course, as a story being told: a person is ready to catch people, save them, rescue them from some trouble they've gotten themselves into. The 'catcher' is named Holden Caulfield, we all know—but I wonder whether the story doesn't tell us about the story-teller [J. D. Salinger], though I don't like it when we in psychoanalysis do this, make guesses that turn out to be wild guesses! This young man, Holden Caulfield, is so vividly brought to the attention of the reader that it's hard not to connect him with his creator—more so, for me at least, than [is the case with] other characters, in fiction.

"I got to know this Holden Caulfield by hearsay before I met him as a reader. My analytic patients spoke of him sometimes as if they'd actually met him; they used his words, his way of speaking. They laughed as if he had made them laugh, because of what he'd said, and how he looked at things. I began to realize that they had taken him into their minds, and hugged him—they spoke, now, not only his words in the book (quotations from it) but his words become their own words (deeply felt, urgently and emphatically expressed). There were moments when I had to be the perennially and predictably pedantic listener, ever anxious, to pin down what has been spoken, call it by a [psychoanalytic] name, fit it into my 'interpretative scheme,' you could call it. I would ask a young man or a young woman who it was just speaking—him, or her, or Holden! Well, I'd hear 'me,' but it didn't take long for the young one, the youth, the teenager, to have some second thoughts! They'd be silent; they'd mull the matter over—and I wasn't surprised, again and again, to hear a quite sensible person, not out of his mind, or her mind (not 'psychotic,' as we put it in staff conferences) speaking of this Holden Caulfield as though they'd spent a lot of time with him, and now had taken up, as their very own, his favorite words, his likes and dislikes, his 'attitude,' one college student, just starting out, once termed it.

"When I asked the student, a very bright one (as he expected I would) what he meant by the word, 'attitude,' I was given a lecture that took up virtually the entire [analytic] hour, to the point that I was reprimanding myself afterwards for giving the young fellow all he needed to avoid [discussing] the important reasons he'd come to see me! But then, I smiled to myself—I realized that what I'd learned about Holden, *his* 'attitude,' was what this young man wanted to understand about himself: why he was so 'skeptical' (his chosen word), why he didn't give people the benefit of the doubt, why he kept to himself, because he was inclined to 'look for trouble' when he met people, was with them (his room-mates, those sitting near him in the cafeteria or in a lecture hall or seminar room). I asked him, naturally, what 'trouble' he was expecting; and he hesitated for a long time, and told me he couldn't easily 'come up with any,' not to mention do so then and there on my analytic couch! He knew I'd press for examples—and then a plaintive excuse: he wanted to swear, as Holden would, but he was worried that I'd be offended, so his tongue was tied!"

In fact, sitting there with Miss Freud, I knew well what Holden had prompted that young man to want to say, to think about, remember, as he spoke his mind, gave his comments, or his "free associations," as they came to him: all the "crap" in this life, all the "goddamn" acts we observe, the statements we hear. (Now I'm using quotation marks to distance myself from those words, even as I didn't choose to mention them in front of the august, illustrious older woman with whom I was talking, and even as she was not about to get specific, speak those words as belonging to a patient, to his favorite novelist.) A moment of awkward silence—whereupon, Miss Freud, true to form, hastened to remind both of us that "there is something to be learned from this book and what it says to those who bring it into their mental life." I am quick to nod, but not all that taken with the phrase "mental life." What I feel like saying is that Salinger's slurs and swear words are not original, but are shocking, because worked so vigorously, adroitly into his lively, arresting, thoroughly enticing, embracing narration—his constant interest in addressing his reader as a "you," and his constant desire, as well, to invoke a moral (yes!) "attitude," to provoke thereby our complacent, maybe to some extent compromised, sense of who we are, what we have done (or left undone).

There *is* a lot of "crap" in this "phony" world, a "goddamn" lot, so I wanted to say, linking arms thereby with Holden, and with any number of young analysands seen in this century by the likes of Miss Freud, and me and my shrink-buddies, so I hear my thoughts aver, their mode of expression deteriorating and becoming unavailable to my vocal cords. As if she saw my lips shut tight, and figured out the give-away reason, Miss Freud observed tersely: "Holden Caulfield says what is forbidden us to

say." I both agree enthusiastically (another obliging nod) and feel uneasy—
well, more irritated than I want to reveal with words or bodily gestures.
But I do hear myself thinking, "What the hell!"—and then I try to speak
by making a critic's summary: "Salinger has Holden cut through a lot of
cant—the 'phoniness' he spots all the time." I'm being heard, but myself
hear nothing. I see those eyes concentrating on mine, the face that holds
them as impassive as ever, the figure so imposing. I hear my voice treasuring,
nourishing that word "phoniness"—as if I had myself become Holden. I
want to run down the field with that word, as he did, raise that voice of
mine, refer to all the "phonies" in the world, escalate to the "frauds"; but I
feel my hands holding the arms of the chair that is holding me, and quickly
my reflexes deliver the goods: in a carefully modulated voice I comment on
a novelist's distinctive capability, his repeated intention—"he cuts through
a lot of cant, Salinger does." Then, as if there is any doubt, I summon a
story's protagonist as the important moral witness: "Holden has a sharp eye
for the hypocrisy and duplicity of everyday life."

Now I am gulping, feeling nervous. Those two tell-tale words, "everyday
life," which in Miss Freud's mind, in mine, in just about anyone's who has
read Sigmund Freud's writing, have a familiar ring—I'm tempted to summon
them as a part of a derivative five-word aside: "the Phoniness of Everyday
Life." In my mind I had played with a celebrated book's title, come up with a
precis of sorts for a celebrated novel—Freud and Salinger's Holden become
joined as the observers of their fellow human beings.

Miss Freud moves us on, moves by my tongue-tied restiveness and
her own struggles with Salinger's created youth, whom she now wants to
approach in an appreciative manner, responsive strictly on her terms: "I
think this Holden Caulfield is very much with us, because he is very much—
well, he is the one who wrote of him." She is evidently aware that she has
made in that sentence a rather sweeping interpretation—her pause in the
middle of the assertion signaled as much, the "well" a cautionary indication
that she was going to take a leap. Then, inevitably for a psychoanalyst who
had distinguished herself by her reluctance to be yet another reductionist
interpreter, ever prepared (gladly, triumphantly) to explain away people and
events through recourse to psychological paradigms, theories, the time had
come for a proper acknowledgment of uncertainty's prevalent importance:
"We can never know where a writer's life has been set aside, in the pursuit of
a talent's expression."

I am moved, impressed—well (to use a word) brought up short by that
renunciation, so poignantly declared (with a characteristic mix of simplicity,
formality, and with a penetrating idiosyncrasy of affirmation). So much for
all too many explanatory or interpretive essays wrought by literary critics,
biographers, psychoanalysts—the constant need to explain, unravel, account

for, get to a definitive bottom of a life, a work of art. In a few seconds (almost as if she is attending her own remarks, being given pleased pause, even wonder-filled pause by them) Miss Freud tactfully moves away from the person of Salinger, from his achievement as a novelist, to the safer and surer ground of her own working experience, and out of it, her memory's sharply instructive lessons: "I've had young analysands speak to me [in her office] as if they were Holden Caulfield, and I needed badly to pay attention to them, to him through them! 'Alright,' I say to them, 'tell me what Holden wants me to know!' It's come to that, actually, a few times; I've joined with them indirectly or implicitly, in turning Holden into a real-life person—as if *The Catcher in the Rye* is a work of biography, rather than fiction. Not that fiction doesn't get us as close to the truth as biography! My father once told me when I was teaching literature [as a young woman in Vienna] that novels are the fantasies of talented people; and he did not mean to show a lack of admiration or respect with those words—quite the contrary." Now a notable silence; the speaker lowers her head ever so slightly, if significantly—as if to pay proper respect to a most talented person whose remarks about "talented people" had just been put on the record. We try to affirm our high regard for Freud by continuing to take the novel we've been discussing seriously, with no lapse into a dismissive discussion of psychopathology. "All of us have our extended spells of fantasy," Miss Freud observes, as if we'd best keep in mind a context, of sorts, for both Holden and his creator. I fear I then slipped, pointed out how often the word "depressed" got used when Holden felt the need to characterize his state of mind. I tell Miss Freud (as if to disown any inclination on my part to call Holden "sick," an all too obvious reflexive posture for me and my kind) about the critics who have not only noted Holden's way of describing himself, but counted the number of times he uses the word "depressed," more than a dozen instances. Her response was lengthy and animated: "Of course this man was 'depressed' at times and said so to himself—though I bet if anyone had called him that, spoke the very words he'd used in his thinking about himself at certain moments, then we'd hear quite something else: an angry refutation, or a surly dismissal conveyed in an angry facial grimace! As I read the novel, I stopped a few times when I came to the word 'depressed,' and I had to think that here was another adolescent who reserved the right to call himself what he wanted—but wouldn't tolerate you or me taking such a liberty, or a critic who was observing him!"

With that remark, Miss Freud showed a second's grimace on her own face, as if she was thinking back through years of difficult, demanding clinical work—so I thought as I wondered what she would say next, and wondered, too, what I might add to her words, which had, actually, in their sum, given me considerably more to consider than I'd guessed would be the case when they first began to be given voice by the one who wanted me to hear them. Suddenly, a sigh, and then a speaker's stiffened resolve: "We have to be sympathetic to our Holdens, but I'm not sure they want that from us—I mean, they are suspicious of just about every adult they know (starting with their parents, of course, and then their teachers!) and so they're ready for all grownups who come their way, certainly including us, whose offices they enter with several chips on their shoulders! I recall a young lad I saw (he had just turned fourteen) and every exchange we had was—oh, I felt we were both working ourselves through a mine-field: he was always prepared to be *doubtful*, even *scornful*, and certainly, *mistrustful*. I wrote those three words down for myself—they echoed through my mind as we tried to converse, session after session, and I tried to understand what was causing his quite evident (and loudly declared) annoyance with people he met at school. I thought of him (of those words!) as I read of Holden—read his remarks about himself and his schoolmates and teachers. Finally, after one especially tense discussion with that lad, I let go of myself, I think it fair to say: I guess I gave him a piece of my mind! I said that I believe we hurt ourselves, bring ourselves down, when we strike out at others all the time, dismiss them with our sharp words or not very friendly judgments, that go unexpressed, but give shape to our looks of contempt, disdain. (By the way, I'm not sure Holden would ever have let anyone speak that way to him!)

"In any event, I kept asking myself this question: why did that lad keep returning to me in my thoughts when I met Holden Caulfield, courtesy of Mr. Salinger? In time I reminded myself (I realized!) that Holden has been very much in the thoughts of many of the adolescents I've seen [in analysis]— he's known in England as well as here [the United States] and when he comes up [in psychoanalytic sessions] I have thought to myself yes, I know this Holden Caulfield very well, indeed; he's everyone's adolescent boy (or young man); he's trying to figure out what's important, who's important (to him!) and why; he's also trying to figure out himself, and learn what causes his moodiness, and his loneliness—a big order for anyone, even those of us who haven't been adolescents for a few decades!"

She stops there to smile wryly—a side of her I always appreciated, very much admired: her singular willingness to align herself with her patients, narrow the psychological distance between herself and them, avoid the emotional and moral smugness that all too commonly threatens, even envelops, some of us who observe others, try to engage with them in an office at home, or under the sponsorship of a clinic. Amid a few seconds of silence, I dare pose questions about Holden Caulfield, about Miss Freud's patients, about my own, and not least, about my students who, again and again, in courses and classrooms, have made mention of that "lad," as I'd just heard him quaintly called. I want to know, especially, the reason for Holden's appeal to so many different youths; but I also want to talk about some students of mine who are inattentive to him, find him uninteresting—or as I've heard him described, "a big bore," or a "pain in the neck."

Now Anna Freud noticeably perks up—and has me struck hard, stunned, by a certain forceful intensity of dislike, some of it couched, if I may use that word, in psychoanalytic speculation, theory: "I'm always being asked what I think about Holden Caulfield, once I admit I've read the book that tells of him—after being told of him by the young patient who has just asked me! I don't dare say that he's a bit bossy and impudent and brash—that he's smitten with himself, a victim of abundant narcissism, some of it out of control, driving him to be self-indulgent, to attribute that [kind of behavior] to others, rather than see it squarely in himself. It is as if, for some young people, for a time, that character in that novel has been a talisman—he signified some elusive truth about what life means, and if you keep talking about him, you'll heal your mind, settle your mind, with his help, because he's been there, where you are, presently: the voice of experience who therefore is a wise advisor. So, the point is to overlook in him what you don't want to acknowledge about yourself—a privileged vanity constantly at work. Remember, he's seeing a psychoanalyst, in a sanitarium, and he calls himself 'sick,' at the end of the book (as I had to notice and haven't forgotten!) when he is looking ahead, but still unsure where he's going and for what reason. *Of course* he'll elicit the interest of his young readers, who have flocked to him—often at the behest of their teachers, who spend so much of their time working with young people beset by worries and confusions, and I should add, plenty of anger and bitterness: life's disappointments that come their way, for all the means their parents possess. The more I hear about Holden, the more I think of those who have enjoyed his company—and that is where I must let the matter rest: that he and his fans belong to the same club!"

With that comment a natural break in her flow of speech, spoken with a good deal of energy, if not emotion. I wait a few seconds, wonder what to say, but want her to continue. Her use of the word "club" is intriguing, for sure. Finally, I make bold to ask her about that word—get up the courage to use it for my own purposes: "Can anyone join that club?"

I've tried to be suggestive, provocative—stress the theme of exclusivity implicit in that way of putting things. Miss Freud quickly turns the discussion over to me: "What do *you* think—I'm not sure I know; I was only thinking of the closeness some young people I've known feel toward this fictional hero of theirs, who lives, at least for a while, in their imagination."

I let my mind have its say by addressing a memory: "I used *Catcher in the Rye* in teaching with high schoolers, down South, before I worked it into college courses up North. My wife, Jane, was a high school teacher, and we both asked a group of high school students, white and black, to read that book in Atlanta, Georgia. Soon we were sorting out the enthusiasm

and interest of some, the indifference and outright annoyance of others—to
the point that we were, each of us, surprised and puzzled. A black youth,
memorably, told us: 'This guy [Holden], he be sweet on himself, all the time,
and he be sour on everyone else.' Jane asked for more, and received a tart,
pointed amplification: 'He be full of himself, he drinks up everything he sees
and he hears, and makes it all his property—like our minister will say, it's
grist for the mill he's got going, this Holden.'"

To that, Anna Freud nodded vigorously, smiled quite appreciatively.
She responded initially with her own muted reservations about Holden, then
more of her frank disapproval—to the point that I felt that I was yet again
being offered a teacher's, a moralist's reprimand: "I believe the issue is not so
much Holden's anger and melancholy [I had been using those two words]
but I repeat, the narcissism—that's the key: what in our profession we'd call
a 'narcissistic personality disorder.' He's quick to turn on others, and he gives
no one the benefit of the doubt, and he's always bringing everything back to
himself ('self-referential' as we'd say in a clinical conference). I hesitate to
overdraw the case, but there is a certain self-assurance in this young man that
slips over—becomes arrogance. One young man I was seeing [in analysis]
told me his friends called him 'cocky' all the time, and then he went on to
associate himself with Holden Caulfield, whose name was a commonplace
of my work for a while—but as you point out, there are many young people
who haven't heard of him, and if he were brought to their attention they'd
yawn, or look for someone else to consider interesting!"

We were getting near matters of class, of race, as they give shape to our
likes and dislikes: Holden Caulfield and his Pencey Prep School, its fancy
white world, readily embraced by certain of Miss Freud's patients, by a few
of mine, or by my students, some of them—one or two well-to-do African-
Americans, by the way: class within race. In a sense, *The Catcher in the Rye* was
a prefiguration of our contemporary psychoanalytic discussion of narcissism
(as Anna Freud years ago anticipated) and of the historian Christopher
Lasch's book, *The Culture of Narcissism*, which summoned theoretical ideas
Sigmund Freud had in mind as he attempted to understand how individuals
get on with others, summoning what anticipations or apprehensions, and
why. Miss Freud, in her own way, had regarded Holden as an aspect of
J.D. Salinger's thinking, if not his preoccupations. She stressed several times
the "significance of brotherhood" in *Catcher*, as she once or twice chose to
abbreviate the novel's title, for the sake of speaking for casual convenience—
though she was never altogether at a remove from interpretive reflection
both serious and formal: Holden is (or is to be) a catcher; he is Caulfield—or
as she put it, "calling others in the field of his life, aiming to hold them."
Immediately, with some charming shyness, even nervousness, she pulled
back, apologized for her "critical excess" (would that the rest of us who teach

and write be given to such second thoughts, I once more caught myself thinking—the embarrassment of one's boastfulness!). Still, like Holden and like his creator and like those who are entranced by them (and by their own possibilities as they get affirmed, asserted in life) Anna Freud hopes to find coherence, give it words that "catch" the attention of others, "hold" them decisively, whatever field they "call" their own, whatever product (whether "rye" or wryness as a point of view) being grown there: "Holden and his brothers and their sister Phoebe, with their 'discontents,' as my father put it—they all seek and welcome our attention, our membership. I think Mr. Salinger had them in mind for us before he planned his famous novel—they catch us, as he was caught by the idea, the story!"

Years later, after Miss Freud's death, I would stumble on a short story J. D. Salinger wrote in the middle of the Second World War, long before his first novel was published—a story that he has never allowed to appear in a book's collection of his fiction. "The Last Day of the Last Furlough" saw the light of day in *The Saturday Evening Post*, way before (July 15, 1944) its author began his writing career at *The New Yorker*. One Vincent Caulfield, a corporal, is soon to go off and fight in battle—and tells this to a sergeant friend: "No good, Sergeant. My brother Holden is missing. The letter came while I was at home." A few lines on, we learn this about Holden from his brother: "I used to bump into him at the old Joe College Club on Eighteenth and Third in New York. A beer joint for college kids and prep school kids. I'd go there just looking for him, Christmas and Easter vacations when he was home. I'd drag my date through the joint, looking for him, and I'd find him way in the back. The noisiest, tightest kid in the place. . . ."

Thus it was for Holden early in his literary career: exclaiming loud and clear his objections, sprinkling them, no doubt, with words such as "goddamn" and "crap," putting the "drag" on us readers, with the result that we become like the "date" his brother Vincent had in the story—fellow seekers eager to spot "phonies," their "phoniness," and so doing, inch ourselves away a bit from this life's seemingly ever-present, sometimes shady ambiguities.

PAMELA HUNT STEINLE

The Catcher in the Rye
as Postwar American Fable

Here's for the plain old Adam, the simple genuine self against the whole world.

—Ralph Waldo Emerson, *Journals*

J. D. Salinger's novel *The Catcher in the Rye* is one of the most significant books in American literature to appear since World War II. The center of heated censorship debates for the past forty years and the cause of some confusion and consternation to American literary critics, *The Catcher in the Rye* has held the attention of popular American readership with a force that can perhaps be best appreciated by a brief review of its publishing history. First published in mid-July 1951 by Little, Brown and Company, *The Catcher in the Rye* was simultaneously published as a Book-of-the-Month Club selection. By the end of July, Little, Brown and Company was reprinting the novel for the fifth time, and by late August *Catcher* had reached fourth place on the *New York Times* best-seller list. Signet Books brought out the first paperback edition in 1953, selling over three million copies in the next ten years. Grosset and Dunlap brought out an edition of their own in 1952, Modern Library in 1958, and Franklin Watts Publishers in 1967. In January of 1960, *Catcher* reappeared on the *New York Times* best-seller list, this time placing fifth among paperback books. All the while, Little, Brown and Company continued reprinting their original edition—completing thirty-

From *In Cold Fear: The Catcher in the Rye: Censorship Controversies and Postwar American Character*. Columbus: Ohio State University Press (2000): pp. 15–28. © 2000 by The Ohio State University.

five printings by 1981. In 1964, Bantam Books brought out their paperback edition and by 1981 had reprinted it fifty-two times. All in all, the total number of copies in print by 1997 was estimated at over ten million, with sustained sales of nearly two hundred thousand copies per year.[1]

Clearly *The Catcher in the Rye* is a landmark book for the post–World War II period in its immediate and sustained popularity. However, publication and printing records alone do not necessarily indicate that a literary work has engaged or become a significant part of the cultural imagination. One might argue that *Catcher* has been so frequently printed in response to its classroom usage—reflecting an appreciation of the novel by English teachers but not necessarily the choice or interest of a voluntary readership. Another interpretation is that sales of *Catcher* have been spurred by its very presence on various censorship lists. While these perspectives certainly bear some truth, the materials of popular culture provide evidence that the success of *Catcher* is broader and of deeper significance than these explanations acknowledge.

Continuing references to *Catcher* in commercial television series and several novels illustrate that the producers of popular media assume a broad base of audience familiarity with the novel.[2] A 1977 novel by Erich Segal, *Oliver's Story*, as well as 1982 episodes of the television series *Sixty Minutes* and *Archie Bunker's Place* all referred to *Catcher* in terms of its status as a controversial text. In another television series, the long-time favorite game show *Family Feud*, as the host reviewed the "correct" answers to an audience-survey question about types of bread, he called out, "Rye," and then quipped, "As in catcher."[3]

Revealing their own esteem for Salinger's work, three authors of contemporary novels have used *Catcher* to move their plot lines forward. In his 1987 teen novel *Can't Miss*, author Michael Bowen assumed and relied on the adolescent reader's familiarity with Holden Caulfield's critique of the "phoniness" of postwar American life to enhance his development of the teenage main character.[4] In the award-winning 1982 novel *Shoeless Joe*, not only did the author, W. P. Kinsella, assume reader familiarity with *Catcher* but the tale itself was written to facilitate an imaginary dialogue with J. D. Salinger. Given the same name as one of Salinger's fictional characters, the novel's protagonist, Ray Kinsella, is a baseball fan who has a vision of a game being played in his cornfields by a literal "dream team" that includes deceased baseball legends—and the very much alive if reclusive J. D. Salinger.

Transforming his cornfields into a ballfield based on the mysterious instructions given by an imaginary ballpark announcer in Ray's vision, the second command requires the real-life presence of Salinger to "ease his pain." Convincing the fictional Salinger that he should leave New Hampshire and come to Iowa with him, Ray tells Salinger, "I've thought about you and baseball. . . . You've captured the experience of growing up in America, the same way Freddy Patek corners a ground ball. *The Catcher in the Rye* is the definitive novel of a young man's growing pains, of growing up in pain. . . . But baseball can soothe even those pains, for it is stable and permanent, steady as a grandfather dozing in a wicker chair on a verandah."⁵

Yet it is Salinger's snug capture of adolescent angst in *Catcher* that is used to soothe the growing pains of a thirteen-year-old girl in popular writer Julie Smith's 1994 detective novel *New Orleans Beat*. At a crucial point in this story, an adult "friend of the family" named Darryl attempts to reach out to a recently returned adolescent "runaway" named Sheila by giving her a book as a gift at a "welcome home" gathering. At first, the title of the book is not disclosed to Sheila—nor to the reader—and she is clearly disappointed that her special adult friend has brought her something that she sees as an impersonal and typical adult-to-adolescent present.

Begrudgingly responding, "I'm not mad. I could . . . read a book," Sheila's disappointment deepens when Darryl tells her the novel is about a boy: "'A boy?' Her (inner) voice said, What on Earth are you thinking of?" Asking her to trust him, "even though it's a book and even though it's about a boy," Darryl then tells Sheila that this book is different, that "it's going to change your life. You're going to read this and think, 'There's somebody out there who understands.'" At this moment the book's title is finally revealed, not by Darryl nor by the unwrapping of the package, but by the larger gathering of adult family members and friends who exclaim in unison before they even see the book: "Catcher in the Rye."⁶

Everyone, it seems, is assumed to understand something about *Catcher*. Exactly what or how much the reader is required to understand is more vague, ranging from the brevity of the first few examples—requiring a "household familiarity" with at least the title *The Catcher in the Rye*—to the complexity of the latter three: to fully enjoy Kinsella's novel, the reader must have some knowledge of both the basic story of *Catcher* and the questions and problems that interested Salinger himself. As both the novels and the television series are geared toward a widespread "middle-American" audience, these references reveal an assumption about *Catcher*'s place in the culture: if people haven't read it for themselves, they are at least familiar with the book's title, its status, and some sense of the story line.⁷

For many of those who have read it, *Catcher* holds an enduring appeal that some readers believe can transcend the cultural gap between generations. When critic Sanford Pinsker sought to define the characteristics of a "formative book" for his literary peers, he chose *Catcher* as his post–World War II exemplar of fiction capable of leading "double lives as cultural statements, fastened as firmly to the here and now as they are to fiction's universals." Noting that formative books have their greatest impact among adolescents, engaging these readers "at a point when options loom larger than certainties, when an admonition to 'change your life' can still have teeth," Pinsker recalled his own youthful response to *Catcher* as a reader "hooked" on Holden Caulfield's "talking" voice.[8]

Similarly, critic Adam Moss, reflecting upon his early reading of *Catcher*, wrote in 1981 that it had become "one of those rare books that influence one generation after another, causing each to claim it as its own."[9] Five years later, the casual remarks of a department store cosmetician in her mid-thirties confirmed and further personalized Moss's point when she commented to me that "*The Catcher in the Rye* was the key thing that got he [her then thirteen-year-old son] and I really talking about reading and how you don't always have to read 'junk.'"[10] Finally, it seems *Catcher* is not only a "formative" book to be shared across generations but a text that is capable of actually transforming its reader, leading Julie Smith to conclude her *Catcher* scene in *New Orleans Beat* with this claim: "Anybody who reads this book . . . can talk any way they want . . . because you can't stop anybody after they've read it, can you? They come out a whole different person, don't they?"[11]

The question then becomes, What is this book, this story that catches the attention and often the affections of so many? Simply told, *The Catcher in the Rye* is the tale of a sixteen-year-old boy, Holden Caulfield, who is flunking out of his third prep school and suffers a breakdown of sorts when he leaves school early to spend three days on his own in New York City. Holden is the narrator of the story, which is told in retrospect from a sanitarium in California, and Salinger maximizes the impact of the narrative by adhering meticulously to the teenage vernacular of the late 1940s–early 1950s. The resulting text is peppered with mild obscenities as Holden expresses his disappointment and, often, disgust with much of the postwar adult world.

Holden's definitive sense of American life is that it is largely "phony"— a term he applies repeatedly throughout the tale to various contemporary definitions of success, ranging from the realms of corporate achievement, conventional marriage, social status, and "belonging" to physical attractiveness, Hollywood glamour, and athletics. The implied "craziness" of his perspective is enhanced by the fact that Holden is well on the way to such success himself if only he would accept it. The novel ends as it begins: with Holden in the sanitarium, expected to return to "normal life" in the near future yet with little indication as to how he will manage the return to normalcy, much less whether he desires to do so.

On the surface, then, *Catcher* appears to be a rather mundane novel with its greatest potential audience among teenagers: the audience most likely to identify with Holden, to find the novel's use of adolescent vernacular familiar, and to appreciate the critique of contemporary adulthood. It is not readily apparent why this particular novel has gained the lasting affection as well as engendered the vehement hostility of adult readers to the degree that they have been willing to debate over it for the past forty-odd years. While other contemporary novels may have found a similarly split audience (Vladimir Nabokov's *Lolita* comes to mind), they have neither spurred such lengthy controversy nor enjoyed the sustained popularity of *Catcher*. It is only by looking more closely at Salinger's carefully drawn characterization of Holden Caulfield and listening through the vernacular and the obscenities that one can isolate the eloquent critique that Salinger presents, catching his audience unaware. The argument is one in the long-standing "determining debate" of American thought and writing that has been given coherent definition in R. W. B. Lewis's *The American Adam*.

*   *   *

In 1955 R. W. B. Lewis put forward his analysis of and argument for a "native American mythology." Pointing out that the salient (and assumedly universal) characteristic of cultural maturation was the generation of a "determining debate over the ideas that preoccupy it: salvation, the order of nature, money, power, sex, the machine, and the like," Lewis believed that such debates were a crucial forum in which "a culture achieves identity not so much through the ascendancy of one particular set of convictions as through the emergence of its peculiar and distinctive dialogue."[12]

Lewis located the American debate in the voices of "articulate thinkers and conscious artists" of nineteenth-century America, and the resulting mythos he isolated was what he called the "American Adam": "the authentic American as a figure of heroic innocence and vast potentialities, poised at the start of a new history."[13] While much of *The American Adam* was devoted to definition and description of this mythological hero as he appeared in American fiction, the heart of Lewis's argument lay in his insistence that this cultural mythology was a motivational source toward human good and, as well, in his mourning of the absence of such a mythology in mid-twentieth-century America: "A century ago, the challenge to debate was an expressed belief in achieved human perfection, a return to the primal perfection. Today the challenge comes rather from the expressed belief in achieved hopelessness. . . . We can hardly expect to be persuaded any longer by the historic dream of the new Adam."[14]

Looking at contemporary American literature from his 1955 vantage, Lewis identified three novels in the post–World War II period as examples of "the truest and most fully engaged American fiction after the second war": *Invisible Man* by Ralph Ellison, *The Adventures of Augie March* by Saul Bellow, and *The Catcher in the Rye* by J. D. Salinger. Lewis saw each of these novels as among the very few to continue the Adamic fictional tradition of solitary experience and moral priority over the waiting world. He applauded the efforts of these mid-twentieth-century writers as they "engender[ed] from within their work the hopeful and vulnerable sense of life that makes experience and so makes narrative action possible," yet who did so by "creat[ing] it from within, since they can scarcely find it any longer in the historic world about them."[15]

Here, Lewis's recognition of the intersection between his own formulation of the "American Adam" as a once dominant yet recently shrinking force in American culture and the story of Holden Caulfield is the first clue as to the source of cultural tension created by *The Catcher in the Rye*. A story of traditional appeal and yet a contemporary oddness, both fit and lack of fit with the historic dialogue are evident when *Catcher* is examined in light of Lewis's argument.

The classic characterization of the American Adam was the nineteenth-century image of a "radically new personality, the hero of the new adventure," "happily bereft of ancestry," and free of the taint of inherited status to stand alone, "self-reliant and self-propelling, ready to confront whatever awaited him with the aid of his own unique and inherent resources." As the nineteenth century drew to a close, this characterization was modified as American literature reflected concurrent perceptions of social and environmental changes in American life: the movement of the "frontier" from forest to barren plain, and ultimately to closure. The American Adam, no longer situated in an Edenic world, found himself instead "alone in a hostile, or at best a neutral universe." Nevertheless, Lewis claimed that the Adamic character remained intact throughout the first half of the twentieth century, "for much of that fable remained . . . the individual going forth toward experience, the inventor of his own character and creator of his personal history."[16]

Bearing these characterizations in mind, at this point I introduce to you Holden Caulfield, as J. D. Salinger did in the first page of *The Catcher in the Rye*:

> If you really want to hear about it, the first thing you'll probably want to know is where I was born, and what my lousy childhood was like, and how my parents were occupied and all before they had me, and all that David Copperfield kind of crap, but I don't feel like going into it, if you want to know the truth. In the first place, that stuff bores me, and in the second place, my parents would have about two hemorrhages apiece if I told anything personal about them. . . . Besides, I'm not going to tell you my whole goddam autobiography or anything. I'll just tell you about this madman stuff that happened to me around last Christmas.[17]

In Holden's statement of introduction, his position as a solitary individual in the Adamic tradition is not only evident but reinforced by the contrast to English literary tradition ("that David Copperfield kind of crap"). The initial assumption is that the mid-twentieth-century reader *wants* to know the family and position of a central character—an assumption that is immediately challenged as irrelevant to the telling of the story itself and as contrary to middle-class expectations of personal and family privacy. Hence, Salinger's introduction of his central character provided an opening defense for the Adamic narrative as well as an implicit jab at the movement of contemporary readers away from that very tradition.

Defense of the Adamic tradition is not surprising in light of Holden's apparent literary lineage. Searching for a fictional representative for his American mythos, "unambiguously treated" and "celebrated in his very Adamism,"[18] Lewis chose James Fenimore Cooper's Natty Bumppo: hero of *The Deerslayer* and, it seems, a direct if unacknowledged ancestor of Salinger's Holden Caulfield. In a central scene in *The Deerslayer*, Natty Bumppo's name is changed as the consequence of his fight with a Huron warrior. In their struggle, Natty kills the warrior, but Cooper characterizes it as a chivalrous battle, ending with the dying man telling Natty that he should now be known as "Hawkeye" instead of the boyish "Deerslayer."[19] In this pivotal moment, Natty takes on the heroic status of the American Adam: "born with all due ceremony during an incident that has every self-conscious quality of a ritual trial . . . [,] Deerslayer earns his symbolic reward of a new name."[20]

If the notion of rebirth is characteristic of the American Adam, it is crucial to the overlapping American narrative of "regeneration through violence" in which acts of violence and destruction are seen as fair practice when they purportedly allow a morally strengthened consciousness to emerge.[21] And it is in keeping with both traditions, then, that early on in *Catcher*, Holden Caulfield purchases a red hunting cap that his prep school roommate calls a "deer-shooting cap." "Like hell it is," Holden retorts, and then clarifies to the reader of his narrative, "I took it off and looked at it. I sort of closed one eye, like I was taking aim at it. 'This is a people shooting hat,' I said. 'I shoot people in this hat'" (22).[22]

Further along, Holden battles an older and stronger classmate to protect the reputation of a female friend and finds himself on the losing end of the fight. Searching for his cap in defeat, Holden comes face-to-face with himself, and it is this critical moment of self-recognition that will lead to his leave-taking of Pencey Prep:

> I couldn't find my goddam hunting hat anywhere. Finally, I found it. It was under the bed. I put it on, and turned the peak around to the back, the way I liked it, and then I went over and took a

look at my stupid face in the mirror. You never saw such gore in
your life. I had blood all over my mouth and chin and even on my
pajamas and bathrobe. It partly scared me and it partly fascinated
me. All that blood and all sort of made me look tough. I'd only
been in about two fights in my life, and I lost both of them. I'm
not too tough. I'm a pacifist, if you want to know the truth. (45)

If the first passage recalls the heroic tradition of Cooper's *Deerslayer*
(Holden donning the symbolic garb of the deer hunter and further
identifying himself by his hawkeyed aim), then the second passage can be
seen as a suggestion for a new errand for the Adamic hero: that of pacifism
except when called to the protection of innocents. His ritual battle endured,
Holden's reversal of the hunting cap brings to mind the cap of a baseball
catcher. Holden is thus implicitly renamed and it is a name he will later
explicitly claim.

Just as the moment of trial and rebirth was the creation of Lewis's
Adamic character, it was his survival through a later "fall" from grace that
brought the character to heroic status. Although the consequences of such
a fall would entail some suffering, the fall itself offered an opportunity for
learning necessary to the character's growth in moral understanding and
conscience to fully heroic stature. In the writing of the elder Henry James,
for example, the hero "had to fall, to pass beyond childhood in an encounter
with 'Evil,'" and "had to mature by virtue of the destruction of his own
egotism." The very act of "falling" opened the path to moral perfection, a
state viewed by James as achievable "not by learning, only by *unlearning*."[23]

Considered within this framework of the "fortunate fall," Holden's
experiences after he leaves Pencey Prep can be seen as necessary to his
developing moral stature: from his introduction to the seamy side of New
York City life via bar flies, stale cabs, hotel pimps and prostitutes to his
confrontation with Mr. Antolini. Antolini is a teacher from one of Holden's
past prep schools, "the best teacher I ever had" (174), and Holden turns
to him for both moral support and physical shelter. Holden's visit to his
home, however, is abruptly terminated when Holden interprets Antolini's
consoling caresses as a homosexual advance.

Holden flees Antolini's apartment, disillusioned, and less innocent
than when he arrived, but before he can depart, Antolini makes a
prediction as to Holden's future: "I have a feeling that you're riding for
some kind of a terrible, terrible fall. But I don't honestly know what
kind," Antolini warns Holden. "It may be the kind where, at the age of
thirty, you sit in some bar hating everybody who comes in looking as if he
might have played football in college." Fearing Holden will compromise
himself in conforming to normative social roles and expectations, Antolini

describes a future of miserable scenarios in which Holden might "pick up just enough education to hate people who say, 'It's a secret between he and I,'" or become a businessman "throwing paper clips at the nearest stenographer" (186).

Holden grasps Antolini's depiction but rejects and amends some of his predictions. Telling him, "you're wrong about hating football players and all. You really are. I don't hate too many guys," Holden asserts his own compassionate perspective: "What I may do, I may hate them for a little while . . . but it doesn't last too long, is what I mean. After a while, if I didn't see them . . . I sort of missed them" (187). Thinking Holden still doesn't understand him, Antolini tries to clarify the future of quiet desperation he fears for Holden:

> This fall I think you're riding for—it's a special kind of fall, a horrible kind. The man falling isn't permitted to feel or hear himself hit bottom. He just keeps falling and falling. The whole arrangement's designed for men who, at some time or other in their lives, were looking for something their own environment couldn't supply them with. Or they thought their environment couldn't supply them with. So they gave up looking. They gave it up before they ever really even got started. You follow me? (187)

In truth, Holden is already struggling against the fall from the idealism that Antolini assumes to accompany the loss of childhood innocence, but Holden is trying as well to maintain *the perception of hope* that is crucial to the struggle itself. It is in this sense that Salinger, in his development of Holden as a hero, perhaps unwittingly draws attention to a paradox within the tradition of the American Adam: heroic status is attained by gaining moral strength through "falling," yet the future role of the hero is to *prevent* (in actuality or figuratively) others from taking the same fall. Hence, in the passage that gives title to the novel, Holden's new-found purpose in life is to be "the catcher in the rye":

> Anyway, I keep picturing all these little kids playing some game in this big field of rye and all. Thousands of little kids, and nobody's around—nobody big, I mean—except me. And I'm standing on the edge of some crazy cliff. What I have to do, I have to catch everybody if they start to go over the cliff—I mean if they're running and they don't look where they're going I have to come out from somewhere and *catch* them. That's all I'd do all day. I'd just be the catcher in the rye and all. (173)

Although he wishes to prevent the fall of others, Holden cannot "catch" himself from his own fall—indeed, the "catcher in the rye" itself is a fantasy. The world of childhood innocence may exist outside of adult society but the inescapable process of maturity will eventually find all children becoming adult "insiders," participants in the larger social context, willing or not. In this sense, Holden's wish to remain "outside" the corrupting influences of adult society is again consistent with the mythos of the American Adam. The very heroism of the Adamic character rests on his ability to participate in and improve upon "society" even as he manages to sustain the moral certitude of his a priori innocence, a paradoxical stance that requires no small amount of skill on the part of the writer to maintain reader credibility.

Salinger manages this paradox through Holden's fearful sensation of "disappearing." In the duality of inside/outside relations, the outside "self" still depends upon the recognition of *other insiders* to validate one's very sense of existence. When Holden decides to leave Pencey Prep School—an action consistent with his outsider status—he painfully acknowledges his need for recognition of his leave-taking by those who remain "inside" Pencey:

> What I was really hanging around for, I was trying to feel some kind of good-by. I mean I've left schools and places I didn't even know I was leaving them. I hate that. I don't care if it's a sad good-by or a bad good-by, but when I leave a place I like to *know* I'm leaving it. If you don't, you feel even worse. (4)

When the necessary "good-byes" are not forthcoming, Holden leaves in a state of limbo, neither insider nor outsider, and the perception of loss of self is palpable as Holden reports that he feels as if he is "disappearing" every time he crosses a road. This sensation is repeated toward the novel's end when Holden again takes flight in a state of near-total anomie in which he fears that he might "never get to the other side of the street" and would instead "just go down, down, down, and nobody'd ever see me again." In his desperation, Holden makes believe that he is talking to his dead brother, Allie, and manages to barely maintain his sense of identity through a series of incantations to Allie, pleading "don't let me disappear" (197–98).

Readers of the novel could construe Holden's sensation of "disappearing" as well as his reliance on his dead brother's support as evidence of incipient insanity rather than an imaginative preservation of self. Holden himself refers to his behavior as "crazy" and "madman stuff" throughout the novel. Yet this craziness is not only the consequence of Holden's alienation from society but also the very expression of that alienation. The only recourse Holden foresees is to "reappear" inside society, in a wholly different circumstance. In an extended fantasy sequence, he envisions himself structurally and functionally inside society while remaining outside in any meaningful sense:

> I'd start hitchhiking my way out West. . . . I'd be somewhere out West where it was very pretty and sunny and where nobody'd know me and I'd get a job. I figured I could get a job at a filling station somewhere, putting gas and oil in people's cars. I didn't care what kind of job it was, though. Just so people didn't know me and I didn't know anybody. I thought what I'd do was, I'd pretend I was one of those deaf-mutes. That way I wouldn't have to have any goddam stupid useless conversations with anybody. (198)

In his fantasy of moving West, Holden is attempting a further "new beginning," in which he will protect his innocence and idealism by physically moving out and away from the inauthenticity of adult society. A course of action that is familiar in American frontier experience, the idea of escaping into the wilderness of the "untracked American forest" is endemic to the American Adam and requires the creation of a fictional environment in which "the world always lies before the hero, and normally, like Huck Finn, he is able to light out again for the 'territories.'"[24]

Holden, however, is not in the midst of the "untracked American forest" but rather in the urban "jungle" of the mid-twentieth century. Salinger's use of this environment emphasizes the coldness of modern institutions and the lack of meaning in contemporary language, as evidenced through his continuing imagery of graffiti and obscenities scrawled over hard exterior surfaces. Time and again, Holden attempts to erase or rub out the obscenities from the walls of a railway station, a museum, and a school. Holden reads these obscenities as expressions of hostility that represent not only the loss of innocence but the perversion of that innocence. When Holden finds "Fuck You" scrawled on the wall of the school attended by his sister, Phoebe, it drives him "damn near crazy" to think that first the "little kids would see it" and "then finally some dirty kid would tell them—all cockeyed, naturally—what it meant," causing them to *think* about it and maybe even *worry* about it for a couple of days" (201).

Consequently, when Holden confronts his own mortality, the perception of hope so crucial to the continuation of the American Adam is dashed by his recognition of the postwar cultural conditions of anonymity and alienation:

> That's the whole trouble. You can't ever find a place that's nice and peaceful, because there isn't any. You may *think* there is, but

once you get there, when you're not looking, somebody'll sneak
up and write "Fuck you" right under your nose. Try it sometime.
I think, even, if I ever die, and they stick me in a cemetery, and I
have a tombstone and all, it'll say "Holden Caulfield" on it, and
then what year I was born and what year I died, and then right
under that it'll say "Fuck you." I'm positive, in fact. (204)

Here, Holden's realization of the apparent futility of attempting to
make his individual life fully distinctive, and the absurdity of trying to prevent
the loss or perversion of innocence, does not stop him from continuing to try
to erase the obscenities he personally confronts. In a revision of the Adamic
plot that reflects the paradoxical sentiments of disillusionment and optimism
prevalent in postwar America, Salinger requires his readers to entertain
notions of Holden's defeat and demise only to salvage Holden's heroic status
by emphasizing the relentless hopefulness of his actions.[25] Signifying the
survival of Holden's optimism, Holden's repeated erasures of the obscene
scrawlings take the form of what critic Ihab Hassan has termed the "rare
quixotic gesture"—an eloquent act of hopefulness by the absurd yet heroic
American character. Arguing that the "unmistakably American flourish" of
the quixotic gesture is rooted in the "quest of American adolescents . . . for
an idea of truth," Hassan believed that such actions were gestures "at once of
pure expression and of expectation, of protest and of prayer, of aesthetic form
and spiritual content," and finally, "behavior that sings."[26]

    While the rubbing out of obscenities is the most self-conscious (and self-
defeating) effort in *Catcher*, the very fantasy of being the "catcher in the rye"
is itself a notion of quixotic hopefulness. Holden's account of his "madman"
days ends with an expression of joy and momentary return to innocence
as he watches his young sister, Phoebe, riding a carousel in the rain at his
encouragement. Phoebe has just returned Holden's red hunting cap, placing it
on his head and effectively acknowledging the temporal nature of his identity
as "the catcher" when she tells him "you can wear it for a while."

    Noting upon reflection that his hunting cap "really gave me quite a lot
of protection, in a way," Holden sits in the rain and gets soaked watching
Phoebe. It is a moment worth the drenching for Holden, who finds himself
feeling "so damn happy, if you want to know the truth. I don't know why.
It was just that she looked so damn *nice*, the way she kept going around and
around, in her blue coat and all." Concluding by telling the reader, "God, I
wish you could've been there," Holden's narrative here implies that while the
preservation of innocence might indeed be impossible, the appreciation of
that innocence is enough to restore the sense of hope (212–13).

    Catcher closes with Holden's summary of his final state of convalescence—
although whether he is recovering from a mental breakdown or physical

exhaustion is unclear. Not surprisingly, the tale ends on a hopeful if enigmatic note as Holden first tells the reader that "if you want to know the truth, I don't know what I think about it. I'm sorry I told so many people about it." In the very next sentence, however, Holden goes on to acknowledge, "All I know is, I sort of miss everybody I told about. Even old Stradlater and Ackley, for instance. I think I even miss that goddam Maurice, leading Holden to warn the reader, "Don't ever tell anybody anything." If you do, you start missing everybody" (213–14). Hence, if Holden at last remains outside society, it is with an enriched sense of his kinship with those *inside*—an affinity ironically recognized through his struggle to distinguish himself from them.

In *The Myth of Sisyphus*, Albert Camus writes of the absurd hero: "The struggle itself toward the heights is enough to fill a man's heart. One must imagine Sisyphus happy."[27] And so do I see Holden Caulfield, as both absurd hero and one ultimately happy at his task, balancing between actions of individual responsibility and engagement in a social community, a hero in the tradition of one of America's central fables. That the postwar context in which *Catcher* was conceived and read is itself a quixotic construction is the subject of the next chapter: a consideration of the perceptions of post–World War II intellectuals that the American errand had gone awry if not failed, and their wish to somehow sustain that selfsame sense of innocence.

Notes

1. I am indebted to Adam Moss's compilation of the publishing history of *Catcher* in "*Catcher* Comes of Age," *Esquire*, Dec. 1981, 56–57, and Michael Kenney's summary "Searching for Salinger," *Boston Globe*, 3 Sept. 1997, sect C1. Some confusion crops up as to the initial copyright date for *Catcher*. Two incidents that appear in *Catcher* were published earlier as segments in two short stories by J. D. Salinger: "I'm Crazy" in *Collier's* (Dec. 1945), and "Slight Rebellion Off Madison" in the *New Yorker* (Dec. 1946). Nevertheless, the first date for the novel as a complete work is July 1951, published by Little, Brown and Co. (New York).

2. The television series are *Sixty Minutes* (CBS), air date 1 Nov. 1982; *Archie Bunker's Place* (CBS), air date 21 Feb. 1982; *Family Feud* (ABC), air date 19 Oct. 1983. The novels are Michael Bowen's *Can't Miss* (New York: Harper and Row, 1987), Erich Segal's *Oliver's Story* (New York: Harper and Row, 1977), W. P. Kinsella's *Shoeless Joe* (Boston: Houghton Mifflin, 1982), and Julie Smith's *New Orleans Beat* (New York: Ivy Books, 1994). These examples came to my attention in the course of everyday experience rather than through an intentional survey—and many more were recounted to me that I did not formally verify.

3. *Family Feud*, host Richard Dawson. For a discussion of the assumed audience and intent of *Family Feud*, as well as its history as a highly successful television game show, see Mark Crispin Miller's essay "Family Feud" in *New Republic*, 18–25 July 1983, 23–27.

4. Bowen 202. In fact, the reference to *Catcher* here is so abbreviated that an unfamiliar reader would likely be more confused than drawn into further identification with Bowen's character: "She sounded like something out of *The Catcher in the Rye*. He gave her a benign smile. '*Phony* is a word I'm not particularly fond of, Rook.'"

5. Kinsella 72. See also 26–34, 51–60, 73–78, and 219–24. In the film version of the novel, *Field of Dreams* (1989), J. D. Salinger is dropped as a character; however, the play on "catcher" and the treatment of baseball as a Zen experience remains focal.

6. Smith 174–75.

7. Further evidence that *Catcher* is assumed to be a part of cultural knowledge exists in its inclusion in the popular 1980s board game Trivial Pursuit (copyright 1981 Horn-Abbot; distributed in the U.S. by Selchow and Righter, Co.). See the Genus edition, card no. 955, "Arts and Literature" category: Q. "What book does Holden Caulfield appear in?" A. "*The Catcher in the Rye.*"

8. Sanford Pinsker, "*The Catcher in the Rye* and All: Is the Age of Formative Books Over?" Georgia Review 1986 (40): 953–67. Of note, Pinsker identifies Kinsella's *Shoeless Joe* as a contemporary contender for "formative book" status.

9. Moss 56.

10. Interview with Monica Bullock, 10 Feb. 1986, Orange County, Calif.

11. Smith 175.

12. R. W. B. Lewis, *The American Adam* (Chicago: U of Chicago P, 1955), 1–2.

13. Ibid., 1. Lewis's reliance on a select body of literature for his analysis combined with his willingness to then generalize that analysis to "a native American mythology" of "our culture" reflects 1950s intellectual assumptions about cultural holism and the value of elite literature. Often referred to as the "myth-symbol-image" school of cultural analysis, this perspective has received just criticism since the late 1960s for its lack of distinction between dominant and subcultural realms of production, familiarity, and adoption of such a mythology. Rather than wholly discounting Lewis's work on the basis of these criticisms, I find *American Adam* to be instructive on two counts: as a primary source for understanding 1950s intellectuals and for his definition of the American Adam itself. Essentially, Lewis's analysis of the American Adam as both mythology and character type remains accurate, if needing a broader range of cultural materials for evidence. Similarly, Lewis's interpretation of that mythology is not so much inaccurate as lacking in address to the question of how such a mythology functions as an ideology, and for whom. Contemporary scholars would perhaps not overlook broader sources nor fail to see the usefulness of the American Adam mythology in attempted justification of otherwise arbitrary, socially constructed inequalities in American life. I have little difficulty, for example, in recognizing the American Adam, alive if unwell, in the 1980s spate of *Rambo* films, literature, and consumer items, and could readily argue the ideological usage of the American Adam mythology in these materials. If Lewis suffered from the "intellectual blinders" of his own time of scholarship, it would be further nearsightedness to disavow what he did elucidate.

14. Lewis 9–10.

15. Ibid., 197, 198.

16. Ibid., 5, 111.

17. J. D. Salinger, *The Catcher in the Rye* (New York: Bantam Books, 1964), 1. Further citations appear parenthetically in the text.

18. Lewis 91.

19. See James Fenimore Cooper, *The Deerslayer* (1841; Albany: SUNY P, 1987), 124–29.

20. Lewis 104.

21. See Richard Slotkin, *Regeneration through Violence* (Middletown, Conn.: Wesleyan UP, 1973), and also Richard Drinnon, *Facing West: The Metaphysics of Indian-Hating and Empire-Building* (New York: New American Library, 1980).

22. Of note, this section of the novel is interpreted by Alan Nadel in *Containment Culture* as evidence that Holden Caulfield is a fictional McCarthyite: "Donning his red hunting hat, he attempts to become the good Red-hunter, ferreting out the phonies and subversives" (71). See my introductory discussion of my disagreement with Nadel's interpretation.

23. Lewis 55, 57.

24. Ibid., 100.

25. Necessary even to his limited consideration of post–World War II writers, this alteration of the classic mythos is what Lewis termed "the matter of Adam: the ritualistic trials of the young innocent, liberated from family and social history or bereft of them; advancing hopefully into a complex world he knows not of; radically affecting that world and radically affected by it; defeated, perhaps even destroyed . . . but leaving his mark upon the world, and a sign in which conquest may later become possible for survivors" (127).

26. Ihab Hassan, *Radical Innocence: Studies in the Contemporary American Novel* (Princeton, N.J.: Princeton UP, 1961).

27. Albert Camus, *The Myth of Sisyphus*, trans. Justin O'Brien (New York: Vintage Books, 1959), 90.

EBERHARD ALSEN

The Catcher in the Rye

I'm quite illiterate, but I read a lot.

Holden Caulfield

J.D. Salinger invented the central character of *The Catcher in the Rye* 10 years before the publication of that novel. The sixteen-year-old Holden Caulfield first appears in the story "Slight Rebellion Off Madison" which Salinger sold to *New Yorker* magazine in 1941 and which he later transformed into Chapter 17 of *The Catcher in the Rye*. "Slight Rebellion" is the story of Holden's relationship with his girl friend Sally Hayes. Holden eventually alienates Sally by calling her "a royal pain" because she doesn't want to run away to the woods of Massachusetts or Vermont with him. *The New Yorker* shelved the story in 1941 but finally published it in 1946. Meanwhile, *Collier's* magazine printed another story about Holden Caulfield, "I'm Crazy" (1945). This story contains what amounts to a plot outline of *The Catcher in the Rye*. It begins with Holden saying good-bye to his history teacher Spencer at Pencey Preparatory School, and it ends with Holden sneaking into his parents' apartment in New York to talk to his sister Phoebe before telling his parents that he's been expelled from yet another school.

Another preliminary study for *The Catcher in the Rye* was "a novelette ninety pages long," so Salinger told William Maxwell, when Maxwell was writing a biographical piece about him for the *Book-of-the-Month Club*

From *A Reader's Guide to J.D. Salinger*. Westport, CT, and London: Greenwood Press, 2002, pp. 53–77. © 2002 by Eberhard Alsen.

News in 1951. Maxwell reports that Salinger had the novelette accepted for publication in 1946 but that he withdrew it at the last minute and "decided to do it over again" (5). That ninety-page draft probably was an expanded version of "I'm Crazy" with "Slight Rebellion Off Madison" spliced into the middle of it.

CRITICAL RECEPTION

The Catcher in the Rye was received enthusiastically by the reading public. Even before its publication, it was adopted by the Book-of-the-Month Club, and it sold fabulously well. Ten years after its first publication, over a million and a half copies had been sold in the United States. It was translated into dozens of languages and put on the reading lists of high schools in America and in several European countries. To this day, the worldwide sales of *The Catcher in the Rye* still total close to a quarter million a year.

Surprisingly, the first reviews of *The Catcher in the Rye* were mixed. Some reviewers praised the novel as a significant success while others panned it as a disappointing failure. Still others were offended by what they called the book's vulgar and obscene language.

On the one hand, the *New York Times*, the *New Yorker*, and the *Saturday Review of Literature* reviewed the book positively. Nash Burger, in the *New York Times*, called *Catcher* "an unusually brilliant first novel" (19); N.S. Behrman, in the *New Yorker*, called it "a brilliant, funny, meaningful novel" (65); and Harrison Smith, in the *Saturday Review*, judged it to be "a remarkable and absorbing novel" (28) and "a book to be read thoughtfully and more than once" (30).

On the other hand, the *New Republic*, the *Atlantic Monthly*, and the *Nation* gave the novel thumbs-down reviews. Anne Goodman, in the *New Republic*, said that "the book as a whole is disappointing" (23). It is "a brilliant tour-de-force, but in a writer of Salinger's undeniable talent one expects something more" (24). Harvey Breit, in the *Atlantic Monthly*, made the point that Holden Caulfield is "an urban, transplanted Huck Finn" (6) but that unlike Twain's *The Adventures of Huckleberry Finn*, *The Catcher in the Rye* ultimately fails because "whatever is serious and implicit in the novel is overwhelmed by the more powerful comic element" (7). And in the *Nation*, Ernest Jones (not the Ernest Jones who was a disciple of Freud's) admitted that *The Catcher in the Rye* is "a case history of all of us," but he said that "though always lively in its parts, the book as a whole is predictable and boring" (25).

The aspect of *The Catcher in the Rye* that caused the greatest disagreement among reviewers is its style. For instance, Riley Hughes, the reviewer in the *Catholic World* complained about an "excessive use of amateur swearing and coarse language" (31), and Morris Longstreth, writing for the *Christian Science Monitor*, found the novel to be "wholly repellent in its mingled vulgarity, naïveté, and sly perversion." Longstreth concluded that *The Catcher in the Rye* "is not fit for children to read" (30). This judgment was shared, a decade later, by parents of high school students in places such as Louisville, Kentucky; Tulsa, Oklahoma; and San Jose, California where the school boards banned the novel because of its language.

More open-minded reviewers analyzed the novel's style objectively and noted the influence of Ring Lardner and Ernest Hemingway. Writing for the *New York Herald Tribune*, Virgilia Peterson said that "had Ring Lardner and Ernest Hemingway never existed, Mr. Salinger might have had to invent the manner of his tale." She described this "manner" by saying, "*The Catcher in the Rye* repeats and repeats, like an incantation, the pseudo-natural cadences of a flat, colloquial prose which at best, banked down and understated, has a truly moving impact and at worst is casually obscene." According to Peterson, the value of the book depends on Holden's "authenticity," that is, on "what Holden's contemporaries, male and female, think of him" (4).

The academic critics didn't have a go at the novel until the mid-fifties. The fact that the novel had become a best seller among adolescents rubbed some critics the wrong way but confirmed the opinion of others that with *The Catcher in the Rye* they had a new classic on their hands. The most positive of the early academic analyses is entitled "J.D. Salinger: Some Crazy Cliff" (1956). It was written by Arthur Heiserman and James E. Miller who bestowed epic grandeur on *The Catcher in the Rye* when they asserted that the novel belongs to the "ancient and honorable narrative tradition . . . of the Quest" (196). The two critics saw similarities between *The Catcher in the Rye* and such masterworks of world literature as Homer's *Odyssey* and James Joyce's *Ulysses* and such American classics as Mark Twain's *The Adventures of Huckleberry Finn* and F. Scott Fitzgerald's *The Great Gatsby*. They said about Holden Caulfield that "unlike other American knights errant, Holden seeks Virtue second to Love," and they explained Holden's quest by saying that he is "driven toward love of his fellow man" (197–198).

At the opposite end of the critical spectrum, George Steiner took issue with the exaggerated praise that other critics had heaped upon *The Catcher in the Rye*. In his article, "The Salinger Industry" (1959), Steiner granted Salinger that "he has a marvelous ear for the semi-literate meanderings of the adolescent mind" (82), and he admitted that Salinger is "a most skillful and original writer" (85). However, Salinger should not be praised "in terms appropriate to the master poets of the world." Salinger falls short of being a writer of the first rank, so Steiner argued, because he "flatters the very ignorance and moral shallowness of his young readers. He suggests to them that formal ignorance, political apathy and a vague *tristesse* are positive virtues" (83).

Subsequently, the critical pendulum swung in Salinger's favor, and since the early sixties, most critics have written appreciative analyses of *The Catcher in the Rye*.

NARRATIVE STRUCTURE AND POINT OF VIEW

In its narrative structure and point of view *The Catcher in the Rye* resembles Mark Twain's *The Adventures of Huckleberry Finn*. Like Twain's novel, Salinger's is told in the first person by an adolescent, the plot is episodic, the central conflict is between an adolescent and adult society, and the reader's interest is generated less by the events of the plot than by the unique personality of the narrator-protagonist.

However, the differences between *Catcher* and *Huck Finn* are more crucial than the similarities. First of all, the events in *The Catcher in the Rye* all occur on one weekend between Saturday afternoon and Monday morning while the events in *Huck Finn* span over two months. Secondly, the episodes in the plot are tied together more closely in *Catcher* than they are in *Huck Finn*. And thirdly, the conflict between Holden and adult society is resolved, whereas the conflict between Huck Finn and adult society remains unresolved. At the end of *Catcher*, Holden is getting ready to go back to school, but at the end of *Huck Finn*, Huck is getting ready to run away again, to "light out for the territory."

The events in *The Catcher in the Rye* follow one another in an almost random order, and the sequence of some of the events at Pencey Prep and the sequence of some of those in New York could be rearranged without damaging the plot. However, the episodes of the plot are strung like pearls on four narrative strands of different lengths. The two longer ones stretch through the length of the entire novel. They are Holden's conflict with the world of adults and his descent into an almost suicidal depression. The two shorter narrative strands are developed only in the second half of the novel. They are the decline of Holden's health and his inner change.

The novel's central conflict is between Holden and the adult world. It is due to Holden's unwillingness to become part of this world because most adults he knows are phonies, that is, people who claim to be something they are not. This central conflict is muted because Holden has more dramatic, face-to-face confrontations with people his own age than with adults. However, those with whom he does have such confrontation are adolescents who have already achieved the phoniness of adults. One such individual is Holden's roommate Ward Stradlater. Stradlater looks like a well-groomed individual but is a secret slob; moreover, in his relationships with girls, he has only one thing on his mind, and that is sexual conquest. Another adolescent who acts like an adult is Holden's girlfriend Sally Hayes, whom he calls "the queen of the phonies" because she is extremely concerned about appearances and, above all, because she acts as though she were already an adult.

During his conflict with Sally Hayes, Holden reveals that the kind of adult future Sally looks forward to is abhorrent to him. This conflict arises when Holden asks Sally to run away with him to the woods of Massachusetts or Vermont. He would get a job, and they would live in a cabin by a brook and maybe even get married. Sally tells Holden that his plan is an unrealistic fantasy because if he didn't get a job they'd both starve to death; besides they're still practically children, and they still have time to do all those things after he goes to college. She says: "There'll be oodles of marvelous places to go to." But Holden says it won't be the same after they are adults. If they wanted to go away they would have to telephone all their family and friends to say goodbye, and when they got to where they're going they would have to send back postcards. But what's worst, he would have to work in an office somewhere in Manhattan, ride to work in buses or cabs, read newspapers, and have other people over to play bridge.

Holden expresses a similar distaste for adult life when his sister Phoebe tells him that he has a very negative outlook and that there's nothing he wants to be when he grows up, not even a lawyer like his father. Holden says that lawyers are all right if they are committed to saving innocent people's lives. But that's not what lawyers do. All they do is make tons of money, play golf, buy expensive cars, and drink Martinis. In short, in Holden's view, even his own father is a phony because he is more interested in making money than in helping others.

Because he can't accept the kind of adult future that he describes to Sally and Phoebe, Holden decides to run away. He plans to hitchhike out West, get a job at a gas station, build himself a little cabin on the edge of the woods, and live there for the rest of his life. He'll pretend to be a deaf-mute so that he does not have to talk to adults.

Holden's conflict with the adult world is resolved because his little sister Phoebe makes him give up his rebellion. When Holden tells Phoebe about his plans to run away, Phoebe decides to skip school and come along with him. She is so persistent that Holden eventually tells her that he has changed his mind and that he is not going away anywhere. At this moment Holden's conflict with the adult world is resolved because he has decided to go home and confront his parents, even though he knows they will probably send him to a very strict military school.

Another pervasive narrative pattern that helps string together the episodes of the plot is Holden's emotional decline. We see the first symptom when he is on his way to say good bye to his history teacher at Pencey Prep. As he is about to cross a highway, he feels that he may disappear when he steps into the road. After he finishes packing his suitcase and gets ready to leave his dorm, he expresses his first death wish. He says that he felt so lonely that he almost wished he were dead. And when he actually walks out of the dorm, he breaks into tears.

Holden's death wish becomes more specific in New York after he gets beaten up by the pimp Maurice. He says he was thinking of committing suicide by jumping out of the hotel window. The next day, when he argues with his girlfriend Sally Hayes, he explains his crankiness by saying that he feels absolutely lousy. Later, that night, in the bathroom of a hotel bar, Holden once again breaks down and cries. And still later that same night, Holden's favorite teacher, Mr. Antolini, makes what Holden considers a homosexual pass at him and Holden says at this point that he was more depressed than he ever was in his entire life. The next morning, as Holden walks up Fifth Avenue toward Phoebe's school, he again has the strange sensation that he will disappear every time he crosses a street.

Holden finally overcomes his depression when he watches Phoebe go around and around on a carousel in Central Park. He says that he didn't care that the rain was soaking him to the skin because he felt tremendously happy, and this happiness almost made him cry. Holden tries to explain this sudden emotional change by saying that Phoebe looked so nice riding the carousel. But that is not much of an explanation. Apparently Holden doesn't understand himself why he is no longer depressed.

The explanation for Holden's sudden emotional uplift lies in his inner change which makes up another narrative strand in the novel. This change begins in the middle of the novel, on Sunday morning, when Holden starts to find out that not all people turn into phonies when they grow up. He finds that out when he gets to know two nuns while having breakfast in an inexpensive restaurant. He is especially taken with the nun who is an English teacher and who shares his fondness for Shakespeare's *Romeo and Juliet*. Holden later thinks of those two nuns when Phoebe accuses him of not liking anything or anybody. Even though he talked to the nuns for only a short while, they are now among his favorite people, along with his dead brother Allie and his favorite teacher Mr. Antolini. Holden's visit with Mr. Antolini also has a lot to do with his inner change because Antolini takes Holden's rebellion seriously and recognizes it as a moral and spiritual crisis. And even though Holden recoils when Antolini expresses his fondness for him by stroking his head, he recognizes that Antolini is a caring individual and not a phony.

Holden completes his inner change when he accepts responsibility for Phoebe. Phoebe threatens to quit school if Holden runs away, and Holden ends his rebellion so that Phoebe will go back to school.

The fourth narrative strand, that of Holden's deteriorating health, not only helps to tie the plot's episodes together, it also lends credibility to

Holden's surrender to the adult world. It could even be argued that at the end of the novel he is simply too sick to rebel any longer. Holden alerts us to the deterioration of his health at the beginning of the novel when he explains why he is in a sanatorium in California: "I practically got t.b. and came out here for all these goddam checkups and stuff" (5). Holden's health seems fine until Sunday night when he gets drunk at a hotel bar and then tries to sober up in the men's room by soaking his head in a sink. Then he walks to Central Park to look for the ducks in the partially frozen lagoon. As ice is forming in his hair, he wonders if he is going to contract pneumonia and die. Then on Monday morning, as he is walking down Fifth Avenue, he begins to perspire heavily, and he feels that he is on the verge of vomiting. When he is at Phoebe's school where he gives the secretary a note for Phoebe, he suddenly needs to sit down because he again feels nauseous. A short time later, while he is waiting for Phoebe in the Metropolitan Museum of Art, he has to go to the bathroom because he feels a bout of diarrhea coming on. But before he can relieve himself, he passes out. Although he feels much better when he comes to, he later makes his condition worse by sitting on a park bench in the December rain while watching Phoebe ride the carousel.

In addition to the four narrative strands of different lengths, what also ties together the novel's episodes is Holden Caulfield's distinctive voice. Salinger's choice of the first person point of view not only gives the novel its special flavor of authenticity, it also allows Holden to express thoughts and feelings that we would not be aware of if the novel were told from an objective third person point of view. The choice of the first person point of view strengthens the reader's identification with the narrator-protagonist and ultimately makes the reader care more about Holden's personality than the events of the plot.

The rightness of Salinger's decision in favor of the first person point of view becomes apparent when we compare a passage from "Slight Rebellion Off Madison" to the reworked version in *The Catcher in the Rye*. In the early story, Salinger uses an objective third person point of view. Therefore, we see Holden only from the outside and hear what he says, but we don't find out what he thinks and feels. In the early story, Holden tells Sally Hayes:

> "You don't see what I mean at all."
> "Maybe I don't. Maybe you don't either," Sally said.
> Holden stood up with his skates slung over one shoulder.
> "You give me a royal pain," he announced quite dispassionately.
> ("Rebellion" 84)

And that's how the scene ends in the short story. We don't find out what Holden thinks. We don't even find out how Sally reacts. Here now is the reworked passage as it appears in the novel:

> "You don't see what I mean at all."
>
> "Maybe I don't. Maybe you don't either," old Sally said. We both hated each other's guts by that time. You could see there wasn't any sense in trying to have an intelligent conversation. I was sorry as hell I'd started it.
>
> "C'mon, let's get outa here," I said. "You give me a royal pain in the ass if you want to know the truth."
>
> Boy did she hit the ceiling when I said that. I know I shouldn't've said it and I probably wouldn't've ordinarily, but she was depressing the hell out of me. (*Catcher* 133)

The major difference between the scene in the story and the novel is that we learn much more about Holden's thoughts and feelings in the novel than we do in the story, and we can therefore identify more with him.

Another aspect of the narrative perspective in the novel is that Holden is occasionally able to step out of his own shoes and look at himself from the perspective of an outsider. Yet in other places, we find that he also has some blind spots in his view of himself.

The occasional objectivity of Holden's point of view is illustrated at the end of the passage in which he describes his fight with Sally Hayes. Holden says that he apologized like mad but that Sally wouldn't accept his apologies. In frustration, Holden did something he knows he shouldn't have done, he began to laugh. He admits that he has a very loud, stupid-sounding laugh, and in a typical Salingeresque non-sequitur, he says that if he ever sat behind himself in a movie theater and heard himself laugh like that, he'd lean over and tell himself to shut up.

On the other hand, there are a number of passages in the novel in which Holden demonstrates a blatant lack of self-perception. For instance, he doesn't even realize in retrospect, when he tells the story, how unrealistic he was when he asked Sally Hayes to run off to the woods with him and live in a cabin. When his money runs out, so Holden said, he'll get a job to support the two of them. Here most readers will shake their heads about Holden's inability to see himself for what he is. Holden has never had to work for his money and probably would not like it at all. He can only entertain such notions because deep down he knows that he can always return to his affluent parents when things don't work out.

Thus the contrast between the blind spots in Holden's self-perception and his occasional ability to see himself exactly the way he is perceived by others is a unique element of the novel's narrative perspective. It helps to develop Holden into a fictional character who is unusually complex.

CHARACTERIZATION AND STYLE

One of the astonishing things about *The Catcher in the Rye* is that adolescents all over the world—boys as well as girls—continue to identify with Holden Caulfield even now, 51 years after the novel was first published. Two reasons for the universal appeal of Holden's personality offer themselves. One is that Salinger subordinated all other aspects of the novel to the development of Holden's character. For instance, it seems that he created the minor characters not to advance the plot but to shed light on Holden's personality, and that he even designed the symbolism to clarify what kind of person Holden is. But the main reason Holden is so believable is that—like most adolescents—he is full of contradictions and ambivalent feelings.

The contradictions in Holden's character are reflected in his appearance. Although he is only sixteen when the events of the novel take place, he is six-foot-two-and-a-half and has a patch of gray hair on the right side of his head. Also, he wears a red hunting hat with the visor turned backwards which contrasts sharply with his sports coat and tie.

Holden is aware of some of the contradictions in his personality. One of these contradictions concerns his age. He sometimes acts as though he were much older than sixteen and sometimes as though he were much younger. On several occasions, Holden tries to pass himself off as older than he is. For instance, he invites two different cab drivers to stop at a bar for drinks and he tells the prostitute, Sunny, and the three girls from Seattle that he is twenty-two years old. But on other occasions, Holden also acts younger than his age, especially when he pretends to be a character in a movie. In one instance, he annoys his roommate Stradlater by tap-dancing all over the bathroom while Stradlater is shaving. Holden says that he is the Governor's son and that his father doesn't want him to be a tap dancer, he wants him to study at Oxford. But he can't help himself because dancing is in his blood. Holden even engages in make-believe when he doesn't have an audience. After he has been beaten up by the pimp Maurice, he pretends that he has been shot in the stomach. As he staggers around in his hotel room, he imagines that he is getting his automatic and that he is walking downstairs to find Maurice. He is clutching his stomach, and he is bleeding all over the stairs, but he finds Maurice and fires six bullets into his hairy belly.

Three other contradictions in Holden's character concern his attitudes toward the movies, literature, and religion. On the one hand, he goes to the movies often, imitates them, and at one point even gives us a long plot summary of a movie he went to see at Radio City, James Hilton's *Random*

Harvest. But he makes the contradictory comment about the film that it was so "putrid" that he could not stop watching it. Elsewhere he says that he hates the movies like poison but that he gets a bang out of imitating them.

About his relation to literature Holden makes this contradictory statement: "I'm quite illiterate, but I read a lot" (18). But when Holden talks about Shakespeare's *Romeo and Juliet*, Thomas Hardy's *The Return of the Native*, Scott Fitzgerald's *The Great Gatsby*, and Ernest Hemingway's *A Farewell to Arms*, we see that he is far from illiterate but has a good understanding of these works.

Holden's comments on religion are also contradictory. He claims that he is an atheist, but then he explains that he likes Jesus but he doesn't like the Disciples because they always let Jesus down. And Holden also shows a better understanding of the personality of Jesus than a Quaker classmate when they disagree about the fate of Judas. Holden says that he believes Jesus never sent Judas to hell. In short, Holden's sensitive comments about Jesus contradict his statement that he is an atheist.

Another major contradiction in Holden's character has to do with his attitude toward money. While he is disdainful of money and generous with it, he also has more respect for wealthy people than for people who are not so well off. Holden's generosity is illustrated when pays for the drinks of the three young women from Seattle with whom he dances on Saturday night and when he gives ten dollars to the nuns for their next collection and later frets that he didn't give them enough. But money itself doesn't mean much to him because he often forgets to pick up his change at restaurants and nightclubs. His disdain for money is also illustrated when he is down to his last four dollars and he uses the coins to skip them across the unfrozen part of the lagoon in Central Park.

Holden's disdain for money and his generosity stand in sharp contrast to statements that show him judging people by how much money they have. For instance, he mentions a roommate at a previous prep school who had very inexpensive suitcases while Holden had genuine cowhide bags from Mark Cross. Holden admits that he tends to dislike people just because they have cheap luggage. A moment later he tells us that one of the reasons he roomed with Stradlater at Pencey Prep is that Stradlater's suitcases were as good as his own. Holden again shows that he looks down on people who don't have much money when he walks behind a father, a mother, and a little boy who just came out of church on Sunday morning. Holden says he could tell they were poor. And then he explains that the father wore the kind of pearl-gray hat that poor fellows tend to wear when they want to look sharp.

And finally, like most adolescents, Holden has conflicting attitudes toward sex. He admits that he thinks about sex all the time and that sometimes he can imagine doing "very crumby stuff" if he had the opportunity. But when the opportunity does come up in New York, and he has a young prostitute in his hotel room, Holden suddenly isn't interested in sex. He says that he knows he is supposed to feel aroused when the girl pulls her dress up over her head, but he doesn't feel that way. Instead of feeling aroused by the girl, Holden feels sorry for her because she looks as if she is only sixteen, Holden's own age. That is why Holden says he felt more depressed than aroused.

Holden even has conflicting attitudes about necking. The previous year he made a rule that he was not going to neck with girls he did not respect. He broke that rule immediately because he spent that night necking with Anne Louise Sherman whom he considered a terrible phony. In short, Holden has the normal sexual urges of an adolescent, but he also has a conscience which tells him not to treat girls as mere sex objects.

Salinger gives Holden's personality additional depth through the secondary characters. Holden's attitudes toward and reactions to these people shed light on his likes and dislikes, especially since a number of the secondary characters seem to be pairs of opposites. Here we see another instance of Salinger's propensity to work in patterns of twos as in the doubling of letters in the names of characters and in his use of double protagonists in some of his early stories and his later novellas.

A pair of characters who reveal much about Holden's values are his older brother D.B., who is a successful writer, and his younger brother Allie, who died of leukemia. Holden's attitude toward D.B. is at best ambivalent and at worst negative. On the one hand, Holden says that D.B. is his favorite author, on the other hand he agrees with Antolini who said that a person who could write like D.B. should not write for Hollywood movies. And although Holden admires D.B. for making so much money, driving a Jaguar, and having a British movie actress for a girlfriend, he does call him a prostitute for selling out to Hollywood. If D.B. were not his brother, Holden would probably even call him a phony.

By contrast, Holden's attitude toward Allie is not only 100% positive but even worshipful. Holden says that Allie was the most intelligent person in the family. But what's even more important, Allie was also the kindest because Holden cannot remember that Allie ever got mad at anybody. Another thing that stands out about Allie is that he loved poetry so much that he copied his favorite poems on his baseball glove so he would have something good to read during the lulls in the games. Allie has remained Holden's favorite person even after his death, and Holden carries Allie's baseball glove around in his luggage as if it were a holy relic. In fact, Holden actually prays to Allie when he is about to cross a street and is afraid that he will disappear: "Allie, don't let me disappear, Allie. Please, Allie" (198). When we compare Holden's attitudes toward his brothers D.B. and Allie, we can see clearly that he respects Allie's kindness more than D.B.'s success.

That Holden ultimately judges people by how kind they are also becomes apparent when we examine his reasons for liking his former English teacher Antolini more than Spencer, his history teacher at Pencey. Holden tries to like Mr. Spencer and he even writes him a note so that Spencer won't feel so bad about flunking him. But when Holden goes to see him, Spencer is sarcastic and nasty while reading Holden's failing history exam back to him. Holden says that he won't ever forgive Spencer for his unkindness because if their roles were reversed, he would never have read that terrible exam out loud to Spencer.

While Mr. Spencer is too unkind to Holden, Mr. Antolini, Holden's English teacher from his previous prep school, is perhaps a bit too kind. One reason Holden likes Antolini is that he cared enough about James Castle, who committed suicide by jumping out of a window, to pick up his body and carry it to the infirmary. Moreover, Antolini is the only adult to take Holden seriously and reassure him that "many men have been just as troubled morally and spiritually as you are right now" (189). But when Holden wakes up on Antolini's couch at night to find Antolini patting his head and stroking his hair, he panics and thinks that Antolini is making a pass at him. Later Holden is no longer sure what Antolini's intentions were and starts thinking that even if Antolini is a homosexual, what counts is that he has been very kind to him.

That Holden tries to be more like Mr. Antolini than Mr. Spencer becomes apparent when we examine his relationship with another contrasting pair of minor characters, his roommate, Ward Stradlater, and his dorm neighbor, Robert Ackley. Ackley has a misanthropic personality, a face full of pimples, and "mossy" teeth. Although Ackley is being ostracized by most of the students at Pencey Prep, and although Holden dislikes his personality, he feels sorry for Ackley and invites him to go out on the town with him on his last night at Pencey Prep. Holden is probably the first person at Pencey to voluntarily spend time with Ackley, and Holden probably does so because unlike many others at Pencey, Ackley is at least a genuine person and not a phony.

By contrast with Ackley, Stradlater is one of the wealthiest, best looking, and most popular students at Pencey Prep, and while Holden can't help admiring him, he ultimately dislikes him even more than Ackley because he is a phony. There are several reasons why Holden thinks Stradlater is a phony. Stradlater always looks well groomed, but he never cleans his rusty razor; he can convince people, especially girls, that he is sincere when he is really lying to them; and he acts as though he likes people even though he is only in love with himself. Holden should therefore despise Stradlater, but instead he lends him his new hounds-tooth jacket and writes an English Composition essay for him. But Holden later gets in a fight with Stradlater because he worries that Stradlater might have seduced Jane Gallagher who is an old friend of Holden's. Holden is concerned, because most of the other boys at Pencey only claim to have had sexual intercourse; but from talking to a couple of girls, Holden knows that Stradlater really did have sex with some of his dates. Thus when Holden says that he hates Stradlater's guts, this may be in part because he envies him.

Yet another pair of minor characters that shed light on Holden's personality are Jane Gallagher and Sally Hayes. The characterization of the two tells us much about Holden's attitude toward the opposite sex. Holden met Jane Gallagher in the summer of 1948 when her family and Holden's were neighbors at a summer resort in Maine. All summer, Holden and Jane played tennis and golf together, and in the evenings they went to the movies or played checkers. Holden's mother didn't think Jane was pretty, and Holden admits that she is "muckle-mouthed," by which he means she distorts her mouth a lot when she talks. But she has a terrific figure and above all a terrific personality. The two things that impress Holden most about Jane are that she always reads good books and that she never uses her kings when playing checkers but always keeps them in the back row because she likes the way the stacked-up pieces look when they are all lined up. Holden and Jane went around holding hands all the time, but they never actually necked. The two times they got close to getting physical were when Jane was crying and Holden kissed her tears away and when Jane suddenly put her hand on Holden's neck while they were watching a movie. Holden thinks that this is a typical thing for adult women to do to their children or their husbands, but if a young girl does it, it is unbearably pretty. In short, Jane Gallagher brings out a deep fondness in Holden, similar to what he feels for his dead brother Allie and for his little sister Phoebe.

We wonder therefore what Holden sees in his girlfriend Sally Hayes who is in many ways the opposite of Jane. For one thing, Sally is extremely good-looking and is very concerned about everybody's appearance. For instance, she tells Holden to grow out his crew cut because crew cuts are getting to be corny. Also, on their date, she wants to go skating at Radio City because she can rent one of those tiny skating skirts that look very good on her. Holden therefore calls Sally "the queen of the phonies" (116). However, when he meets her at the Biltmore Hotel for their Sunday date, Holden is overwhelmed by how gorgeous she looks. He even says that as soon as he saw her, he felt he wanted to marry her. But in retrospect, he admits that this was a crazy idea because he didn't even like her very much. Aside from her phoniness, another one of the reasons Holden doesn't like Sally much is that she has a loud, embarrassing voice. But then Holden adds that Sally can get away with that kind of voice because she is so good-looking. Even though Holden finds Sally irritating, he starts necking with her as soon as they get in the back of a taxicab. Holden even tells Sally that he loves her, but then he explains to us that he was lying when he said that but that he meant it at the time. The reason Holden briefly feels he loves Sally is, of course, that she is willing to play kissing and groping games with him.

Holden can no longer overlook the differences in his and Sally's personalities when he finds out that she is actually looking forward to becoming an adult and living the kind of conformist upper-middle-class life that Holden rebels against. This is why he finally tells her that she gives him "a royal pain in the ass" and why he lets her go home by herself. He says that he should not have done that but that has he was totally fed up with Sally. Without being aware of it, Holden here affirms a mature preference for substance over appearance, for the terrific personality of Jane Gallagher over the terrific looks of Sally Hayes.

The most important minor character in the novel is Holden's ten-year-old sister Phoebe. She is so important because she brings out a belated sense of responsibility in Holden and makes him end his rebellion. Holden mentions Phoebe early on in the novel and says about her that she is extremely smart and pretty. She is "roller-skate-skinny" and has red hair similar to that of Holden's dead brother Allie. She gets straight A's in school, and she likes to write novels that she never finishes about a girl detective named Hazle Weatherfield. Holden considers Phoebe one of the very few people who really understand him. Phoebe's only fault, so Holden says, is that she is sometimes a bit too affectionate.

When we finally see Phoebe for the first time, we find that she is unusually perceptive and mature for a ten-year-old. Because Holden is home early for Christmas vacation and sneaks into the apartment, Phoebe figures out at once that Holden must have flunked out of yet another private school. When Holden tells her that he plans to hitchhike out West to work on a ranch in Colorado, Phoebe doesn't approve but gives him her Christmas money for travel expenses. Moreover, she also senses that Holden feels very depressed and lonesome. She therefore leaves school, packs her suitcase, and insists on coming along with Holden. Although Holden is moved by Phoebe's unconditional love, he won't allow her to run away with him. At this point Holden exhibits a sense of responsibility that we have not seen in him before. He accepts that he is his sister's keeper and that he must make sure Phoebe goes back to school. He therefore gives up his plan to run away and promises to go home and face his parents.

The way Holden Caulfield talks reveals just as much about the contradictions in his character as what he does. The silliness of Holden's speech mannerisms contrasts with his astute insights and his strongly held values. Taken out of context, almost any long quotation of what Holden is saying must seem insipid. For instance, Holden keeps attaching meaningless phrases such as "and all," "or something," and "or anything" to the end of many statements, as in "it's a pretty good book and all," "we could get married or something," and "there was no sun out or anything."

Moreover, like many adolescents who want to seem tough by sneering at the world, Holden attaches emphatic negative adjectives to nouns, adjectives such as "lousy," "goddam," "stupid," "crazy," "crumby," "corny," or "phony." For instance, on the first page of the novel, Holden says that he won't talk about his "lousy childhood" because he doesn't want to tell us his "whole goddam autobiography." And a few pages later, he talks about the "crazy cannon" on top of a "stupid hill" at Pencey Preparatory School.

Another speech mannerism is Holden's habit of attaching the adjective "old" to the names of people. This makes sense when he speaks of "old Spencer," his history teacher who is close to retirement. It does not make sense when he speaks of "old Phoebe," his ten-year-old sister. However the adjective "old" is not a term of endearment, as in Jay Gatsby's beloved phrase "old sport." Holden applies the adjective equally to people he likes and people he hates. For instance he talks about "old Maurice," the pimp who beats him up, and about "old Sally" who gives him "a royal pain in the ass."

And finally, Holden keeps repeating two statements that he is very fond of. One of them is "if you want to know the truth" and the other one is that something or someone "really kills me."

Since the style of *The Catcher in the Rye* is so distinctive, it begs to be parodied. And indeed, one of the reviews of the novel was written as a parody of its style. Here is part of the opening paragraph:

> This girl Helga, she kills me. She reads just about everything I bring into the house, and a lot of crumby stuff besides. She's crazy about kids. I mean stories about kids. But Hel, she says there's hardly a writer alive can write about children. . . . It depresses her. That's another thing. She can sniff out a corny guy or a phony book as quick as a dog smells a rat. This phoniness, it gives old Hel a pain if you want to know the truth. That's why she came hollering to me one day, her hair falling over her face and all, and said I had to read some damn story in *The New Yorker*. Who's the author? I said. Salinger, she told me. J.D. Salinger. Who's he? I asked. (Stern 2)

SETTINGS AND SYMBOLS

The time and locations of the settings in *The Catcher in the Rye* can be established from information that Holden mentions in passing. The narrative begins on Saturday afternoon, the 17th of December 1949 at the Pencey Preparatory School for Boys in Pennsylvania, and it ends on Monday morning, the 19th of December, in New York City. Even though it is winter, there are almost as many scenes that take place outdoors as indoors. Most of the outdoor scenes occur in New York, and the most memorable one is the scene of Holden watching Phoebe ride the carousel in Central Park in the pouring rain.

Like Salinger's earlier fiction, *The Catcher in the Rye* provides only sketchy, impressionistic descriptions of its physical settings. A typical example is the description of the home of Mr. Spencer, Holden's history teacher at Pencey Prep. After Holden rings the bell and Mrs. Spencer opens the door, Holden says: "They didn't have a maid or anything, and they always opened the door themselves. They didn't have too much dough" (5). And all that Holden mentions about the inside of the Spencers' house is that Mr. Spencer, who had the grippe, was sitting in a big leather chair, wrapped in a blanket, and that "there were pills and medicine all over the place, and everything smelled like Vicks Nose Drops" (7). As this example shows, the social milieu seems to be more important in the settings of *The Catcher in the Rye* than the physical details.

What almost all the indoor settings—except for the Spencers' home—have in common is that the social environment is upper middle class. First of all, Holden says about the social milieu of Pencey Prep that quite a few of his fellow students come from very wealthy families. When he goes home to talk to his sister Phoebe, we find that his parents' apartment house is located in one of the most expensive areas of Manhattan, on 71st Street just off Fifth Avenue, and that the family has a live-in maid. Later, Holden visits his former English teacher, Mr. Antolini, and says that he lived in a "very swanky apartment" and that his wife "was lousy with dough." The only indoor settings in New York that are not upper middle class are the hotel where Holden meets the young prostitute Sunny and the restaurant where he meets the two nuns.

There are three settings in the novel that are important because they cannot be associated with social class and because they have symbolic significance. One of these settings is the room with the dioramas in the Museum of Natural History. That room is symbolic because Holden's fondness for it reveals his desire to have things always stay the same. Another of these symbolic settings is Phoebe's elementary school, the same school where Holden went when he was younger. That school also symbolizes the kind of stability that Holden likes, and he is very much upset when that stability is threatened by obscene graffiti.

A third symbolic setting is an imaginary one. It is the cabin by a brook to which Holden wants to escape with Sally Hayes. Later in the novel, we get another version of that cabin to which he wants to escape by himself.

The Catcher in the Rye develops its meaning chiefly through its major symbols and through the change in the connotation of the central metaphor of the catcher in the rye. Like the symbolic settings in the novel, most of the symbolic objects contribute to the characterization of Holden Caulfield. Six major symbols in the novel are the ducks in Central Park, Holden's red hunting cap, the glass cases in the Museum of Natural History, the cabin by the woods to which Holden wants to escape, the obscene graffiti, and the carousel in Central Park. An analysis of these symbols clarifies the inner change that Holden experiences.

Before discussing the novel's symbols, it is necessary to analyze the novel's central metaphor, Holden wanting to be the catcher in the rye. Holden comes up with the idea when his little sister Phoebe tells him that he doesn't like anything or anybody and that he doesn't even know what he would like to be when he grows up. Holden replies that he does know what he wants to be when he grows up. He says when he heard the song, "If a body catch a body coming through the rye," he decided that that's what he wants to be, the catcher in the rye. Phoebe corrects him and says that the line goes, "If a body meet a body coming through the rye," and that it is not from a song but from a poem by Robert Burns. This information doesn't make a difference to Holden, and he explains that he keeps picturing thousands of little children playing in an enormous field of rye which has a steep cliff at one end, and there are no adults around except for him. He says that if the little kids are running and not looking where they are going, "I have to catch everybody if they start to go over the cliff" (173). That's all he wants to do all day; that's the only thing he would really like to be, the catcher in the rye.

The way Holden explains why he wants to be the catcher in the rye shows the kindness and unselfishness of his character. However, the surreal nature of the metaphor also reveals Holden's unwillingness to face the real life choices he needs to make now that he is approaching adulthood. By the end of the novel, Holden realizes that children won't grow up if there's always someone there to protect them from all potential harm. He therefore gives up his dream of being the catcher in the rye and is ready to make a realistic choice of what he wants to do with his life.

As far the symbols in the novel go, the most obvious one is Holden's hat. Holden describes it as a red hunting hat with a very long visor. When Holden's dorm neighbor Ackley tells him that where he comes from, people wear that kind of hat to shoot deer in, Holden replies that his is not a deer shooting hat but a people shooting hat.

Holden's hat is a complex symbol because it suggests several interpretations of its meaning. For one thing, it can be seen as a badge of Holden's deliberate nonconformity. He bought it because it clashes with the rest of his getup, his sports coat and tie. Also, he likes to draw attention to the incongruous hat by wearing it with the visor turned backward. By turning the visor backward Holden suggests that his values are the reverse of what everybody else's are. It is also the way that baseball catchers wear their caps. Therefore Holden's turning the visor of the hat to the back can be seen as foreshadowing his desire to be the catcher in the rye. And finally, because Holden calls it a people shooting hat, it symbolizes his dislike of most of the people around him. This dislike is very obvious to those who know Holden well. For instance, both his sister Phoebe and his favorite teacher Antolini tell him that he hates more people than he likes.

Near the end of the novel the hat disappears temporarily because Holden gives it to Phoebe. It is significant that Holden does not have the hat when his inner change occurs, when he decides not to run away. The hat reappears on Holden's head—this time with the visor facing front—in the carousel scene where it gives Holden protection while he is sitting on a park bench in the pouring rain.

Symbols that illustrate a more positive aspect of Holden's character than the hunting hat are the ducks in Central Park. Holden thinks of them for the first time while his history teacher is talking to him. He says he was not paying attention to Mr. Spencer because he suddenly started to wonder where the Central Park ducks go when the lagoon freezes over. Holden mentions the ducks in Central Park several more times and even asks two New York cab drivers if they know what happens to the ducks when the lagoon freezes. Holden's obsession with the ducks has been interpreted in a number of different ways. It has been suggested that the ducks represent Holden who also feels he has no place to go and is being "frozen out." Another view is that the mystery of the disappearance of the ducks can be likened to the mystery of people's disappearance into death. Still another interpretation of the meaning of the ducks picks up on Holden's idea that maybe some park employee came with a truck and took them to a zoo for the winter. Thus, when Holden wonders about the fate of the ducks, he is really wondering if there is some benevolent authority, some God, that takes care of humans just as the zoo employee takes care of the ducks. But the most common sense interpretation is simply that Holden's concern for the well-being of the ducks illustrates an important character trait, his compassion for all living things.

Another important symbol in *The Catcher in the Rye* is the glass cases in the Museum of Natural History. These dioramas display life-size figures of Indians weaving blankets and Eskimos catching fish. They are what Holden likes best in the museum because even if he went there a thousand times, the Eskimo would still be catching the same two fish and the Indian squaw would still be weaving the same blanket. They would not be different even though he, Holden, would have changed. Holden concludes that certain things should always stay the same: "You ought to be able to stick them in one of those big glass cases and just leave them alone" (122). Here we realize that Holden is troubled by change in general. He knows that he himself can't help changing as he grows up, but he wants the things he likes to be exempt from change. But eventually, at the end of the novel, during the carousel scene, he overcomes this desire for immutability.

A symbol that illustrates a more adult side of Holden's character than the glass cases with the Indians and Eskimos is the cabin in or on the edge of the woods. At a first glance, this symbol seems to represent only his wish to escape from the world of the phonies and from the kind of upper-middle-class future his parents have mapped out for him. But a close analysis shows that there is more to the symbol than that.

The cabin appears in two versions. Holden comes up with the idea of escaping to a cabin in the woods for the first time when he tries to get Sally Hayes to run away with him to Massachusetts or Vermont. He tells her that they will stay in a cabin camp until their money runs out. Then he will get a job somewhere, and they will live by a brook, and eventually they might get married. At this point, Holden's escape plan is still very sketchy. Later, he comes up with a more elaborate plan which includes the second version of the cabin. This time he plans to hitchhike to somewhere way out West where it is very pretty and sunny and where nobody knows him. He will get a job at a filling station, and he will pretend to be a deaf-mute. That way, he won't have to have "any goddam stupid useless conversations with anybody" (198). If someone wants to talk to him, the person has to write him a note on a piece of paper. With the money he earns at the gas station Holden plans to build himself a little cabin on the edge of the woods but not right in the woods because he wants the cabin to be in a place that is sunny all the time. He will do all his own cooking, and later on, he will meet a beautiful girl who is also a deaf-mute, and they will get married. If they have any children, they will hide them and home-school them. Holden imagines that he will not want to come home to New York until he is about thirty-five or until someone in the family gets very sick and wants to see him before the person dies. That will be the only reason for him to leave his cabin. He plans to invite his family to come and visit him in his cabin, but if any of them do anything phony, he won't let them stay.

In retrospect, Holden realizes that the part of his plan about pretending to be a deaf-mute was crazy, but he stresses that he really did decide to go out West. We therefore need to take his plan seriously. When we do, we realize that both versions of his dream of living in a cabin away from society involve his plan to eventually get married. In other words, Holden is realistic enough to know that once he is an adult, he will not want to live alone. This aspect of the cabin symbolism reveals that despite his dream of escape, Holden is on the verge of accepting adulthood.

When Holden crosses the threshold between adolescence and adulthood, two symbols help us understand his inner change. Both symbols show up near the end of the novel. One is the obscene graffiti and the other is the carousel in Central Park. In both cases, we see a change in Holden's attitude toward those symbols.

Holden's initial response to the obscene graffiti is to erase them, to pretend that they were never there. The first "Fuck you" that Holden sees on a wall in Phoebe's school is written in crayon, and so he has no trouble rubbing it out. But the second "Fuck you" is scratched into a wall with a knife, and Holden can't erase it. At this point Holden comes to the realization that even if he had a million years, he could not erase half the "Fuck you" signs in the world. And then he sees another "Fuck you" in one of his favorite places of refuge in New York, the Metropolitan Museum of Art. This is very depressing to him, and he realizes that he will never find "a place that's nice and peaceful" because there aren't any such places. He says that even if you think you have found such a place, "somebody'll sneak up and write 'Fuck you' right under your nose" (204).

The graffiti can be seen as symbols of all the negative things that Holden wants children to be protected from. But he comes to realize that they cannot be protected from all of them. When Holden still thought he wanted to be the catcher in the rye, he believed he could rub out all the "Fuck you" signs in the world. By the end of the novel he knows he can't. Moreover, he also knows that he cannot escape to a place that is free from "Fuck you" signs. In short, the ubiquitousness of the "Fuck you" signs is one of the reasons Holden gives up his dream of escaping to a cabin by the woods.

The carousel in Central Park is a symbol that also suggests a change in Holden, but it is a more complex symbol than the obscene graffiti. There's an obvious aspect to the meaning of the carousel, an aspect that Holden seems to be aware of, and a less obvious aspect that he seems unaware of.

The less obvious aspect of the carousel's meaning has to do with Holden's telling Phoebe that he changed his mind and that he is not going away anywhere. They are walking out of the zoo at Central Park and toward the carousel, and it is starting to rain. Holden hears the carousel music long before the carousel comes into sight. The song is "Oh, Marie!" which Holden says he heard "about fifty years ago" when he was a little kid (210). This is one thing he likes about carousels, he says, they keep on playing the same songs. Here Holden is still associating the carousel with his childish desire to have things always stay the same, like the dioramas in the Museum of Natural History.

But when Holden and Phoebe come to the carousel, Holden's attitude changes. Phoebe wants the two of them to take a ride together, but Holden tells her that he'll just watch her. Then he buys Phoebe a ticket and sits down on one of the benches surrounding the carousel where the parents of the other children on the carousel are sitting. When the rain starts coming down hard, the other adults seek shelter, but Holden continues sitting on his bench. He gets very wet, but he says he didn't bother to get out of the rain because he suddenly felt very happy about watching Phoebe ride the carousel. He explains: "It was just that she looked so damn *nice*, the way she kept going around and around in her blue coat and all" (213).

The carousel is therefore a symbol that has more than one level of meaning. Although it awakes childhood memories in Holden, it helps him define himself as being no longer a child. Watching Phoebe ride the carousel brings Holden a vicarious enjoyment similar to that of the parents of the other children on the carousel. It seems that he is enjoying his first taste of what it is like to be an adult and that he is enjoying it so much that he doesn't mind getting soaked to the skin in the heavy December rain.

All this is confirmed by what Holden actually realizes about the symbolism of the carousel. On this particular carousel the children are supposed to lunge upward and try to pull down a golden ring. Holden says that he is afraid Phoebe might fall off the carousel horse, but he stops himself from doing or saying anything. He has come to understand that when children want to go for the golden ring, we should not stop them. He says: "If they fall off, they fall off, but it's bad if you say anything to them" (211). Holden here realizes that the carousel represents life and grabbing for the gold ring represents the chances that children must take in order to grow up. When we see Holden allow Phoebe to take her chances, we realize that he no longer wants to be the catcher in the rye and that he has come to accept adulthood.

THEMES AND INTERPRETATIONS

There aren't many twentieth-century novels that have been more frequently analyzed in print than *The Catcher in the Rye*. Among the hundreds of interpretations, four trends stand out. One is an historical approach which relates *The Catcher in the Rye* to Mark Twain's *The Adventures of Huckleberry Finn*. Another is a sociological approach which treats the novel as social criticism. A third approach is psychological and focuses on Holden's transition from adolescence to adulthood. And a fourth approach examines the moral and religious implications of the novel.

The first systematic comparison of *The Catcher in the Rye* and *The Adventures of Huckleberry Finn* is Edgar Branch's essay "Mark Twain and J.D. Salinger: A Study in Literary Continuity." Branch says that "the two novels are clearly related in narrative pattern and style, characterization of the hero and critical import" (217). Moreover, Branch argues that "*Huckleberry Finn* and *The Catcher in the Rye* share certain ethical and social attitudes. Yet Salinger's critical view assumes a cultural determinism that in *Huckleberry Finn*, although always present, permits freedom through self-guidance" (216). Like many early critics, Branch sees the ending of *The Catcher in the* Rye as pessimistic and that of *Huckleberry Finn* as optimistic. He writes: "*Huckleberry Finn*, in short, recognizes both necessity and freedom, the restrictions limiting moral accomplishment and its possibility. *The Catcher in the Rye* leaves us doubtful that the individual, even assisted by the analyst's best efforts, can ever truly escape the double trap of society and self" (214–215). What further contributes to the "underlying despair of Salinger's book," so Branch says, is that Holden has not matured or learned anything by the end of the novel and that "Holden wants to remain forever the catcher in the rye" (215).

Unlike Edgar Branch and most early critics, Carl F. Strauch sees the ending of *The Catcher in the Rye* as optimistic. In his essay, "Kings in the Back Row: Meaning Through Structure—A Reading of Salinger's *The Catcher in the Rye*," Strauch says that "the conclusion is neither pessimistic nor, for that matter, ironical in any sense perceived thus far" (47). Strauch argues that by the end of the novel, Holden has "miraculously wrought his own cure" (48) because he has accepted a sense of responsibility. Strauch says: "The conclusion is, therefore, optimistic and affirmative" (48).

As Strauch describes it, the meaning of the novel is both psychological and philosophical because *Catcher* is a story of an irresponsible young neurotic who dies a figurative death and is reborn as a new, healthy, and responsible individual. The support for this reading of the novel comes from a detailed analysis of what Strauch calls its "interlocking metaphorical structure" (48). This structure consists of four stages in the novel, Holden's "neurotic deterioration," his "symbolical death," his "spiritual awakening," and his "psychological self-cure" (48).

Several later interpretations have analyzed *The Catcher in the Rye* in more rigid psychoanalytical terms. James Bryan's essay, "The Psychological Structure of *The Catcher in the Rye*" is a Freudian analysis which defines Holden's neurosis as "a frantic need to save his sister from himself" (107). Bryan bases this notion on the psychoanalytical axiom that "a sister is often the first replacement for the mother as love object, and that normal maturation guides the boy from the sister to other women." However Holden has a serious problem because "Holden's sexuality is swaying precariously between reversion and maturation" (107). Fortunately, so Bryan contends, "Phoebe's responses to Holden's secret needs become the catalyst for both his breakdown and his recovery" (111).

More recently there have been Adlerian and Lacanian readings of *The Catcher in the Rye*. In the essay, "Adlerian Theory and Its Application to *The Catcher in the Rye*—Holden Caulfield," R.J. Huber explains that Adlerian psychoanalysts are always interested in knowing whether an individual "feels competent or inferior, and whether [s/he] strives with or without social interest in mind" (47). Huber's conclusion is that Holden "reveals deep-seated inferiority feelings and a compensatory striving for grandiosity" (48).

The most fashionable psychological study of the novel is James Mellard's essay "The Disappearing Subject: A Lacanian Reading of *The Catcher in the Rye*." Mellard shares Carl Strauch's view that Holden eventually cures himself. According to Mellard, Holden passes through the Lacanian stages of "alienation" and "separation" from the "Other" but eventually achieves symbolic wholeness with that "Other" (203–204). Here is how Mellard describes the moment when Holden becomes whole again: "Restored to the only sort of fullness that shall ever be available to one who has acceded to the Symbolic, Holden is gripped by joy at this moment. Sitting on a bench in the sudden rain, watching Phoebe go around on the carousel, at this final moment of the main narrative, Holden feels unbounded pleasure, perhaps a Lacanian *jouissance*" (211). Reacting to the argument of earlier critics that when Holden tells his story, he is a patient in a mental institution, Mellard says that "on the evidence of the story he tells, he no longer has any real need for therapy. He would appear to be as healthy, as 'whole,' as sane as anyone ever might be" (211).

Many critics have assumed that when Holden tells his story, he is a patient in a mental institution. But as early as 1963, Warren French pointed out that there's no textual proof for that assumption. In his book *J.D. Salinger*, French says: "Even though Holden acknowledges being attended by a psychoanalyst at the end of the book, his breakdown is clearly not just—or even principally—mental" (108). French points out that Holden is physically ill and that "his run-down physical condition magnifies the pain" of his "emotional and intellectual problems" (109). French describes the plot as being partially Holden's quest for sympathy for his physical condition and for a place of peaceful refuge. Being denied this sympathy and refuge, Holden physically collapses. But as French notes, there is another story intertwined with that of Holden's physical breakdown and that is "the story of the breaking down of Holden's self-centeredness and his gradual acceptance of the world that has rejected him" (115). What Holden learns from his experiences is "the injunction that we must all love each other" (116). But French does not believe that Salinger develops "the idea of universal compassion" convincingly in the novel: "The trouble with compassion is that, although without it one cannot be a decent human being, it cannot by itself provide a person with the means of making himself useful. . . . Being simply a saint requires no education" (118).

The notion that Holden is some kind of a saint or even a Christ figure is advanced in several interpretations of *The Catcher in the Rye*. For instance, in his essay "The Saint as a Young Man: A Reappraisal of *The Catcher in the Rye*," Jonathan Baumbach argues that what Holden wants is "to be a saint—the protector and savior of innocence. But what he also wants . . . is that someone prevent *his* fall" (56). For this reason, so Baumbach says, "Holden's real quest throughout the novel is for a spiritual father" (56). However, Holden does not find such a spiritual father: "The world, devoid of good fathers (authorities), becomes a soul-destroying chaos in which his survival is possible only through withdrawal into childhood, into fantasy, into psychosis" (57). Holden's savior turns out not to be a father figure but his ten-year-old sister Phoebe. Baumbach concludes: "The last scene, in which Holden, suffused with happiness, sits in the rain and watches Phoebe ride on the merry-go-round, is indicative not of his crack-up, as has been assumed, but of his redemption" (471).

Although some critics have noted that Holden is not an average adolescent because he comes from a very wealthy family, it wasn't until the mid-seventies that we got a socioeconomic interpretation of *The Catcher in the Rye*. In the essay "Reviewers, Critics, and *The Catcher in the Rye*," Carol and Richard Ohmann offer a Marxist interpretation of the novel. They call *The Catcher in the Rye* "a case study in capitalist criticism" (119) and note that "Salinger wrote about power and wealth and reviewers and critics about good and evil and the problems of growing up" (122). The Ohmanns agree with previous critics that "Holder's sensitivity is the heart of the book," but they disagree with everyone else when it come to the question "What does he reject?" (129). Yes, it is phoniness that Holden rejects, but the Ohmanns contend that "this phoniness is rooted in the economic and social arrangements of capitalism, and in their concealment" (130). The two critics cite a number of passages to prove that "the novel's critique of class distinction may be found, not just between the lines of Holden's account, but in some of his most explicit comments on what's awry in his world" (131).

The Ohmanns conclude with a speculation as to what response Salinger expected from his readers: "Given Salinger's perception of what's wrong, there are three possible responses: do the best you can with this society; work for a better one; flee society altogether" (134). The Ohmanns fault Salinger for Holden's response to this choice: "When Holden imagines an adult self he can think only of the Madison Avenue executive or the deaf-mute, this society or no society" (134). And yet, the two critics give Salinger credit for creating an accurate picture of social reality in mid-century America: "*The Catcher in the Rye* is among other things a serious critical mimesis of bourgeois life in the Eastern United States, ca. 1950—of snobbery, privilege, class injury, culture as a badge of superiority, sexual exploitation, education subordinated to status, warped social feeling, competitiveness, stunted human possibility, the list could go on" (135).

The Ohmanns here map out a list of socioeconomic themes that could be profitably pursued in further interpretations of *The Catcher in the Rye*, but very little such criticism has been published in the meantime. In fact, since the mid-seventies, very little has been written about the novel that has not been said before. In addition to the Lacanian interpretation of James Mellard that I mentioned before, the only notable studies have been essays on the reception of *The Catcher in the Rye* by readers in foreign countries and by female readers in the United States.

A little known fact in Salinger lore is that *The Catcher in the Rye*—in the translation of Nobel Laureate Heinrich Böll (*Der Fänger im Roggen*)—was required reading in the West German secondary schools for over 20 years. In an article entitled "Jerome D. Salinger's Novel *The Catcher in the Rye* as Required Reading in Upper Level German Classes" (1968), Fritz Kraul defends that choice. Kraul notes that "Salinger's novel continues a narrative tradition which was based on novels of social criticism by writers such as Upton Sinclair and Sinclair Lewis." As Kraul describes it, *The Catcher in the Rye* "depicts the conflict between the individual and society, and in particular the difficulties which face today's American adolescents" (79). The novel is valuable because "it affords a picture of contemporary American society" and because Holden Caulfield's story is that of a "protest against society" (81). The chief targets of the protest are society's "conformity and the pressure to succeed" (83). As positive values the novel holds up "the selflessness of the two nuns, the courage of James Castle, and the patience of Holden's late brother Allie" (86).

More recently, *The Catcher in the Rye* has become the subject of gender criticism. In her essay, "Holden Caulfield: C'est Moi," Mary Suzanne Schriber points out that almost all previous criticism on *The Catcher in the Rye* was written by males. She cites a number of critics who admit that they identify with Holden and therefore assume that Holden's experiences and view of life are universal. Therefore, "the popularity and the ascription of broad significance and exceptional literary importance to *The Catcher in the Rye* can be traced to . . . assumptions that the male is the normative" (235). These assumptions, so Schriber argues, have led male critics to accord *The Catcher in the Rye* the status of a classic of American literature. Schriber disagrees because she claims that female readers do not identify with Holden the way male readers do because "an adolescent male WASP is not automatically nature's designated spokesperson for us all" (236). In short, Schriber argues that once the responses of female readers are considered, *The Catcher in the Rye* will no longer be rated as highly as it has been in the past.

CONCLUSION

Despite some feminist protests, there is almost universal agreement that *The Catcher in the Rye* is a classic of twentieth-century American literature. The novel deserves that distinction because it is an extremely well constructed piece of verbal art. But like all human creations, it is by no means perfect. What grates on some readers is that in two separate scenes taking place the same evening Holden's roommate Stradlater and his dorm neighbor Ackley both happen to trim their finger and toe nails in Holden's presence, that Holden pointlessly summarizes a "putrid" movie he has seen, that Mr. Antolini pontificates too much and says too little, and, above all, that Holden incessantly repeats phrases such as "it really kills me" and "if you want to know the truth." But these are quibbles over what not everyone thinks of as weaknesses. What makes up for these weaknesses (if they are such) are the novel's strengths in narrative structure, characterization, and symbolism.

While early critics of the novel stressed the episodic nature of the plot and were unable to see any development in Holden's character, it has by now been firmly established that the episodes of the plot are held together by several strands of narrative development and that one of them is a pattern of character change. In short, Holden is not a static character but experiences an inner change, and this change is a movement from adolescence to adulthood, from his immature desire to be the catcher in the rye to his mature understanding that if children want to grab for the gold ring, we should not stop them but let them take the risk of falling.

Another strength of the novel is the characterization of Holden as a very complex human being who is at once generous and materialistic, illiterate and well-read, an atheist and a fan of Jesus. Despite these contradictions, one thing stands out about him and that is his unusual kindness. This kindness extends to pimply fellow students, to ugly girls, to underage prostitutes, to nuns who will never eat at swanky restaurants, and to the freezing ducks in Central Park. And even though the minor characters are designed chiefly to bring out specific personality traits in Holden, most of them assume a life of their own in the reader's imagination, from the "muckle-mouthed" Jane Gallagher who keeps her kings in the back row during checkers to the hairy-bellied pimp Maurice who snaps his fingers very hard at the crotch of Holden's pajamas before beating him up.

Perhaps the most important and the most impressive aspect of the novel is its symbolism. None of the symbols are artificial, all of them occur naturally in the scenes in which they appear, and most of them allow several different interpretations. The most notable examples are Holden's hunting hat and the ducks in Central Park. Moreover, some of the symbols are constructed in such a way that the change in their meaning parallels the change in Holden's outlook. This is the case with the obscene graffiti in Phoebe's school and with the carousel in Central Park. Parallel to the change in the meaning of those symbols, the central metaphor of the catcher in the rye also changes its connotation from positive to negative.

Because of the multi-layered narrative structure, the complex characterization of Holden Caulfield, the many memorable minor characters, and the rich symbolism, *The Catcher in the Rye* allows more interpretations than the average novel. This thematic richness is the ultimate proof that this novel is a work of art of the first rank.

Twenty-five years after the publication of *The Catcher in the Rye*, a critic noted that so much criticism had been written about it that it was hard to imagine that anyone could say anything new. And yet that same year, in 1976, Carol and Richard Ohmann published a Marxist analysis and pointed out a number of socioeconomic themes that had not yet been pursued.

At this writing—51 years after the publication of *The Catcher in the Rye*—some of the themes pointed out by the Ohmanns still have not been explored, for instance the theme of social class and privilege and the theme of education subordinated to status. Also, we do not yet have any good psychological analyses of the novel. What we have so far are efforts to use the novel to illustrate psychological concepts rather than efforts to use psychological concepts to interpret the novel. Another approach to *The Catcher in the Rye* that has been neglected so far is the reader response approach. This is an approach that the novel definitely calls for because Holden Caulfield not only addresses a specific kind of reader, but his narrative is full of gaps for the reader to fill.

Works Cited

Baumbach, Jonathan. "The Saint as a Young Man: A Reappraisal of *The Catcher in the Rye*." *Modern Language Quarterly* 25 (December 1964): 461–472. Rpt. in Salzberg 55–64.

Behrman, N.S. "The Vision of the Innocent" [Review]. *New Yorker* (11 August 1951): 64–68.

Branch, Edgar. "Mark Twain and J.D. Salinger: A Study in Literary Continuity." *American Quarterly* 9 (Summer 1957): 144–58. Rpt. in Grunwald 205–217.

Breit, Harvey. "Reader's Choice" [Review]. *Atlantic Monthly* 188 (August 1951): 82. Rpt. in Marsden 6–7.

Bryan, James. "The Psychological Structure of *The Catcher in the Rye*." *Publications of the Modern Language Association* 89 (1974): 1065–1074. Rpt. in Salzberg 101–117.

Burger, Nash K. "The Catcher in the Rye" [Review]. *New York Times* (16 July 1951): 19.

French, Warren. "The Artist as a Very Nervous Young Man." In *J.D. Salinger*. New York: Twayne, 1963, 102–129.

Goodman, Anne. "Mad About Children" [Review]. *New Republic* 125 (16 July 1951): 20–21. Rpt. in Salzberg 23–24.

Grunwald, Henry A., ed. *Salinger: A Critical and Personal Portrait.* New York: Harper, 1962.

Hassan, Ihab. "Rare Quixotic Gesture: The Fiction of J.D. Salinger." *Western Review* 21 (Summer 1957): 261–280. Rpt. in Grunwald 138–163.

Heiserman, Arthur, and James E. Miller. "J.D. Salinger: Some Crazy Cliff." *Western Humanities Review* 10 (Spring 1956): 129–137. Rpt. in Grunwald 196–205.

Huber, R.J. "Adlerian Theory and Its Application to *The Catcher in the Rye*—Holden Caulfield." In *Psychological Perspectives on Literature: Freudian Dissidents and Non-Freudians.* Ed. Joseph Natoli. New York: Archon, 1984, 43–52.

Hughes, Riley. "The Catcher in the Rye" [Review]. *Catholic World* 174 (November 1951): 154. Rpt. in Salzberg 31.

Jones, Ernest. "Case History of All of Us" [Review]. *Nation* 173 (1 September 1951): 176. Rpt. in Salzberg 24–25.

Kraul, Fritz. "Jerome D. Salingers Roman 'Der Fänger im Roggen' als Pflichtlektüre im Deutschunterricht der Oberstufe." *Der Roman im Unterricht* 20 (1968): 79–86.

Longstreth, Morris. "Review of *The Catcher in the Rye.*" *Christian Science Monitor* (19 July 1951): 7. Rpt. in Salzberg 30–31.

Marsden, Malcolm, ed. *If You Really Want To Know: A Catcher Casebook.* Chicago: Scott Foresman, 1963.

Maxwell, William. "J.D. Salinger." *Book-of-the-Month Club News* (July 1951): 5–6.

Mellard, James. "The Disappearing Subject: A Lacanian Reading of *The Catcher in the Rye.*" Rpt. in Salzberg 197–214.

Ohmann, Carol, and Richard Ohmann. "Reviewers, Critics, and *The Catcher in the Rye.*" *Critical Inquiry* 3 (Autumn 1976): 15–37. Rpt. in Salzberg 119–140.

Peterson, Virgilia. "Three Days in the Bewildering World of an Adolescent" [Review]. *New York Herald Tribune Book Review* (15 July 1951): 3. Rpt. in Marsden 3–4.

Salzberg, Joel, ed. *Critical Essays on Salinger's The Catcher in the Rye.* Boston: G.K. Hall, 1990.

Schriber, Mary Suzanne. "Holden Caulfield: C'est Moi." In *Critical Essays on Salinger's The Catcher in the Rye.* Ed. Joel Salzberg. Boston: G.K. Hall, 1990, 226–238.

Smith, Harrison. "Manhattan Ulysses, Junior" [Review]. *Saturday Review of Literature* 34 (14 July 1951): 12–13. Rpt. in Salzberg 28–30.

Steiner, George. "The Salinger Industry." *Nation* 189 (14 November 1959): 360–363. Rpt. in Grunwald 82–85.

Stern, James. "Aw, the World's a Crummy Place" [Parody/Review]. *New York Times Book Review* (15 July 1951): 5. Rpt. in Marsden 2–3.

Strauch, Carl F. "Kings in the Back Row: Meaning Through Structure—A Reading of Salinger's *The Catcher in the Rye.*" *Wisconsin Studies in Contemporary Literature* 2 (Winter 1961): 5–30. Rpt. in *Salinger's "Catcher in the Rye": Clamor vs. Criticism.* Ed Harold P. Simonson and Philip E. Hager. Boston: D.C. Heath, 1963, 46–62.

SUGGESTIONS FOR FURTHER READING

Costello, Donald P. "The Language of *The Catcher in the Rye,*" *American Speech* 34 (October 1959): 172–181. Rpt. in Salzberg 44–53.

Lundquist, James. "Against Obscenity: *The Catcher in the Rye.*" In *J.D. Salinger.* New York: Ungar 1979, 37–68.

Oldsey, Bernard. "The Movies in the Rye." *College English* 23 (December 1961): 209–215. Rpt. in Salzberg 92–99.

Seng, Peter J. "The Fallen Idol: The Immature World of Holden Caulfield." *College English* 32 (December 1962): 203–209. Rpt. in Marsden 73–81.

Shulevitz, Judith. "Holden Reconsidered and All." *New York Times Book Review* (29 July 2001): 23.

Vanderbilt, Kermit. "Symbolic Resolution in *The Catcher in the Rye*: The Cap, the Carousel, and the American West." *Western Humanities Review* 17 (Summer 1963): 271–277.

Weinberg, Helen. "J.D. Salinger's Holden and Seymour and the Spiritual Activist Hero." In *The New Novel in America: The Kafkan Mode in Contemporary Fiction*. Ithaca, NY: Cornell UP, 1970, 141–164.

CARL FREEDMAN

Memories of Holden Caulfield—
and of Miss Greenwood

Two years ago, the fiftieth anniversary of J. D. Salinger's *The Catcher in the Rye* took place. The book is almost exactly the same age I am. To be precise, it's about three months younger: I appeared in April 1951, the novel—after a much longer gestation period—in July. Inevitably, a good many essays about it have recently been published, and, though they indicate little consensus about the exact meaning or value of the novel, they do generally agree that it is still, in some sense, an extraordinary text. At the height of Salinger's reputation—the 1950s and 1960s—his was in many ways the dominant voice in contemporary American fiction, despite his slender output, and it was not unusual for him to be discussed in tones that suggested a genius almost on the order of Shakespeare's or Tolstoy's to be at stake. His stature has long since assumed much more modest proportions. Few, I suppose, would maintain now that *The Catcher in the Rye* belongs in the absolute first rank of the modern novel: on a level, that is, with Conrad's *Nostromo* (1904) or Lawrence's *Women in Love* (1920) or Joyce's *Ulysses* (1922) or Faulkner's *Absalom, Absalom!* (1936) or Pynchon's *Gravity's Rainbow* (1973). Yet if it is, in this strict sense, a work of the second rank, it is also a novel that possesses a remarkable hold on its readers, or at least on a good many of them. There are more than a few of us for whom *The Catcher in the Rye* still feels less like a canonical book than like a personal experience, and one of the most powerful

From *Southern Review* 39, no. 2 (Spring 2003): pp. 401–17. © 2003 by Louisiana State University.

of our lives. Though I earn a living chiefly by producing materialist criticism of literary texts (on the page and in the classroom), I think of this text mainly as a part—a phase, really—of my personal history, and of its protagonist as someone I know, or once knew: attitudes that do not necessarily exclude a properly critical approach but that by no means inevitably make for one either. Accordingly, though what follows will certainly have its critical moments, it is at least as much a memoir as a critical essay, a memoir of the Holden Caulfield I knew and of an earlier self, both of whom are now long in the past but also still with me.

But this must also be a memoir of Miss Greenwood. No, I do not mean Sylvia Plath's Esther Greenwood, protagonist of *The Bell Jar* (1963) and the most memorable, perhaps, of all the many fictional characters conceived under the direct influence of Holden Caulfield. The real Miss Greenwood was my eighth-grade English teacher and my first teacher who was also, in some important way, a friend. Not that I had gotten along badly with my earlier teachers—quite the contrary. But before Miss Greenwood a teacher was no more to be counted as a friend than was a parent, a doctor, or a rabbi. Teachers were all just adults, authority figures, and one took it for granted that they inhabited a world different from one's own. Miss Greenwood, somehow, was different. Doubtless this was at least partly because she was quite young herself, no more than a year or so out of college. It is a somewhat staggering thought that, during the time I am remembering, she was thus only slightly older than the seniors I teach today, and younger than nearly all of my graduate students. It is even more staggering to think that, if she and I were to meet today, we would be, for most practical purposes, about the same age. In the eighth grade, of course, the gulf was much wider—and yet bridgeable in a way that the age gulf between an adult and me had never quite been before.

I still have before me a fairly clear mental image of Miss Greenwood. She was thin, of about average height, with brown hair cut relatively short and a pleasant, freckled face. Her looks were not those of a bombshell or head-turner, but I expect that a fair number of men would have found her—I expect that a fair number of men *did* find her—attractive, and increasingly attractive as they got to know her better. But you would probably have had to be in love with her to call her beautiful. I was in love with her, though it is a love that I recognized as such only many years later. I am pretty sure that, at the time, I never consciously thought of Miss Greenwood in a romantic or even a sexual way, and in retrospect that seems a curious omission. After all, I was a horny, virginal fourteen-year-old boy, and I was preoccupied with sex in that intense, yearning way typical of my age and gender; but, as far as I can recall, the guest stars in my lustful fantasies tended to be either female classmates my own age or else generically "good-looking" women whose images were based on models and movie stars. Why not Miss Greenwood? She was pretty enough for the role. Perhaps I just respected her too much. Perhaps it was just that, in those more innocent days, the idea of "doing anything" with Miss Greenwood was literally beyond (conscious) comprehension.

In retrospect, however, it seems clear that nothing short of sexual love could have driven me to do what I frequently did during the eighth grade: namely, to *stay* in the school building after the final bell had rung, to use some of those precious hours of freedom between the end of school and dinner at home to talk with a teacher whose class I had been required to attend earlier in the day. Miss Greenwood was often in her classroom for a while after classes had ended, doing various chores—cleaning blackboards, arranging papers, and the like—and I got in the habit of dropping by. I would help her to the extent I could, and we would chat about various things. Some of these talks were brief—no more than ten or fifteen minutes—but others went on for an hour or even more. My house was within walking distance of the school, but sometimes, especially after one of our longer chats, Miss Greenwood would give me a lift home in the used, battered Volkswagen bug that she had recently purchased and about whose mechanical soundness she was, as I remember, a bit nervous. She took some consolation in the relatively low number on the odometer, and was mildly alarmed when I told her that odometer readings could be faked. Our relations were by no means completely informal. It was always clear that we were teacher and pupil, and certainly I never called her anything except "Miss Greenwood" (with the result that today I am not sure of her first name, though I once knew it well—Mary, perhaps?). But we were definitely friends.

Our conversations were mainly about two of our strongest common interests, politics and literature, which, as it happens, are the two main fields about which I write professionally today. We probably talked more about politics than about literature. The school year was 1964–65, and we shared happiness and relief that, in the presidential election, Lyndon Johnson defeated Barry Goldwater so resoundingly, though Miss Greenwood, I believe, was somewhat discreet about her political preferences (doubtless a prudent habit for any schoolteacher, but especially wise since the school principal was widely thought to be a rather unbalanced right-winger). I think the first political bet that I ever made—and won—in my life was with Miss Greenwood. In January 1965, Hubert Humphrey was inaugurated as vice-president and so had to give up his seat in the Senate, where he had been the Democratic whip. Several senators competed to succeed him, with the frontrunners generally agreed to be John Pastore of Rhode Island and Russell Long of Louisiana. Miss Greenwood liked Pastore's chances—a choice she shared with most journalistic pundits and by no means a stupid one, for

Pastore's political profile resembled Humphrey's own, and his northeastern liberalism seemed in tune with the (very brief) moment of triumph that American liberalism was then enjoying. But I already knew a fair bit about how the Senate worked, and I reckoned that the southerners—still the dominant force in that body, despite the huge defeat they had recently suffered when the Civil Rights Act of 1964 was passed—would prove strong enough to win the post for one of their own. As indeed they did.

Long's victory brought him a position for which he never displayed much aptitude and which he lost to Edward Kennedy four years later. But it brought me the copy that I still possess of Salinger's fourth (and, as things now seem to have turned out, last) book, the one that collected the long stories, "Raise High the Roof Beam, Carpenters" and "Seymour—An Introduction." The volume was already out in hardcover, and Miss Greenwood and I agreed that the loser of the bet would buy the winner a copy of the paperback as soon as it appeared. It was a logical choice, for there was nothing we shared more intensely than our common admiration for Salinger. I think that I vaguely knew who Salinger was even before meeting Miss Greenwood—I browsed through the current paperbacks frequently, and those Salinger paperbacks, with their covers nearly blank save for title and author, were hard to miss—but I had never read his work until Miss Greenwood recommended *The Catcher in the Rye* to me. I didn't realize at the time how typical an enthusiasm for Salinger was among intelligent college students of her generation, nor did it occur to me that, in urging me to read *The Catcher in the Rye*, Miss Greenwood was running something of a risk. Salinger's novel was one of three strictly banned throughout our public school system (Aldous Huxley's *Brave New World* [1932] and George Orwell's *Nineteen Eighty-four* [1949] were the others); and, though recommending it to a single student in an after-school chat was not, presumably, a transgression on the order of assigning it to a whole class, I'm sure she could have gotten into some trouble if, for instance, my parents had been the sort to make a fuss. Looking back, I suspect that, out of college and living on her own in a new city, Miss Greenwood was missing companions with whom she could discuss her favorite writer, and so she took a chance on me.

Her recommendation was about as successful as a recommendation can be. The book just knocked me out, as Holden himself would say. Today it seems clear to me that, technically, the main source of the novel's overwhelming power is its almost unparalleled mastery of voice. Except for *Huckleberry Finn* (1884)—often enough proposed as the chief precursor text of *The Catcher in the Rye*—there is not a novel in American literature, perhaps not a novel in the world, that more convincingly invents and sustains a young colloquial voice, page after page after page, with virtually not a single false note, and while managing to avoid both sentimentality and condescension

on the part of the unseen author. If it is difficult to believe that Holden
Caulfield is "just" a literary fabrication, it's because the reader seems to
hear an entirely real human being talking to him or her for more than two
hundred pages without interruption. But at the age of fourteen, of course, I
was less struck by Salinger's technique than by the reality that his technique
appeared to convey. Simply put, Holden seemed absolutely *right* to me—in
some ways the rightest human being I had ever encountered. His world was
basically similar to my own—never mind the differences between an upper-
class northeasterner in the late 1940s and a middle-class southerner in the
mid-1960s—and, at two or three years older than me, he was just young
enough to be a peer and just enough older to seem automatically savvier and
more worldly wise. Again and again Holden hit off exactly what a morass
of mendacity the world had prepared for children in the process of leaving
childhood behind; again and again he articulated, with painful but exuberant
and wonderful accuracy, the essential inauthenticity of bourgeois American
society that I myself was just beginning to be able to name.

Take Holden's roommate Stradlater, for instance: crude, obtuse, brash,
outgoing, handsome, athletic, and, Holden believes, one of the few boys
at Pencey Prep who actually succeeds in "giving the time" to the girls that
he dates. I knew the type, and I resented the all-but-universal envy and
admiration that the type attracted from his fellows. Who but Holden would
have had the clear-sightedness and courage to dismiss him simply as "a
stupid bastard"? And who, really knowing the type, could deny that Holden
was exactly right? Or take Mr. Spencer, the history teacher who pompously
and uselessly lectures Holden about his future: "Life *is* a game, boy. Life *is*
a game that one plays according to the rules." I heard this sort of thing all
the time, and Holden knew exactly what it was worth: "Game, my ass. Some
game. If you get on the side where all the hot-shots are, then it's a game, all
right—I'll admit that. But if you get on the *other* side, where there aren't any
hot-shots, then what's a game about it? Nothing. No game."

Or take "this guy Ossenburger," the wealthy mortician and Pencey
alumnus after whom Holden's dorm is named:

> The first football game of the year, he came up to school in
> this big goddam Cadillac, and we all had to stand up in the
> grandstand and give him a locomotive—that's a cheer. Then, the
> next morning, in chapel, he made a speech that lasted about ten
> hours. He started off with about fifty corny jokes, just to show us
> what a regular guy he was. Very big deal. Then he started telling
> us how he was never ashamed, when he was in some kind of
> trouble or something, to get right down on his knees and pray to
> God. He told us we should always pray to God—talk to Him and

all—wherever we were. He told us we ought to think of Jesus as our buddy and all. He said *he* talked to Jesus all the time. Even when he was driving his car. That killed me. I can just see the big phony bastard shifting into first gear and asking Jesus to send him a few more stiffs.

Though at the age of fourteen I had never even set eyes on a school precisely similar to Pencey, this passage seemed to sum up practically every school assembly I had ever been forced to attend; and future assemblies were made a little more bearable for knowing that at least one other person saw them for exactly what they were.

Sometimes it seemed to me that there was almost no variety of phony that Holden had not managed to spot and expose, from the insufferably pretentious pseudo-intellectual Carl Luce, an old schoolmate with whom he has an extended conversation in a bar, to the young naval officer ("His name was Commander Blop or something") he meets briefly in Ernie's nightclub: "He was one of those guys that think they're being a pansy if they don't break around forty of your fingers when they shake hands with you. God, I hate that stuff." Though most of Holden's insights are delivered in this ad hoc manner, there are a few more synoptic passages. Perhaps the best is the summary of Pencey he offers to Sally Hayes, herself an excruciating phony—the sort who appears much more intelligent than she is because she knows "quite a lot about the theater and plays and literature and all that stuff" and whom Holden finds harder to shake than most phonies because she is physically very attractive and usually willing to make out with him.

> "You ought to go to a boys' school sometime. Try it sometime," I said. "It's full of phonies, and all you do is study so that you can learn enough to be smart enough to be able to buy a goddam Cadillac some day, and you have to keep making believe you give a damn if the football team loses, and all you do is talk about girls and liquor and sex all day, and everybody sticks together in these dirty little goddam cliques. The guys that are on the basketball team stick together, the Catholics stick together, the goddam intellectuals stick together, the guys that play bridge stick together. Even the guys that belong to the goddam Book-of-the-*Month* Club stick together. If you try to have a little intelligent—"

Sally is technically correct, as Holden himself agrees, when she interrupts him to object, "Lots of boys get more out of school than *that*." But no matter—Holden has Pencey, and the world, dead to rights.

Holden's wisdom seemed all the more impressive to me because there is no trace of superiority about it. He is never the detached, self-sufficient bystander, coolly and ironically observing life from its foyer; instead, he is passionate and disappointed, always newly indignant at every fresh instance of phoniness that life offers. It is also true that he is therefore extremely unhappy—an aspect of the book that I rather glossed over in my first few readings. I was able to see that Holden almost never seems to be having a good time, but I was not particularly unhappy myself—allowing for the fact that hardly any fourteen-year-old can be unambiguously called happy—and I hesitated to attribute to such a powerfully kindred spirit the extreme degree of psychic misery that now seems to me one of the principal features of Holden's character. Or to put it another way: The almost unerring acuteness of Holden's insights, and the superb colloquial vigor with which he could express them, seemed to make for a kind of intellectual high spirits that I could not, at the age of fourteen, easily reconcile with underlying pain. To see phonies so clearly could not exactly be a recipe for happiness in a world where phonies were so numerous, but surely, I felt, truth itself had its own consolations.

Not everyone has felt such a deep affinity with Holden as I did. Some readers—most prominently Mary McCarthy—believe that Holden is too harsh in his judgments of others, that he is too much the pitiless phony-spotter. "I was surrounded by jerks," says Holden of his fellow patrons at Ernie's, and for some this sentence sums up almost the entirety of Holden's world view. Miss Greenwood to some extent held this opinion. Indeed, one of the things that slightly divided us in our shared passion for Salinger was that for me, then as now, Salinger was first and foremost the author of *The Catcher in the Rye*, whereas Miss Greenwood preferred his stories about the Glass family. Looking back, I suspect that this difference of opinion was largely a gendered one. Holden's outlook is intensely masculine (though never macho), and I suppose that from the other side of the gender divide it might well often seem suffocatingly masculine. But this point never occurred to me at the time, and I doubt it did to Miss Greenwood either. The problem with Holden, she once said to me, is just that you get the idea he probably wouldn't like you very much—whereas Buddy Glass, Holden's successor as Salinger's principal narrator and alter ego, was Miss Greenwood's idea of a very nice guy indeed.

I now think that Holden's supposed pitilessness in judging others has been greatly exaggerated. It has become conventional to say that he likes nobody except his three siblings; and, since one of them, his younger brother Allie, is dead, and since another, his older brother D. B., seems, as an evidently successful Hollywood screenwriter, to be in danger of becoming a bit of a phony himself, only his kid sister Phoebe ("himself in miniature or in glory," as McCarthy insisted) would be left as an unambiguously Good Person, a certified nonphony, in the land of the living. But in fact Holden likes quite a lot of people: people of both sexes and of various ages, and chance acquaintances as well as old friends. He immensely likes Jane Gallagher, sort of his girlfriend but not exactly, who always kept her kings in the back row whenever they played checkers. He equally likes his old English teacher Mr. Antolini, even though he is understandably disconcerted when Mr. Antolini makes what appears to be a homosexual pass at him. He likes the nuns he meets in a sandwich bar, and he likes Mrs. Morrow, the mother of a classmate, whom he meets on a train. He even likes Selma Thurmer, the daughter of the headmaster at Pencey, despite her big nose and her falsies and her fingernails bitten bloody. He likes children in general, and so tries to rub out dirty words scrawled where children might see them; and, of course, he fantasizes about being the catcher in the rye, spending every day keeping children safely in the field of rye and away from the cliff's edge. He likes the ducks in the Central Park lagoon, and worries about what happens to them when the pond freezes solid in winter. Furthermore, Holden (unlike the Hemingway heroes with whom McCarthy so unjustly compares him) usually manages a good deal of concrete human sympathy even for those whom he cannot bring himself to like: his obnoxious, pimple-squeezing schoolmate Ackley, for instance, and Sunny, the prostitute who cheats him out of five dollars. His encounter with the latter makes for one of the book's most memorable scenes. At the end of a very long, very lonely, and frequently horny evening, Holden accepts a pimp's offer to send a whore to his hotel room. But when Sunny (who is "[n]o old bag," just as the pimp Maurice promises) actually arrives, Holden is so overcome with sadness at the thought of her life that his enthusiasm for losing his virginity evaporates into thin air and he offers to pay Sunny full price for just a few minutes of conversation.

In the eighth grade it did not occur to me to point out this deeply sensitive and compassionate side of Holden's character in reply to Miss Greenwood's criticism of him as too astringently judgmental. Nonetheless, her (perhaps not wholly intentional but clear enough) implication—that Holden might not like *me*—bothered me very little. It was not so much that I disagreed with her suggestion as that it somehow seemed beside the point. Maybe Holden wouldn't necessarily like me, but so what? Holden *was* me. And indeed, Holden by no means expresses invariable liking for himself throughout the long monologue that constitutes the novel. Though most readers have, I think, failed to notice the fact, he frequently confesses to acts of phoniness on his own part. Precept, as Samuel Johnson said, may be very sincere even when practice is very imperfect, and the fact that Holden—as sturdy a moralist, in his own way, as Dr. Johnson—is capable of self-criticism, that he can recognize his own involvement in the whole system of phoniness from which he recoils so bitterly, only made (and makes) him all the more admirable and all the more right in my eyes.

Whatever Holden might have thought of me, though, Miss Greenwood had an explanation for why I liked Holden and *The Catcher in the Rye* so much more than her own favorite, Buddy Glass, and the stories centered on his family. She once commented that people closer to her own age—people in their late teens, I believe she meant—often liked *The Catcher in the Rye* because people that age often felt rebellious toward society (this conversation took place, remember, just as the 1960s were coming into focus as a political and cultural era). She suggested that I myself was feeling that kind of rebelliousness, at an earlier age than was typical. At the time, I recall, I felt slightly uncertain as to exactly what Miss Greenwood's attitude toward my supposed rebelliousness was, though I took her remark as basically flattering, if only for the precocity it implied. Today, especially in view of the fact that I did not, at that point, overtly fit the usual profile of the school rebel—I had never, by the eighth grade, detonated firecrackers in the school bathroom, or brought a subversive petition to class, or smoked marijuana, or even grown my hair long—hers must surely be counted as a pretty shrewd, prescient judgment of a fourteen-year-old boy who grew up to become a Marxist literary critic.

But it must also be pointed out that Holden himself is not really a rebel. True enough, his acute penetration into the life of his society could in principle supply the basis for rebellion, but Holden is never able to take the step from diagnosis to action, or even to serious planning. The only action he ever even contemplates is a strategy not of rebellion but of withdrawal: He imagines leaving civilization (like Huck Finn at the end of Mark Twain's novel, though in Holden's America the frontier has been long closed) and living somewhere out west in a cabin on the edge of the woods, pretending to be a deaf mute in order to avoid conversations with phonies. Even this is pure fantasizing, as Holden at heart always knows. Not only is Holden not a rebel, but (like Hamlet, who is in many ways almost as much Holden's predecessor as Huck is) he even has great difficulty acting meaningfully in *any* way. Etymologically, the opposite of an actor is a patient—someone who is acted upon—and it is no accident that a patient is precisely what Holden is during the time present of the novel. It is also significant that, though everyone knows that Holden tells his story from some sort of medical institution ("this crumby place," as he calls it), there has been considerable disagreement among readers as to exactly what sort of hospital it is and why Holden is there. Is it because he is threatened by tuberculosis and needs a long rest in a sanatorium? Or because he has suffered some sort of mental collapse and requires psychiatric help? The source of the confusion is that Salinger definitely allows both explanations. Holden is a mess, physically *and* psychologically.

Holden, then, might be seen as basically pathetic, someone who, despite all his advantages (intelligence, eloquence, evident good looks, family money), is essentially incapable of coping with life—hence his removal not to an isolated Thoreauvian cabin where he can practice Emersonian self-reliance, but to an expensive private hospital where a professionally trained staff is on call twenty-four hours a day to tend to his physical and emotional weaknesses. This was not, needless to say, an interpretation that occurred to me during my first reading of the novel, or my second, or even my third. But by about the fourth reading—undertaken when I was eighteen or nineteen, and so about as much older than Holden as I had been younger when in Miss Greenwood's class—I did begin to see Holden less as a hero or a kindred spirit than as a pathetic weakling. I remember some feeling of loss when I began to view him in this way, but on the whole I welcomed my changed perception: It seemed to me a more adult perception, and I considered the fact that I could now look down on Holden to be a sign of my own increasing maturity. One of the advantages of middle age, however, is that it often allows us to see how much more wisdom there usually is in even the most callow idealism of adolescence than in the superior "knowingness" of young adulthood. Yes, Holden is defeated by life, at least temporarily, and we don't know what path he will take "after" the end of the novel. He might begin to act on the insight that Mr. Antolini (quoting the psychoanalyst Wilhelm Stekel) tries to convey to him—"The mark of the immature man is that he wants to die nobly for a cause, while the mark of the mature man is that he wants to live humbly for one"—though it is also conceivable that he will gradually abandon his revulsion from phoniness and learn to "adjust" better to the latter. The incontestable point is that Holden's defeat is an honorable one, and honorable defeats are in the scheme of things more valuable than most victories. I think that I was right, at the age of fourteen, to gloss over the pain and weakness in Holden's character, for at that stage of life I probably couldn't have taken the full pressure of those things and still properly appreciated just how right Holden is.

Proust suggests somewhere that the "first edition" of a book ought to mean the edition in which one first happened to read it, and it may seem that I am now advocating a somewhat similar privileging of the first reading, at least insofar as my own first reading of *The Catcher in the Rye* is concerned. Though I do indeed maintain the essential validity of my original pro-Holden and indeed "Holdencentric" interpretation (it is noteworthy that Holden dominates his text as relatively few great characters other than Hamlet and Huck Finn have done), I am not actually proposing an emulation of Peter Pan. Growing up can have its virtues. When I first read the book, I gave little thought to the historical contexts of Holden's character, because for me Holden's "context" was simply life itself, life as I knew it. But as a professional critic and teacher, I now insist that a more specific and rigorous analysis of context can enhance rather than diminish one's appreciation of Holden.

One such context, for example, is the Second World War. As part of the revival of interest in America's last "good war" that has in recent years played such a prominent role in American popular culture, the notion that *The Catcher in the Rye* is in some sense about that war—that it is, as Louis Menand suggested in a fiftieth-anniversary essay published in the *New Yorker*, more a book of the 1940s than the 1950s—has gained a certain currency. It has some biographical plausibility. Like several of his characters—D. B. Caulfield, Seymour Glass, the unnamed American soldier who narrates "For Esmé—with Love and Squalor"—Salinger did serve in the war. He landed on Utah Beach during the fifth hour of the Normandy invasion and in the following months took part in some of the fiercest combat of the twentieth century; his daughter Margaret (author of a fascinating and remarkably even-tempered memoir called *Dream Catcher* [2000]) has said that he was among the first American soldiers to enter a liberated Nazi concentration camp. As a result of his combat experience he suffered something like a nervous breakdown—but only after the German army had surrendered—and, again according to his daughter, has remained forever after possessed by memories of the war and by a sense of his own identity as a soldier. It is often said that the truest and most sincere pacifists are combat veterans, and there may well be a direct connection between Salinger's experience of war at its most ferocious and Holden's description of himself as "a pacifist, if you want to know the truth."

But there are no combat scenes in *The Catcher in the Rye*. A brief mention of D. B.'s military service is the most explicit indication the novel gives that World War II even took place. But perhaps it is the professional writer D. B. who himself supplies the best clue to reading the book as a war novel. Holden well remembers the occasion on which Allie suggests to D. B. that at least one advantage of D. B.'s time in the army must be that it gave him a good deal of material about which to write; D. B. replies by asking Allie to compare Rupert Brooke with Emily Dickinson and then to say who ranks as the greater war poet. The correct answer, as Allie sees at once, is of course Emily Dickinson. If Dickinson is indeed the great poet of the American Civil War—and if, for that matter, Virginia Woolf's *Mrs. Dalloway* (1925), with its unforgettable portrait of Septimus Smith, is one of the great World War I novels—then in much the same way *The Catcher in the Rye* can be read as a record of the war against Hitler. One way to express the gap between Holden's shrewd perceptions and his pathetic inability to act effectively is to say that he (again like Hamlet) just takes everything a little too hard. Wealthy and privileged as his background may be, Holden's world is every bit as bad as he says it is; but nothing plainly in it, not even Allie's death from leukemia, *quite* accounts for the extreme degree of pain and loneliness and psychic dislocation that often seems to lie just beyond Holden's awesome powers of self-expression. Life appears to have a kind of wrongness for Holden that neither he nor Salinger can ever completely verbalize, and it may be that this wrongness is finally to be identified with the inexpressible barbarism of the Second World War.

Doubtless what is at issue here is not only the war in general but the Holocaust in particular, and at this point a war-centered reading of the novel may shade into an ethnic one. Again biography seems pertinent. Salinger's own ethnic make-up—of Jewish background on his father's side and Irish Catholic background on his mother's, just like the seven Glass children—was pretty unusual in his generation, and he is said to have felt severely dislocated by his mixed heritage, especially as regards his being, yet not being, Jewish. One can easily understand that, under these circumstances—and especially given the fact that during the 1920s, the 1930s, and well into the 1940s, anti-Semitism existed in the United States at levels that are practically unimaginable today—the annihilation of European Jewry was bound to be a deeply complex and traumatic event for him, especially after seeing some of the machinery of extermination with his own eyes: "You never really get the smell of burning flesh out of your nose entirely, no matter how long you live," he told Margaret. A further complexity was that he evidently had a tense, distant relationship with his father (who vainly wished that young Jerry would join the family business, a prosperous firm that imported kosher meats and cheeses), but a warm, loving one with his mother, to whom *The Catcher in the Rye* is dedicated: a situation perhaps reflected in Salinger's giving Holden an Irish surname and a home address not on the (stereotypically Jewish) Upper West Side of Manhattan, where he himself was raised, but on the (stereotypically Gentile) East Side—while also, however, supplying a note of Jewishness in the name of the Caulfields' next-door neighbors, the Dicksteins.

The context of war and ethnicity—the two categories intimately and complexly linked by the mediating term of the Holocaust—thus enters the novel as a determinate absence. We do not get overt scenes of combat or extermination, but instead something like the negative imprint of the unspeakable physical violence visited upon the world during the decade or so prior to 1951, the period during which Salinger worked, on and off, toward the completion of his novel. This context may well illuminate Holden's sadness and mental instability, though it hardly says much about his intelligence and sensitivity. Another context, however, and one that illuminates both these sides of his character, is presented far more explicitly: the context of class relations under capitalism, which constitute a different kind of violence.

Though Holden is constantly talking about the injuries of class, this dimension of the book has been astonishingly—or maybe not so astonishingly—ignored by journalistic and academic Salinger critics, as Richard and Carol Ohmann show in "A Case Study in Canon Formation: Reviewers, Critics, and *The Catcher in the Rye*" (perhaps the single most perceptive critical treatment of the novel to date, at least insofar as my own—fairly extensive though far from exhaustive—reading of the secondary literature goes). Class, of course, has been the great taboo subject in American discourse for more than half a century, a taboo so strong that it extends, to some degree, even into the overtly "progressive" circles of institutionalized cultural studies, where elaborate attention to race and gender is taken for granted. Still, it seems extraordinary that Salinger criticism has been able so thoroughly to erase a subject with which Salinger himself deals so overtly and so often.

Consider, for instance, Mr. Haas, the headmaster at Holden's old prep school Elkton Hills, who bears the remarkable distinction of being, in Holden's opinion, "the phoniest bastard I ever met in my life." Mr. Haas's general practice is to ingratiate himself as much as possible with the parents of his pupils, and he normally turns on as much charm as he can. But he does make exceptions:

> I mean if a boy's mother was sort of fat or corny-looking or something, and if somebody's father was one of those guys that wear those suits with very big shoulders and corny black-and-white shoes, then old Haas would just shake hands with them and give them a phony smile and then he'd go talk, for maybe a half an *hour*, with somebody else's parents. I can't stand that stuff. It drives me crazy. It makes me so depressed I go crazy.

Holden understands that, in the American upper bourgeoisie at the middle of the twentieth century, a fashionable suit and pair of shoes are *de rigueur* for a man, as a trim, elegant body is for a woman. He understands, too, that Haas cares nothing for his pupils or their parents as individuals: He is interested only in toadying up to those who unambiguously appear to be members in good standing of the class with which he identifies and toward which, probably, he aspires. Or consider—again—the successful businessman Ossenburger, who has amassed a fortune through a chain of cut-rate mortuaries ("these undertaking parlors all over the country that you could get members of your family buried for about five bucks apiece"). Holden has not, perhaps, read his Max Weber as carefully as he might have, and so fails to remark that Ossenburger's speech suggests the links between capitalist acquisitiveness and Protestant spirituality as clearly as any Weberian sociologist could wish. But he does plainly see that Ossenburger is considered important enough at Pencey to rate a cheer at the football game and a speech in the chapel simply and solely because of his ability to throw large sums of money around: "[H]e gave Pencey a pile of dough, and they named our wing after him." Holden also possesses a shrewd sense of the routine fraudulence that so typically underlies capitalist success in modern America: "You should see old Ossenburger. He probably just shoves them [i.e., the remains of his customers] in a sack and dumps them in the river."

Haas and Ossenburger, then, are especially odious because of the relative purity, so to speak, with which they incarnate the market-based relations of the capitalist class structure. Conversely, the nuns that Holden meets at the sandwich bar are admirable not so much for their religious vocation (Holden admits to being "sort of an atheist"), but because they have chosen to live outside the class system to the maximum extent feasible. It is not merely that they spend their lives teaching school and collecting money for charity. Holden, after all, has known plenty of phony teachers, and charity can be practiced by those of his own high-bourgeois background—his mother, for instance, and his aunt (who is "pretty charitable—she does a lot of Red Cross work and all"), and Sally Hayes's mother—but when such women perform good works it is with no renunciation, or even qualification, of their privileged place in the socioeconomic hierarchy. Holden's aunt may help out the Red Cross, but "when she does anything charitable she's always very well-dressed and has lipstick on and all that crap. I couldn't picture her doing anything for charity if she had to wear black clothes and no lipstick while she was doing it"—that is, if she had to abandon, even temporarily, the uniform of her class position. As for Sally's mother, she (like her daughter) craves attention as a spoiled child does, and "[t]he only way *she* could go around with a basket collecting dough would be if everybody kissed her ass for her when they made a contribution." Otherwise, "[s]he'd get bored. She would hand in her basket and then go someplace swanky for lunch." But the nuns are genuinely different: "That's what I liked about those nuns. You could tell, for one thing, that they never went anywhere swanky for lunch." Holden immediately adds that he is saddened by the nuns' inability to enjoy the swankiness that is routine for his own people—he does not sentimentalize the poverty they have chosen—but at the same time their integrity remains an inspiration in a world so heavily populated by those obsessed with scrambling up, or staying on top of, the class ladder.

Even before striking up a conversation with the nuns (who turn out to be moving from a convent in Chicago to one in New York), Holden notices that they have with them a pair of cheap suitcases, "the ones that aren't genuine leather or anything," and this observation provokes what is perhaps the most remarkable meditation on class in the novel. Holden thinks back to his roommate at Elkton Hills, Dick Slagle, who, like the nuns, had cheap suitcases, whereas Holden's own "came from Mark Cross, and they were genuine cowhide and all that crap, and I guess they cost quite a pretty penny." Holden finds Dick to be smart and funny, and the two are capable of having a good time together. But their relationship is soon poisoned by class. Dick is resentful and envious of the superior class position that the Mark Cross suitcases symbolize: He ridicules Holden's suitcases as "bourgeois" (an adjective he then extends to Holden's fountain pen and other possessions) while also pretending to other people that the Mark Cross suitcases really belong to him. Holden is baffled as to what to do. He tries stuffing his suitcases out of sight under his bed, and is perfectly willing to throw them away or even to trade suitcases with Dick, if doing so will save the friendship. But nothing avails, and within two months both boys ask to be moved. Holden sadly sums up the lesson:

> The thing is, it's really hard to be roommates with people if your suitcases are much better than theirs—if yours are really *good* ones and theirs aren't. You think if they're intelligent and all, the other person, and have a good sense of humor, that they don't give a damn whose suitcases are better, but they do. They really do. It's one of the reasons why I roomed with a stupid bastard like Stradlater. At least his suitcases were as good as mine.

On personal grounds, Holden likes and admires Dick, and despises Stradlater, but such purely personal factors are finally less powerful than the social realities of class.

So the reality Holden confronts—the reality whose phoniness he so acutely diagnoses—is not "the human condition" or "the pains of adolescence" or any of the other ahistorical clichés that have dominated Salinger criticism; it is, rather, the specific historical conjuncture of a particular time and place. What I find especially remarkable—and this is a point that even the Ohmanns, to whose excellent analysis I am much indebted, do not, I think, sufficiently emphasize—is the extent to which Holden, while perched near the top of capitalist America's class hierarchy, is nonetheless capable of understanding how much misery class relations cause. *The Catcher in the Rye* is about as far from being a proletarian novel as a novel can be, and it would sound odd to describe Salinger as a political writer. But the novel demonstrates that the standpoint of the proletariat is not the only one from which the injustices of capitalism can be glimpsed, and Holden's situation irresistibly suggests an impeccably Marxist point: namely, that any comprehensive system of oppression corrupts the quality of life for *everyone*, even for those who materially gain the most from it. In the eighth grade, of course, I was hardly capable of constructing a class analysis of a work of literature—though I strongly suspect (especially in view of Miss Greenwood's evident prescience as regards my political tendencies) that the sheer *rootedness* of Holden's outlook, the historical concreteness of his insights, did subliminally contribute to my spontaneous sense that Holden saw things as they really were. In any case, today this concreteness helps to confirm my sense that I was always justified in seeing Holden as simply right, and, though in chronological age he is only a few years older than my own daughter is now, there are important ways in which he remains for me a kindred spirit and even a hero. Miss Greenwood was clearly a far-seeing teacher—but could she have guessed anything like the actual impact on me of being introduced to J. D. Salinger?

And what, you may ask, became of Miss Greenwood herself? I have almost no idea. Not long after she taught me, she got married—becoming, after the all-but-universal fashion of the time, Mrs. Walker—and soon after that she left the school, probably because she and her new husband moved out of town. She is most likely a grandmother today—yet another staggering thought. I am tempted to try to get in touch with her, though it is not clear to me that this is feasible. How much, after all, do I have to go on? One possible—and very common—first name, two common Anglo-Saxon surnames, and the certain knowledge that, for a brief time in the mid-1960s, she taught English at Leroy Martin Junior High School in Raleigh, North Carolina. The evidence is scant, and the trail very cold. Still, I suppose a professional detective could do the job, and, given the resources of the telephone and the Internet, even an amateur might have a reasonable shot. But, beyond the question of whether the thing could be done, there is also the question of whether it would be a good idea. Such reunions sometimes produce much pleasure and even joy—such, indeed, has been my own personal experience—but one hears that sometimes they yield little but disappointment and embarrassment. It is possible that, in the aging grandmother I now imagine Miss Greenwood to be, I would plainly see traces of the skinny kid just out of college who once so enchanted my much younger self. But it is also possible that her whole manner and personality would seem utterly different and unfamiliar to me, whether because of actual changes in her, or because of flaws in my adolescent perceptions of more than three and a half decades ago, or because of the tricks that memory can play. Perhaps she would not even remember me except after detailed prompting, or—most humiliating possibility of all—not even *with* such prompting. So I remain undecided about trying to see Miss Greenwood again. One of the most startling and disconcerting things about living in a world with other human beings is the thousand and one ways they have of turning out to be different from what one had thought or assumed or expected or remembered them to be. The Miss Greenwood of this memoir may or may not (still) exist. But—and this is, of course, one of the most magical things about art—I am quite certain that for me Holden Caulfield will always, *always*, be there.

YASUHIRO TAKEUCHI

The Zen Archery of Holden Caulfield

Many have considered the deep influence of Zen Buddhism on J. D. Salinger,[1] but the perspective afforded on Salinger by Eugen Herrigel—the German philosopher who wrote on Zen and his experience of Japanese archery—has somehow escaped the attention of critics. Yet Herrigel's account of what he calls the "Great Doctrine" of Japanese archery offers substantial insight into *The Catcher in the Rye*, for the novel is intimately concerned with both Zen and hunting, two themes that converge in the Japanese art of the bow. The mystical "shooting" technique of the master Japanese archer illuminates the Zen-informed way in which Holden Caulfield is at once the catcher in the rye and the children he protects, the "shooter" of phonies and a phony himself, and finally a figure in whom binary oppositions merge in a state of transcendent aimlessness.

Salinger's short story "Seymour—An Introduction" evinces the author's direct engagement with Japanese archery. In this story, Seymour Glass's younger brother Buddy is "playing curb marbles" on the street. Seymour offers Buddy advice that is seemingly contrary to the goal of marble throwing, suggesting that he not target his opponent's marble: "Could you try not aiming so much?"[2] But Seymour's counter-intuitive advice is to be understood in light of the technique of a Japanese master archer:

From *English Language Notes*, vol. XLII, No. 1 (September 2004): pp. 55–63. © 2004 by the Regents of the University of Colorado.

> When he [Seymour] was coaching me [Buddy], from the curbstone across the street, to quit aiming my marble at Ira Yankauer's . . . I believe he was instinctively getting at something very close in spirit to the sort of instructions a master archer in Japan will give when he forbids a willful new student to aim his arrows at the target; that is, when the archery master permits, as it were, Aiming but no aiming. (241–42)

Salinger's understanding of Buddy's "master archer in Japan" likely reflects specifically the teachings of Kenzo Awa, the master archer who served as mentor to Herrigel. Salinger would have been familiar with Awa through his ties to renowned Zen master Daisetz Suzuki, to whom Herrigel was also linked.

To review the circumstances of these connections, Herrigel stayed in Japan from 1924 to 1929, teaching philosophy at Tohoku Imperial University (now Tohoku University). After returning to Germany, he published a lecture on Zen, "Die ritterliche Kunst des Bogenschiessens" (The Gallant Art of Archery), in 1936, the Japanese translation of which was published in the same year.[3] Herrigel later published an expanded version of this work as *Zen in der Kunst des Bogenschiessens* (Zen in the Art of Archery), in 1948 (three years prior to the publication of *Catcher*). The preface to the English translation of Herrigel's book, published in 1953, was written by Zen master Daisetz Suzuki, with whom Salinger had "become friends," according to Salinger's daughter Margaret. In Margaret's view, Salinger was well informed on the subject of Zen through Suzuki by the time he wrote *Catcher*.[4] Given his special interest in Zen together with his command of German,[5] it is likely, once again, that Salinger was familiar specifically with archery master Awa's teachings to Herrigel.

This speculation on Salinger's knowledge of Awa is particularly suggestive considering the significance of hunting in Salinger's *Catcher*: the defining motif of the novel is a catcher (in a hunting hat) whose job is to catch and save children. For many, to be sure, hunting is one thing and saving is quite another; Trowbridge, for instance, maintains that Holden's calling his hunting hat "a people shooting hat" reflects a hostile attitude towards others (though to be fair, Trowbridge demonstrates a shrewd understanding of Holden's "double vision, . . . his love–hate for humanity").[6] Yet for Jesus Christ, a frequent presence throughout *Catcher*—indeed, the novel is set during the Christmas season—these two acts, shooting/hunting/catching and saving are synonymous. At the lake of Gennesaret, to cite a familiar Bible story, Jesus tells the fisherman Simon to "let down your [Simon's] nets for a draught." Though Simon has caught nothing all night, he quickly catches "a great multitude of fishes" through Jesus's grace. Simon is frightened, but

Jesus says, "Fear not; from henceforth thou shalt catch men" (Luke 5:4–10). Thus, Jesus plays the role of Simon's fishing master, and in this role employs the metaphor of fishing (hunting)—and specifically the word "catch" in English-language Bible translations—to represent saving.

Salinger makes use of the hunting/catching trope not only through the catcher in the rye motif, but throughout the novel. For instance, Salinger chose Phoebe as the name for Holden's younger sister; in Greek mythology, Phoebe is a name for Artemis, goddess of the hunt and protector of children. Although Phoebe has also been the goddess of the moon and a Titan, the association of the name of Holden's sister with Artemis resonates particularly with the catcher of the novel's title, for it is Phoebe Caulfield who acts as Holden's master in the art of hunting/catching leading up to the novel's climactic carousel scene, as I have discussed elsewhere.[7] In view of this understanding of the hunting/catching trope, one senses little hostility in Holden's description of his hunting hat: "This is a people shooting hat. . . . I shoot people in this hat".[8] Rather, one relates Holden's shooting to his dream of being a catcher in the rye.

Holden's way of "shooting" people is further illuminated by the master archer's mystical way of shooting at a target, as understood by Herrigel:

> For them [Japanese master archers] the contest consists in the archer aiming at himself—and yet not at himself, in hitting himself—and yet not himself, and thus becoming simultaneously the aimer and the aim, the hitter and the hit. . . . Then comes the supreme and ultimate miracle: art becomes "artless," shooting becomes not-shooting.[9]

This ambivalent way of shooting, shooting-but-not-shooting, accords with Seymour's advice to Buddy that he "try not aiming so much," as does a similar teaching that Herrigel relates, that "the archer should hit without taking aim, [and] that he should completely lose sight of the goal and his intention to hit it."[10] Holden's dream of catching/saving people, viewed from the perspective of the paradoxical way of Zen archery, is consonant with his strange unwillingness to touch or otherwise contact the people he wishes to catch/save. One senses the resonance of Holden's "no-shooting" way of catching/saving in his reluctance to throw a snowball at a snow-covered car and hydrant; the very act of not throwing the snowball preserves, or saves, their pristine, "nice and white" (48) condition. One also senses this resonance in his avoidance of "saying hello to" or calling up Jane (40, 42, 77, 82, 137, 151, 175, 195, 262), the embodiment of innocence (i.e. she is "nice and white") for Holden. Moreover, one senses it in his childhood memory of a rule against touching museum exhibits ("one of the guards would say to you,

'Don't touch anything, children'" [157]), which works to reinforce Holden's own desire: "certain things they should stay the way they are" (158).[11] The not-aiming of Zen archery similarly informs the admonition that Phoebe, as goddess of the hunt, directs at Holden when—desperate to connect with her as the novel approaches its climax—he tries to catch her, literally, by the arm: "keep your hands to yourself" (272), Phoebe responds. Holden thus learns that to succeed, catching must ultimately become not-catching, just as "shooting becomes not-shooting" for Master Awa.

This understanding enables a new reading of the well-known carousel scene at the close of the novel, during which Holden lets Phoebe face the risk of falling from the carousel (273–74). Leaving Phoebe to face this risk does not necessarily mean that Holden has given up his catcher dream and accepted the need to grow into adulthood, as many critics have argued.[12] It simply means he has mastered the art of hunting/catching. Thus when the goddess Phoebe returns from the carousel, she puts the red *hunting* hat on Holden's head (274) as an act of coronation.

Beyond the implications of the principle of not-aiming, Japanese archery illuminates a mysterious yet recurring phenomenon in *Catcher*, a sense of oneness between the catcher and the caught. In his 1936 lecture on archery, Herrigel describes Awa's experience of becoming one with the target. As Herrigel relates it, Awa observed that when he no longer took aim at the target, he felt the target itself drawing closer and closer, until he became one with it.[13] In other words, in shooting at the target, Awa shot himself. In *Zen in the Art of Archery*, Herrigel describes this state as "becoming simultaneously the aimer and the aim, the hitter and the hit."[14] In *Catcher*, Holden tries to shoot/catch characters who can be described as fallen in either a physical or moral sense, and with whom Holden himself is identified through a variety of literary devices.[15] The fallen constitute three groups: the dead (Holden's brother Allie and the suicide James Castle); children at risk of losing their innocence (Phoebe and Jane); and a number of "phonies," including Holden's own brother D. B., who as a screenwriter in Hollywood is a literary "prostitute" (4).

The third of these groups—the phonies—offers an intriguing example of how Holden is identified with his prey, that is, of how the catcher is identified with the caught. Some critics have already pointed out that Holden is himself a phony—that although Holden criticizes/attacks/ shoots phonies he is himself guilty of the very behavior that he criticizes; for instance, French observes that "Holden obviously fails to see that his criticisms apply to himself."[16] But in a number of instances, Holden evinces a clear awareness of his own phoniness, rendering problematic the views of those who ascribe Holden's apparent hypocrisy to a lack of self-awareness resulting from "immaturity"[17] or "mental instability."[18] Rather, Holden's contradictory phoniness/anti-phoniness should be understood as a conscious reflection on Salinger's part of the oneness of the shooter and the shot, a central notion in Awa's teachings. For instance, soon after criticizing his roommate Stradlater for "snowing his date in this quiet, *sincere* voice" (64), Holden says that he "gave him [Ackley] a big, phony handshake" (65) and that he spoke "in this very sincere voice" (66). Stradlater and Holden, both speaking in a "sincere voice," practice the same phoniness. Other examples of Holden's phoniness also resist interpretation in terms of "immaturity" or "mental instability." At one point, Holden defines a "dumb" story as follows: "One of those stories with a lot of phony, lean-jawed guys named David in it, and a lot of phony girls named Linda or Marcia that are always lighting all the goddam Davids' pipes for them" (70). Soon after this, Holden asks a lady on a train if she would "care for a cigarette," and gives her "a light" (72). Beyond reflecting hypocrisy or a lack of self-insight, Holden's giving someone a light in proximity to this story equates the novel itself—Salinger's story—to the "dumb" (phony) sort of story that Holden describes. This structural gesture seems more strictly to concern Salinger's intention of identifying Holden (catcher/shooter/saver) and the phonies (caught/shot/fallen), than simply to model Holden's psychology.

An exchange of roles between Stradlater and Holden early in the novel offers the most striking example of the identity Salinger asserts between Holden and the phonies. Stradlater, in the course of getting ready for a date, asks two favors of Holden: that Holden lend him his hound's tooth jacket, and that Holden write an English composition in Stradlater's name. It soon emerges that Stradlater's date is Holden's former girlfriend, Jane Gallagher, and this means that Stradlater, in Holden's jacket ("He [Stradlater] put them [a pack of cigarettes] in his coat pocket—*my* coat pocket" [44; emphasis original]) and with Holden's Vitalis on his hair ("Old Stradlater was putting Vitalis on his hair. *My* Vitalis" [41; emphasis original]), is doing something that Holden probably should do. Soon after, Holden writes Stradlater's composition for him, using, interestingly enough, Stradlater's typewriter (51). Stradlater does Holden's job using Holden's possessions, and Holden does Stradlater's job using Stradlater's possession. Considering that Holden presumably imitates Stradlater's voice to write Stradlater's composition, and that Stradlater wears Holden's jacket, essentially disguising himself as Holden, the two characters effectively merge.[19] Stradlater, perhaps the most prominent embodiment of phoniness in the novel, and Holden, denouncer of phoniness, thus become one.

Beyond catching-but-not-catching and the identity of the catcher and the caught, the Great Doctrine of archery that Master Awa taught Herrigel offers a further insight that informs the character of Holden Caulfield: the identity of the shooter/catcher/saver and the Divine. As Master Awa explained of the Great Doctrine, "when the target and I become one, it also signifies that

I become one with Buddha. . . . You [Herrigel] should aim not at the target but at yourself. Then you will succeed in shooting yourself, Buddha, and the target all at the same time."[20] Hence, Salinger may well have become aware of this spiritual, if not specifically Zen Buddhist, identification of opposites that informs Holden's character through Japanese archery. This possibility lends support to my argument that at the close of *Catcher* Salinger identifies Holden with the Jesus Christ of Carl Jung's conception, who also embodies the oneness of opposites, of fisherman (catcher) and fish (caught).[21]

The Great Doctrine and *Catcher* also take similar views of the condition that ensues upon the transcendent fusion of opposites wherein a subject as an active center of logical being evaporates. Through archery, Herrigel at last experiences such transcendence directly, an experience during which, in Awa's words, "the bowstring has cut right though you [Herrigel]"; Herrigel both shoots and is shot simultaneously. Later, Herrigel is at a loss, hardly knowing what to say about his experience: "I'm afraid I don't understand anything more at all, . . . even the simplest things have got in a muddle. . . . Do 'I' hit the goal, or does the goal hit me?"[22] Having transcended the binary oppositions which comprise our "knowledge" of the world, Herrigel cannot put into words what he has experienced. Yet this is precisely the nature of mastering the Great Doctrine, and at this point, Awa acknowledges that Herrigel has mastered the "artless art" of archery.[23] After the final, climactic rain scene of *Catcher*, in which Holden experiences oneness with his dead brother Allie, with the falling Phoebe, and with the phonies around him[24]—that is, after Holden too has been hit by his own arrow—Holden finds himself unable to understand or explain what he has experienced: "D. B. asked me what I thought about all this stuff I just finished telling you about. I didn't *know* what the hell to say. If you want to know the truth, I don't know what I think about it" (276–77; emphasis original). Finally, Holden respects the principle of the Zen adept, who "shuns all talk of himself and his progress" and "regards it [such talk] as a betrayal of Zen."[25] Reflecting on, presumably, his narration of the novel, Holden blurts out (concludes), "I'm sorry I told so many people about it" (277).

Having achieved transcendence, Holden no longer takes aim at anything, and thus he finds it absurd for the doctor to ask if he is going to apply himself when he returns to school after recovering from the breakdown he has apparently suffered (276). For Holden, this is "a stupid question" because he has already moved beyond the stage of consciously pursuing goals, in other words, of taking aim. If Holden were to take aim—or to speak directly of his goal/target—he would miss his aim as surely as the novice archer straining at his bow. An understanding of this adds nuance to Holden's final words, the final words of the novel: "Don't tell anybody anything. If you do, you start missing everybody" (277).

NOTES

1. See, for example, Bernice and Sanford Goldstein, "Zen and Salinger." *Modern Fiction Studies* 12.3 (1966): 313–24; and Dennis McCort, "Hyakujo's Geese, Amban's Doughnuts and Rilke's Carousel: Sources East and West for Salinger's *Catcher*," *Comparative Literature Studies* 34.3 (1997): 260–78.

2. J. D. Salinger, "Seymour—An Introduction," *Raise High the Roof Beam, Carpenters*, and *Seymour—An Introduction* (Boston: Little, Brown, 1963) 241–42.

3. Eugen Herrigel, *Nihon no Kyujutu* ("The Gallant Art of Archery"), trans. Jisaburo Shibata (Tokyo: Iwanami, 1982) 101, 110–11.

4. Margaret A. Salinger, *Dream Catcher* (New York: Washington Square Press, 2000) 11.

5. For a discussion of Salinger's interest in German speaking writers such as Rilke and Kafka and his experience in wartime Germany, see Ian Hamilton, *In Search of J. D. Salinger* (London: Heinemann, 1988) 85–93, 108.

6. Clinton W. Trowbridge, "Character and Detail in *The Catcher in the Rye*," *Holden Caulfield*, ed. Harold Bloom (New York: Chelsea House, 1990) 77–78.

7. Yasuhiro Takeuchi, "The Burning Carousel and the Carnivalesque: Subversion and Transcendence at the Close of *The Catcher in the Rye*," *Studies in the Novel* 34.3 (2002): 328–29.

8. J. D. Salinger, *The Catcher in the Rye* (Boston: Little, Brown, 1951) 236. Further citations will be made parenthetically.

9. Eugen Herrigel, *Zen in the Art of Archery*, trans., R.F.C. Hull (New York: Vintage Books, 1989) 5–6.

10. Herrigel, *Zen in the Art of Archery* 73.

11. For an extended discussion of these episodes, see Yasuhiro Takeuchi, "Salinger's *The Catcher in the Rye*," *The Explicator* 60.3 (2002): 164–66.

12. See, for example, Warren French, *J. D. Salinger* revised ed. (Boston: Twayne, 1976) 122; and Sanford Pinsker, *The Catcher in the Rye: Innocence Under Pressure* (New York: Twayne, 1993), 94.

13. Eugen Herrigel, *Nihon no Kyujutu* ("The Gallant Art of Archery"), trans. Jisaburo Shibata (Tokyo: Iwanami, 1982) 42–43.

14. Herrigel, *Zen in the Art of Archery* 5.

15. For an extended discussion of how Salinger conveys these identities, and in particular those between Allie and Holden and between Phoebe and Holden, see Takeuchi, "The Burning Carousel and the Carnivalesque," 326–31.

16. Warren French, *J. D. Salinger* revised ed. (Boston: Twayne, 1976) 109–10. For similar instances, see Duane Edwards, "Don't Ever Tell Anybody Anything," *ELH* 44.3 (1977): 554.

17. French 110.

18. Edwards 556.

19. For other instances of role changes through lendings and borrowings of clothes, see Takeuchi, "The Burning Carousel and the Carnivalesque," 325.

20. Herrigel, *Nihon no Kyujutu* 43. The English translation of this quotation is my own, from the Japanese.

21. Takeuchi, "The Burning Carousel and the Carnivalesque," 330. See also Jung, *Aion*, trans. R.F.G. Hull, 2nd ed. (Princeton: Princeton UP, 1969) 112–13.

22. Herrigel, *Zen in the Art of Archery* 61.

23. Herrigel, *Zen in the Art of Archery* 64.

24. See Note 15.

25. Herrigel, *Zen in the Art of Archery* 10.

MYLES WEBER

Augmenting the Salinger Oeuvre
by Any Means

In February 1977, *Esquire* magazine ran an unsigned short story with the Salingeresque title "From Rupert—With No Promises." Its appearance triggered widespread speculation that J. D. Salinger authored the work, thereby ending twelve years of nonpublication. Reports surfaced within weeks, however, that *Esquire*'s fiction editor, Gordon Lish, wrote the piece himself. "My feeling," Lish later explained, "was that if Salinger was not going to write stories, someone had to write them for him" (Alexander 248).

Efforts to pad Salinger's oeuvre without the knowledge or cooperation of the author extend beyond his fiction. In 1982, an aspiring writer named Steven Kunes submitted to *People* magazine the transcript of a purported interview with the author (the two never actually spoke). Before the interview could run, however, Salinger filed suit against Kunes in U.S. District Court. Salinger had received reports of counterfeit letters on falsified letterhead distributed by Kunes buttressing claims of authenticity for the interview. In his signed affidavit, Salinger objected not only to the illegality of the forgeries but also to their quality, which he found "dreadfully conceived and written" (Williams C2). Salinger, a native New Yorker then as now resident in Cornish, New Hampshire, hypothesized in the affidavit about his recurring victimhood. "I publish my fiction seldom," he wrote. "I have tried, all my professional life, to live and work in privacy. It may be precisely

From *Consuming Silences: How We Read Authors Who Don't Publish*. Athens: The University of Georgia Press (2005): pp. 88–116. ©2005 by the University of Georgia Press.

because I live and work as quietly and as remotely as I do, that I have from time to time been the mark for opportunists" (Williams C1).

Salinger's hypothesis about his predicament is sound. It is precisely because he publishes seldom—since 1965, never—and remains remote and inaccessible that bootleggers, forgers, critics, and editors have had a financial incentive to supplant the void left by the author's withdrawal and feel compelled to extend his aborted career narrative. Salinger's aversion to publicity ultimately gives rise to the journalistic stakeout, usually of Salinger's home or the local post office; the ambush photograph; harassing questions shouted at the fleeing author; the forged story, letter, or interview; and attempts to excerpt, paraphrase, or otherwise bring to light extant documents penned by Salinger, particularly letters dating from his apprenticeship as a professional author. At the very least, these badgering efforts ultimately succeed in eliciting public statements in the form of legal affidavits and depositions. The journalists and biographers cannot fail, then: either they concoct secondary texts for and about Salinger, or they force the author to supply them himself in his attempt to frustrate their designs.

In most of these cases, the pursuers have no qualms about their methods. According to a 1988 article in *Newsday*, Frank Devine, editor of the *New York Post*, regarded as "nonsense" the notion that Salinger had a right to be left alone. When Salinger swung his fist ineffectually at a *Post* photographer who blocked the author's car in a New Hampshire parking lot, Devine complained that the "subject"—Salinger—was "interfering with the photographer doing his job" (Collins 10). Lish was likewise unrepentant about his Rupert story. "I did not see that fiction as a hoax," he later wrote, "so much as an attractive plausibility" ("Fool" 409). Most famously, Ian Hamilton believed he was on secure ethical and legal footing when he included long excerpts from unpublished Salinger letters in a proposed biography of the author in 1986. But the courts ruled differently, blocking the book's publication and demanding the removal even of paraphrasings of those excerpted passages. (Two years later, Random House published a curious work by Hamilton, *In Search of J. D. Salinger*, the focus of which was its author's quest for and failure to deliver a satisfying biography.)

The singularity of Salinger's authorship and its trappings routinely trips up critics and other writers who apply conventional expectations of productivity and public interaction to all famous living authors. In 1981, Thomas LeClair grouped Salinger, Don DeLillo, Thomas Pynchon, and William Gaddis together as a clique of relatively homogeneous, publicity-shy authors. "For them," he wrote, "talking, with its instantaneousness and simplification, is the exact opposite of writing fiction" (50). What all four authors fear, he claimed, is the inevitable process by which bad language— literary gossip, celebrity chatter, discussion of advances and other forms of remuneration—drives out good language. "The invisibility necessary for Salinger and DeLillo to write is also one way they, along with Pynchon and Gaddis, preserve the integrity, the strange discreteness, of their novels," LeClair observed (51). But Salinger's case was unlike the others': he no longer published new work. A former author, he simply avoided listening to chatter and refused to generate his own. In 1970, Salinger repaid with interest a seventy-five-thousand-dollar advance from Little, Brown for a proposed fifth book; in 1974, he told a *New York Times* reporter that he derived great satisfaction from writing only for himself (Fosburgh 1); and since then, he has published no new fiction and removed himself from the arenas of public discourse. His four extant books, to which his publishers retain rights, remain in print.

J. D. Salinger's author persona, therefore, is ultimately unlike any other, with the near exception of Harper Lee's (see the conclusion). Katherine Anne Porter, Ralph Ellison, and Truman Capote each went a decade or considerably longer without publishing a book of fiction, but each also wrote book reviews and other essays or sat for interviews, therein commenting on their progress drafting, respectively, *Ship of Fools*, a follow-up to *Invisible Man*, and the ultimately uncompleted *Answered Prayers*. DeLillo, Pynchon, and Gaddis may have shunned publicity and therefore been subjected to incidents of journalistic ambush or subterfuge similar to those Salinger has suffered, but they spoke to the reading public through their major works of the 1970s, 1980s, and 1990s. And whereas countless unknown or failed writers neither publish books nor generate secondary texts, these authors have not gone missing in any specific sense. Salinger's notoriety as the author of *The Catcher in the Rye*, *Nine Stories*, *Franny and Zooey*, and *Raise High the Roof Beam, Carpenters* and *Seymour—An Introduction* guarantees that the critical establishment will speculate on his whereabouts and the condition of his unnervingly static oeuvre.

There are numerous authors whose string of published works ended abruptly—Flannery O'Connor, Nathanael West, and F. Scott Fitzgerald come immediately to mind—but a perfectly reasonable explanation exists in these cases: they died. Jerome David Salinger, born 1 January 1919, is by all reports alive and healthy; the condition of J. D. Salinger the author, however, is a source of contention, mainly between Salinger himself and the literary community, which insists on the author's existence beyond his textual demise and concerns itself with filling what Lish calls "Salinger's gigantically perfect silence" ("Fool" 415). If Jerome David Salinger is not going to produce more texts, the literary community reasons, then someone has to produce some for him, which at the very least means attributing to him volumes of strategically shaped silence. Lish's offhand remark attempting to justify his faux-Salinger story is indicative of the pervasive attitude toward

Salinger; Lish's methods for expanding Salinger's stunted canon were simply more proactive than that of the majority of journalists, critics, and scholars who have treated Salinger's extended period of nonpublication as text ripe for critical interpretation—that is, as a deliberate (and cunning) extension of his authorship. As a strategy for filling the Salinger void, this is only somewhat less manipulative than the puckish or illegal methods employed by Lish and Steven Kunes. The critical establishment, denied access for decades to whatever pages Salinger is actually accumulating in his desk drawer, simply will not permit Salinger to depart the active literary scene. Rather than disappear, he is reconfigured as a prolific, nearly conventional author inundating the marketplace with silence.

"For the past two decades I have elected, for personal reasons, to leave the public spotlight entirely," Salinger stated in court documents supporting his 1986 suit filed to block publication of Hamilton's biography. "I have shunned all publicity for over twenty years and I have not published any material during that time. I have become, in every sense of the word, a private citizen" (Alexander 280). When the 1987 ruling of the United States Court of Appeals for the Second Circuit came down in Salinger's favor, it was widely feared in publishing circles that the decision would curb First Amendment rights and have a chilling effect on future scholarship. But Salinger's lawyers insisted there was nothing ominous about the ruling. They maintained that an author, too, has First Amendment rights, including "a right *not* to speak" (Margolick 44).

Most members of the literary community who analyze Salinger's fiction have rejected that assertion, at least implicitly. Their working assumption is that Salinger, a professional author for more than two decades, cannot revert to private-citizen status. He remains a public figure issuing texts, even if he does not actually publish or otherwise address the public directly or willingly. As such he clearly has no right *not* to speak. He is helpless, in fact, to block their close textual analyses of the nonexistent works through which they believe he communicates.

"I am sometimes made to wonder where it is Salinger's mind has kept itself going to—now that we no longer have even the coded record the fellow used to mark down for us of the turnings of its travel," Lish wrote in 1986 as a prelude to indulging in idle speculation. "But there I go again," he admitted in the same essay, "guessing about Salinger with nothing to go on to back me up" ("Fool" 408). This literary guessing game elicits the participation of numerous scholars, who focus their analyses on the few public statements Salinger *has* made, in an effort to decode the subsequent workings of the uncommunicative author's mind.

In his 1999 biography of Salinger, Paul Alexander picked over the brief author's notes included on the inside flaps of Salinger's final two books to try to unlock the puzzle of his withdrawal and attribute to the author a careful, premeditated design to his silence. In the second author's note, from 1963, Salinger explained that his decision to collect "Raise High the Roof Beam, Carpenters" and "Seymour—An introduction" in a single volume was made "in something of a hurry" to avoid close chronological contact with new material in his series of works on the Glass family: "There is only my word for it, granted, but I have several new stories coming along—waxing, dilating—each in its own way, but I suspect the less said about them, in mixed company, the better" (Alsen 238). Because only one subsequent work, "Hapworth 16, 1924," appeared in print, Alexander attributed deceitful intent to Salinger in these notes, the textual and biographical evidence of which he parsed with single-minded humorlessness. ("What exactly did he mean by 'mixed company'?" [225].) Alexander was suspicious of nearly every phrase Salinger penned; the majority he deemed deceptive or disingenuous.

Alexander was building a case supporting the accusation that Salinger's seclusion is elaborately designed to initiate a dialogue with the audience and fuel the publicity machine, the workings of which the conniving recluse in truth welcomes rather than resents. It is the same accusation that Ian Hamilton, smarting from his failed legal wrangling with Salinger in the mid-1980s, made in the quasi biography Random House ultimately issued. In fact, a dialogue of sorts *has* been initiated and maintained, not by Salinger, but by journalists, critics, scholars, biographers, and readers who believe Salinger is speaking to them.

In 1975, C. David Heymann published an article in the *Village Voice* about his efforts to find out more about Salinger by trekking to New Hampshire. "My approach was from the side," he reported of his arrival at Salinger's Swiss chalet-style home. "The door appeared to be locked; a large curtained picture window to the left of the door was dark. I knocked and called hello. My voice trembled. I was scared" (35).

Salinger does not make an appearance at this point in Heymann's narrative, but his dog does; it barks when Heymann raps on the door. "It was a miserable whine, empty-sounding and hollow, and it shattered the perfect silence," wrote Heymann. "I waited and listened." Finally, Heymann turned to leave, but the whining continued. "As I walked back down the slippery hill to my car I could still hear the dog baying in the background. I could hear it as I backed the car out of the driveway and into the road. It echoed among the hills as I drove down the road away from the house and toward the town. It stayed with me all the way into town. It was, I reflected, an unpleasant, forbidding sound" (35).

This strikes me as an inordinately detailed and nuanced account of a guard dog doing what guard dogs are supposed to do: bark at intruders. It suggests that nonresponses from Salinger to contact initiated by outsiders are imbued with undue importance and meaning, even assigned a mood ("unpleasant, forbidding") and a tone ("hollow," "empty-sounding," "miserable"). Reports such as this demonstrate that, upon significant reflection, we can gain some understanding of the life that the author J. D. Salinger leads. For one thing, it is sad. And it must therefore follow that his silence calls out to us from that unhappy place.

Ron Rosenbaum made the pilgrimage to Cornish for *Esquire* magazine. In a 1997 article, he reflected on his visit from the vantage point of Salinger's driveway, where he claimed the author's mailbox beckoned to him. "It's not a passive silence," he commented on the wall of inaccessibility and reclusion Salinger has built around himself, and his refusal to publish; "it's a palpable, provocative silence" that speaks to the reader and exerts power over him. "Something draws us to it, makes us interrogate it, test it," Rosenbaum explained. "[W]hen a writer won't break his silence, we think of ways to break into it" (50).

Apparently Salinger's mailbox beckons to innumerable others; how else to explain the 2002 collection *Letters to J. D. Salinger*, edited by Chris Kubica and Will Hochman and published by the University of Wisconsin Press? Hochman explains in his postscript that the volume "shows readers 'talking' critically and creatively" to an author whose response is fully muted, and whose status as a publishing author has lapsed (243). A majority of the correspondents in the book are professional writers, editors, and academics (including Tom Robbins, George Plimpton, and Sanford Pinsker) solicited by Kubica. "Would you consider publishing a letter to Salinger," he asked them, "in a collection of such letters for all of us to read and to save it, in effect, from Salinger's nearest landfill?" (xvii). Some seventy-eight solicited contributors were willing to do just that, knowing that the exchange was not with a human writer but with a Foucauldian author function largely of their own design, but who was no less legitimate for being so. Novelist Jessica Treadway praised the author for the revelatory truth of *Nine Stories* (44). Poet and fiction writer David Huddle apologized for writing in a style too closely imitative of Salinger's (37). The editors also opened up the exchange to unsolicited e-mailers, who submitted their letters via Kubica's Web site. Among the seventy-one such items selected is a letter from David Miller questioning the rightness of the project itself: "I think to attempt to write or visit J. D. Salinger betrays what Salinger has stood for, for the past 50 years" (200). But the vast majority of correspondents played along with the conceit of directly addressing J. D. Salinger and offered thanks, praise, or puzzlement at his disappearance.

With Salinger's ultimate status as an author uncertain, readers reject his withdrawal from the public sphere and its attendant duties, like reading fan mail. In this light, *Letters to J. D. Salinger* can be viewed as an attempt to return the missing author to his rightful place as an accessible figure who welcomes adulation and responds to querying from the reading public. In a related fashion, Warren French has twice reworked his book-length study of Salinger. First published in 1963, *J. D. Salinger* was issued in revised form in 1976 to incorporate, one might have thought, analysis of a new work of Salinger fiction, "Hapworth 16, 1924," which appeared in 1965. But in fact the revisions largely addressed Salinger's withdrawal from public life and his eleven-year silence. In *J. D. Salinger, Revisited* (1988), French returned again to the same unchanged canon of Salinger works, with no purpose other than to acknowledge—to "revisit"—the expanding silence the author was emitting, and to speculate on its sources and meaning, as if Salinger were an author whose list of published works continued to expand.

Of course, not all critics engage in a hermeneutics of Salinger's silence. "I have no idea why Salinger has not in recent years graced us with more stories," wrote Robert Coles in a 1973 "Reconsideration" of Salinger in the *New Republic*. "It is no one's business, really" (32). In his contribution to *Letters to J. D. Salinger*, Andy Selsberg concurred: "You don't have to publish. You don't have to read the letters or reviews. You don't have to explain. We've got what we need. Don't say another word" (Kubica and Hochman 40). But the fact that Selsberg's comments are written in second person, directly addressing an author whose disappearance he condones, suggests just how strong is the tendency to confront the author's silence and reclusion and analyze them, either as acts of manipulation or, in the words of Dipti R. Pattaniak, as "a conscious intellectual and spiritual stance worthy of sober critical attention" (114).

In the early 1960s, novelist Herbert Gold and a coeditor were preparing an anthology of American short stories and requested permission to reprint one of Salinger's. "You wrote a short note to deny us the privilege," Gold stated in his contribution to *Letters to J. D. Salinger*. Though he has since lost the actual note, its mysterious concluding sentence remains fixed in Gold's memory. "It read: 'I have my reasons'" (Kubica and Hochman 33).

Salinger's reasons for refusing anthologization of previously published work are open to speculation. The same is true of his reasons for exiting the literary world altogether a few years later. "It's because he can't stand any criticism," Salinger's sister, Dorris, told her niece (Margaret Salinger 428). According to novelist Tom Wolfe, Salinger "seems to be a classic burnt-out case" who has exhausted his "small, precious talent" (60). In the same vein, British novelist Emma Forrest suggested in a 2001 collection of essays focused on this very topic that the author, unlike Philip Roth, may not have been "good enough" to sustain a career that would build toward ever-greater accolades and popular success and therefore retreated to avoid failure (61). Joel Stein, in the same volume, emphasized Salinger's discomfort at receiving attention, which sounds more like a rephrasing of the question of why the author withdrew than an attempt at an answer (171).

Much speculation of this sort conflates Salinger the nonpublishing author with Salinger the recluse, who, according to Jonathan Yardley, defends his privacy "with a tenacity that at times has spilled over into something more like lunacy" (C1). The apparently irrational extent to which Salinger protects his privacy has given rise to the most extreme and intrusive hypotheses for his silence, such as one offered in Alexander's biography: that Salinger had "a penchant for young women that he did not want to reveal to the public" (312–13). More often, though, Salinger's "lunacy" generates less offensive if no less fanciful explanations for his retreat from the world. Two of the many suggested by Hamilton are, one, that Salinger, a fledgling actor in his adolescence, is now sinking his teeth into the role of a lifetime, that of a reclusive artist (*In Search* 22); and, two, that the author—an egotistical, ill-tempered, unforgiving man—wants so badly to be canonized that he has invented a Salinger-like character named Seymour Glass, "a saint who writes beautiful poetry" (Salinger writes prose), "who has a breakdown in the war" (as did Salinger), "who marries the wrong woman" (Salinger's short-lived marriage to a war bride seemed doomed from the start), "who commits suicide" (Salinger has not killed himself, but has made himself semiposthumous by not publishing or even addressing the public for four decades) (*In Search* 150).

The religious aspect of Hamilton's second hypothesis moves the focus of the discussion away from biographical or psychological speculation toward at least a fleeting consideration of the content of Salinger's works, something I do at greater length later in this chapter. The characters populating Salinger's later novellas—members of the Glass family—are heavily schooled in, and at times obsessed with, spiritual matters, particularly those addressed by Vedanta Hinduism, Zen Buddhism, and Eastern Orthodox Christianity. Supported by the biographical information available about Salinger, the widespread assumption has been that the author himself began seriously to focus on such matters in the 1950s, which might explain his professional self-removal a decade later. "The holy man, the initiate, withdraws not only from the temptations of worldly action; he withdraws from speech," George Steiner explained (*Language* 13). James Lundquist, reasoning that Zen Buddhism exploits the virtues of logical nonsense in the form of riddles rather than conventional logic (33), thought this applicable to Salinger's career: What could be more nonsensical than a diligent author who chooses not to publish? And even Ron Rosenbaum, contemplating the compelling void one confronts from the bottom of Salinger's driveway, described the eerie nonresponse as "the deliberate silence that represents some kind of spiritual renunciation" (53).

Lost on none of the scholars interpreting the author's silence is the apparent irony that the more Salinger insists on anonymity, the more famous he becomes; the lengthier and more remarkable his period of nonpublication grows, the louder his text of silence speaks. For some, including his two biographers, it is only a short leap from making such observations to voicing the accusation—neither provable nor disprovable—that Salinger knowingly designed his career this way, to elicit greater acclaim and remuneration.

Observations about Salinger's inescapable celebrity status began early, while the author was still publishing. He had from the start avoided the usual trappings of literary publicity, refusing to sit for interviews, demanding that his photograph be removed from the cover flap of his novel, insisting that his publisher, Little, Brown, send out no review copies of the book, and departing New York City, America's literary epicenter, for rural New Hampshire in January 1953, the year his second book, *Nine Stories*, was published. At first, critics responded to the talented author's personal quirks with fond bewilderment or outright admiration. But by 1960, David Leitch had decided that Salinger's desire for anonymity was "almost an affectation" (70). That same year, Harvey Swados observed that Salinger had so sedulously avoided publicity that he had "aroused the liveliest curiosity about himself" (12). In Don DeLillo's 1991 novel *Mao II*, a Salingeresque character explains this phenomenon in terms of a fickle creator: "When a writer doesn't show his face, he becomes a local symptom of God's famous reluctance to appear" (36).

In *Before the Great Silence*, Maurice Maeterlinck spoke similarly of how familiar but unavailable persons—specifically, the dead—assume a fixed identity in our minds that supersedes the living and approaches the sublime power of the divine. "When I think of my mother, my father, my two brothers, or five or six friends of mine who are dead, they still exist, they live as distinctly as when they were alive" (84). In fact, he claimed, they are more clearly recognizable than when they were living. "They no longer change," he reported. "They have lost all their little defects, and are always smiling, as though they had returned from the most beautiful country" (85). In contrast: "The majority of the living weary us, or are strangers to us. We truly know and love only the dead" (195). Salinger's inaccessibility may likewise do more than merely pique the public's curiosity. It may permit them to perfect their mental image of the author and attribute a similar perfection to his recent work—the sublime silence of nonpublication—whose power is unlike that of any conventional book. "So long as a man is alive one does not know what he is or what he will do," Maeterlinck added. "We have unwavering confidence only in the dead" (195). Similarly, public confidence in J. D. Salinger may outstrip public confidence in any publishing author, the quality of whose prose may suddenly dip, whose personality may shift alarmingly, or who may begin to repeat himself to an annoying extent. Ironically, should a posthumous Salinger publish new works, public confidence may be shaken. But a living Salinger committed to silence and privacy is, for these purposes, safely and vividly dead.

Thomas LeClair warned that, in addition to the obvious paradoxes of seclusion ("The less a writer is visible, the more he is pursued"), there is a deeper danger that "the condition necessary for writing can become the novelist's subject: purification, obsession, silence" (52). But, professionally speaking, where is the danger in that? As Warren French concluded about Salinger in 1988, "His long silence has not affected his reputation" (*Revisited* 122). Similarly, Daniel M. Stashower observed in 1983 that Salinger's isolation "has done nothing to damage but rather has strengthened the claim of some literary critics that Salinger is one of the more important American writers in the postwar era" (375).

Because Salinger's silence and seclusion have been perceived as solidifying his professional reputation, some writers detect cunning deliberation in the author's behavior. As early as 1967, Howard M. Harper Jr. described the relationship between Salinger and his critics as "something of a cat-and-mouse game, the roles interchanging with each installment of the Glass saga" (95). Not everyone who views Salinger's behavior as calculating has been censorious. Som P. Ranchan congratulated Salinger for infusing his manipulation of the literary world with exemplary Hindu symbolism and mythology. "It is my conviction that Salinger is a mischievous mystic who has played an interesting game with critics," Ranchan wrote. "In this metaphysical game he has used primarily the Vedantic frameworks inlaid with Zen and shakta values" (v). But Salinger's two biographers, Ian Hamilton and Paul Alexander, made clear their intention was to expose not a playful mystic but a greedy fraud.

Even before Salinger sued to block publication of his book, Hamilton found the author's behavior inconsistent, his comments about not wanting to be contacted "flirtatious" and "teasing" (Field 63). An angry letter Salinger wrote berating Hamilton for contacting Salinger's sister and son was rejected as "somewhat too composed, too pleased with its own polish for me to accept it as a direct cry from the heart." Hamilton showed the letter to a friend in the literary business, who assured him it was really a come-on; he suggested that Salinger's helpless statement "I can't stop you" should best be translated as "Please go ahead" (*In Search* 7), which is precisely what Hamilton did, only to face litigation, after which the gloves came off. In his revised manuscript, Hamilton did not limit himself to the standard ironic observations—"He was famous for not wanting to be famous" (4)—but plainly and paradoxically accused the author of cheapening his talent by not selling his new works. "He said he wanted neither fame nor money and by this means he'd contrived to get extra supplies of both—much more of both, in fact, than might have come his way if he'd stayed in the marketplace along with everybody else" (8).

Salinger's suit against Hamilton and his publisher, Random House, was set in motion when an advance copy of the galley proofs got into the hands of Salinger's agent (Margolick 45). Eleven years later, Renaissance Books prudently released Paul Alexander's biography with little advance publicity and, in a Salingeresque twist, sent out no review copies (Quinn 26). Subjected to no revenge-inducing legal hassles, Alexander was still suspicious of his subject's true designs. "[S]imply because he turned into a recluse does not mean he didn't want fame," Alexander reasoned. "In fact, one could argue that by taking the position he did—and keeping it—he ensured he *would* remain famous for being a recluse" (26). The manner in which Salinger handled supposedly unwanted publicity seemed to Alexander a bit too contrived to get attention, just as it had to Hamilton. "The whole act," as he called it, "felt as if it were being put on by a master showman, a genius spin doctor, a public-relations wizard hawking a story the public couldn't get enough of" (302). And the author's ultimate motivation for this elaborate performance was again assumed to be pecuniary. When Salinger sought to block inclusion of his unpublished letters in Hamilton's original biography manuscript, Alexander asserted, he was concerned not so much about his copyright as his trademark: "[P]art of what Salinger was protecting by filing his lawsuit against Hamilton was the image he had created over the years, an image that promoted sales of books" (284).

Neither biographer offered statistical evidence to support his claims, nor could he: even if one tabulated actual worldwide sales of Salinger's four books, how would one then estimate, for the purpose of comparison, the hypothetical annual sales of a nonreclusive, actively publishing author who goes on television to hawk his books and sells film rights to Hollywood? Serious analysis is beside the point: this is an argument based on conjecture. It is an attempt to shape a compelling author persona where none exists outside reader expectations. Just as a dearth of published works prompted critics to produce some on the author's behalf, an absent author elicited a replacement figure, whose gaze remains fixed on the reader, and who is very self-aware. "He's a media animal," assumed one contributor to *Letters to J. D. Salinger*. "He's creating an icon, and he's smart enough to know it" (Kubica and Hochman 223).

The issue of public-relations savvy surfaces whenever Salinger is mentioned in the media. In 1998, Joyce Maynard published *At Home in the World*, a memoir that chronicled in embarrassing detail her nine-month relationship with Salinger. The following year, she placed at auction fourteen personal letters written by Salinger just before and during the affair. Included in the cache, which Sotheby's sold for $156,500, was the initial letter, dated 25 April 1972, written in response to Maynard's *New York Times Magazine* essay "An 18-Year-Old Looks Back on Life" (Smith B1). "No one forced J. D. Salinger in the spring of 1972 to initiate an epistolary relationship with an 18-year-old college freshman," wrote Joyce Carol Oates in a 1999 *New York Times* op-ed piece, published amid a flurry of bad press against Maynard, who was labeled a "leech" and a "highly skilled predator" the next day in the same newspaper (Dowd A23). "[N]o one forced the 53-year-old writer, at the height of his perhaps sufflated fame, to seduce her through words, and to invite her to live with him in rural New Hampshire" (Oates, "Words" A23). Brooke Allen, writing in the *National Review*, concurred. Salinger "should have had the good sense, if not the good taste, to keep his mitts off of impressionable young girls," she wrote. Allen took special note of the fact that the pair were ludicrously mismatched: in stark contrast to Salinger, Maynard is an exhibitionistic writer "who spills her guts in public about everything from her sexual dysfunctions to her breast implants" (34).

Both Allen and Oates questioned the judgment of an author whose chief fear is unwanted publicity, but if one approaches the incident from the inverted perspective of Hamilton and Alexander, the affair makes perfect sense. No longer is Salinger a lonely middle-aged recluse trading on his celebrity status to elicit the company of a young woman, ultimately causing his own downfall through inadvertent exposure. Instead, the author is a manipulative genius who introduces an uninhibited writer into his inner circle precisely so that, twenty-seven years later, she will raise a storm of controversy by violating his privacy, thereby extending the Salinger myth and selling yet more copies of his extant books.

But available evidence fails to support the accusation that Salinger is engaging in an elaborate publicity stunt. Every few years, Salinger approaches one of the fans or journalists who stake out his home and asks politely to be left alone. He returned a call to a *New York Times* correspondent in 1973 to voice his displeasure at the recent appearance of the pirated edition of his early stories. In 1980, in response to a pleading letter with accompanying photographs, he drove to town to meet an attractive young woman named Betty Eppes but fled once it became apparent she was conducting a formal interview for publication. He filed the 1981 suit against forger Steven Kunes and won. He filed the 1986 suit against Ian Hamilton for copyright infringement and won. And in 1997, he contracted with Orchises Press to publish in book form his final *New Yorker* story, "Hapworth 16, 1924," but publication was indefinitely suspended.

In every case but the last, someone other than Salinger initiated contact, but that means nothing if one assumes the author deliberately lured the intruders into his world. What determines if Salinger's behavior over the past four decades constitutes a public-relations coup or a largely successful attempt at self-seclusion is, I believe, the reader's understanding of suspended authorship. If a writer, by ceasing to publish, likewise ceases to exist as a public entity, then Jerome David Salinger has merely disappeared into the private world of his own free will. Attempts to break into that world are therefore affronts to his privacy. But if an author is doomed to fulfill his natural life span, publicly and against his will, then Salinger is still a writer concerned primarily about his career. That is, he remains a publicity hound taking pains not to lose his readership or access to their money.

Theories claiming that J. D. Salinger has deliberately attempted to remain viable as a public figure through silence do not hold up well under scrutiny. When the case of *J. D. Salinger v. Random House Inc. and Ian Hamilton* got extensive newspaper coverage in 1987, Andrew Delbanco wrote, "J. D. Salinger is back in public view because he has made another effort to keep himself out of it" (27). The implication of Delbanco's comment is that the unfettered appearance of Hamilton's original biography, with page after page of excerpts from Salinger's personal letters, would not have put Salinger back in public view, whereas the lawsuit to block the book's publication did. Hamilton agreed with Delbanco's analysis, summing up the media fallout from the lawsuit thus: "Salinger was getting more feature-length attention in the press than would surely have resulted from the unimpeded publication of my 'writing life'"—that is, of his original manuscript (*In Search* 209). Yet Hamilton's research methodology, which he outlined in the opening chapter of his book, suggests who is actually guilty of manipulation in this case.

Hamilton explained that he initiated his research on the book in 1984 by writing a letter to Salinger to request an interview and to assure the author that he, Hamilton, was a serious critic and biographer not to be confused with the fans and magazine reporters who had been approaching him for decades. "All this was entirely disingenuous," Hamilton admitted.

> I knew very well that Salinger had been approached in this manner maybe a hundred times before, with no success. . . . I had not, then, expected a response to my approach. On the contrary, I had written just the sort of letter that Salinger—as I imagined him—would heartily despise. At this stage, *not* getting a reply was the essential prologue to my plot. . . . The idea, or one of the ideas, was to see what would happen if orthodox biographical

> procedures were to be applied to a subject who actively set himself
> to resist, or even to forestall them.... It would be a biography,
> yes, but it would also be a semispoof in which the biographer
> would play a leading, sometimes comic, role. (*In Search* 3–4)

What Hamilton outlined, of course, was the biographer's equivalent of a perjury trap, set for an absent, inaccessible author, and designed to elicit a response in keeping with *how Hamilton imagined him*. When a writer abdicates his role as author, he loses most of the control that he—or his work, his publisher, his agent, his publicist—would normally exert over the shaping of his public persona, which falls instead into the hands of critics and readers who, ironically in some cases, insist the abdication never took place.

It is difficult if not impossible to refute conclusively a hypothesis as speculative and steeped in conspiracy as that emanating from Salinger biographers and critics. But it seems to me that Salinger's efforts to curb exposure of his personal life have largely succeeded, not deliberately backfired. The case involving novelist W. P. Kinsella is illustrative. His 1982 novel *Shoeless Joe* includes a character named J. D. Salinger whom the protagonist kidnaps, but the film adaptation of the novel does not. In *Letters to J. D. Salinger*, Kinsella wrote to the author, "When my book appeared my publisher's lawyers received a grumbling letter from your attorneys saying that you were outraged and offended to be portrayed as a character in my book, and that you would be very unhappy if the work were transferred to other media. Hollywood didn't have the balls to use you as a character in the movie *Field of Dreams*, opting instead for a generic black reclusive author that you couldn't claim was a thinly disguised you" (Kubica and Hochman 111). A hit feature film, of course, affords exponentially greater exposure than does a novel by a midlevel author; Salinger's efforts to remove himself from the narrative and thereby avoid additional publicity worked precisely as intended.

Even Ian Hamilton subsequently voiced reservations about his project and its guiding premise. "I was perhaps over-disposed to be skeptical about Salinger's reclusiveness," he admitted in a reflective essay published two years after his Salinger book finally appeared. "I didn't really believe that he wanted to be left alone. It didn't fit with what he'd written" (*Keepers* 19). What Salinger has written—or rather what he has *authored* (as opposed to copyrighted letters, which he refuses to publish)—should probably be treated as the only reliable source material on J. D. Salinger the silent author. That sounds like a tautology, but I believe it is worth stating in this case. Since 1965, Salinger's few public utterances have comprised either curt responses to would-be journalists or statements issued to block others from publishing his work. A reliable reading of the author's silence must originate from an examination of his published fiction, which constitutes the only statements offered by Salinger to the public voluntarily and unprovoked.

The advantages to such a reading are numerous. Most important, one is thereby directed away from reading the author's post-1965 period of nonpublication as a text that speaks ominously of his frustration, sadness, trickery, insanity, peacefulness, arrogance, spirituality, or whatever attribute one wishes to project onto the pliable, unresponsive private citizen named Salinger. Such a reading still gives consideration to the author's silence and places it in context, but the silence itself would remain merely what it is: not a text, but an absence of texts—a full suspension of the author's voice.

Such a reading would build on the work of Mark Silverberg, who examined Ian Hamilton's failed attempt to "find Salinger" within the text of silence and concluded that such an effort uncovers not the mysterious author but rather "the impossibility of ever accurately locating Salinger," at least among the "potent rhetorical entities" that surface from disparate sources unregulated by a central authority. "Rather than a biography," Silverberg wrote, "Hamilton's work is best seen as anti-biography which subverts the efficacy of the whole genre and opens a void similar to the ones opened by Barthes and Foucault in their discussions of the disappearance of the Author" (223). Hamilton's account, Silverberg concluded, suggests that an objective reading of Salinger of the kind Hamilton attempted is impossible because "the author's name has become tightly entwined not only with his works, but also with a whole network of accounts, assumptions, stories and beliefs from which the name can never be completely disentangled" (228). My goal is precisely to disentangle that confusing network.

In "Literature and Biography," Boris Tomaševskij expressed disdainful resignation toward the author legend one found threaded through most authors' oeuvres. Had he and Salinger been contemporaries, Tomaševskij might have been especially irritated by Salinger's fiction, which according to the critical consensus is marred by the author's overt interference in the narrative. James Lundquist wrote in 1979 that Salinger had a tendency "to talk *through* his characters rather than making them seem as if they are speaking *for* themselves" (116). In 1958, Paul Levine summed up recent Salinger works, including "Franny," "Raise High the Roof Beam, Carpenters," and "Zooey": "The stories hold the reader's attention not through the revelation of character but through the revelation of author" (114). Salinger himself, in the dust-cover notes for *Franny and Zooey*, described Seymour's brother, the fictional fiction writer Buddy Glass, as his "alter-ego and collaborator" (Alsen 237); for his part, Buddy claims credit for authoring not only the novellas he narrates or introduces but also such Salinger works as "Teddy," "A Perfect Day for Bananafish," and *The Catcher in the Rye*.

The British novelist David Lodge noted that Salinger's fiction has "a disorienting effect on the reader" because Buddy Glass cites criticism of his fiction and rumors about his private life that are nearly identical to those provoked by Salinger himself (241). John Wenke classified the effect as one of displacement: the fictional conceit that a real-life Buddy Glass is the actual author furthers Salinger's disappearing act, he claimed (66). My reading is the opposite: the effect is not a displacement of Salinger by the narrator, but rather a displacement of the character Buddy by the author. In the end, there is no Buddy Glass left in the narratives; there is only Salinger.

There may in fact be no Glass family members left at all. In "Seymour— An Introduction," Buddy admits that the Seymour described in "A Perfect Day for Bananafish," the earliest Glass story, "was not Seymour at all but, oddly, someone with a striking resemblance to—alley oop, I'm afraid—myself" (*Raise High* 113). The absurdly long and sophisticated letter that comprises the majority of "Hapworth 16, 1924," ostensibly composed by a hyperprecocious seven-year-old Seymour, seems similarly to be the imaginative work of an intrusively adult Buddy, who claims to be reproducing the original document word for word. And the long conversations and private moments recorded among Franny, Zooey, mother Bessie, and even Franny's boyfriend, Lane, in *Franny and Zooey* are reconstructed by a narrator, Buddy Glass, who was nowhere near at the time. It would seem that Salinger, by his own admission, is Buddy, and that Buddy in turn is omniscient, embodying or at least speaking for everyone. Mary McCarthy came to a similar conclusion in her blistering attack on *Franny and Zooey* in 1962. "[W]ho are these wonder kids but Salinger himself, splitting and multiplying like the original amoeba?" she asked of the seven Glass siblings. "In Hemingway's work there was hardly anybody but Hemingway in a series of disguises, but at least there was only one Papa per book. To be confronted with the seven faces of Salinger, all wise and lovable and simple, is to gaze into a terrifying narcissus pool" (39).

All of this is merely to say that there is a strong justification for ascribing to the author the concerns and prejudices of the major characters. By presenting Buddy Glass as alter ego and collaborator, Salinger has directed us to do just that. Holden Caulfield and the Glass children are judgmental of outsiders, impatient with social niceties, and scornful of gratuitous displays of talent. The author persona that emerges from these works is likewise uncomfortable with society as it normally functions and has a similar ambivalence toward the sharing of creative works with the public.

Moreover, obvious connections can be drawn between the author's aborted career and his characters' specific observations about silence and artistic reticence. In *The Catcher in the Rye*, Holden imagines pretending to be "a poor deaf mute bastard" in order to avoid having "goddam stupid useless conversations with anybody" (198). He is offended by the adulation heaped on

Ernie, "a big fat colored guy that plays the piano" in a Greenwich Village club (80). "I swear to God, if I were a piano player or an actor or something and all those dopes thought I was terrific, I'd hate it," Holden states. "I wouldn't even want them to *clap* for me. People always clap for the wrong things. If I were a piano player, I'd play it in the goddam closet" (84).

Four years later, in "Franny," the reluctance of the title character, a promising actress, to flaunt her artistic gifts must be read in the context of newly explicit religious concerns apparently shared by both author and character. One problem with such a reading, however, is that "Salinger's Big Religious Package," to use Stanley Edgar Hyman's dismissive phrase, is a wide-ranging mixture so varied as to make most critical analyses meaningless. "Zooey" alone, Hyman noted, includes references to "the Upanishads, the Diamond Sutra, Meister Eckhart, Dr. Suzuki on *satori*, saints, *arhats*, *bodhisattvas*, *jivanmuktas*, Jesus, Gautama, Lao-tse, Shankaracharya, Hui-neng, Sri Ramakrishna, the Four Great Vows of Buddhism, God's grace, the Jesus Prayer, *japam*, Chuang-tzu, Epictetus, and the Bible" (126), all intended to put Franny's spiritual crisis in context or, coming from Zooey's mouth, lift her malaise, which in fact they appear to do by story's end. In "Seymour—An Introduction," Buddy explains that the family's roots in Eastern philosophy, including Zen Buddhism, are "planted in the New and Old Testament, Advaita Vedanta, and classical Taoism" (208), thereby narrowing the field of references somewhat but preserving a range of influences on Salinger's characters and of potential sources for their epiphanies.

Placing Salinger's silence in meaningful context amid such a diffuse smorgasbord of religious influences requires that one adopt a vaguely Orientalist analysis of the kind presented by Yasunari Kawabata in his Nobel Prize acceptance speech, in which he spoke of a generically Eastern tradition that seeks enlightenment through "a discarding of words" (55). "Here we have the emptiness, the nothingness, of the Orient," he stated in 1968, before Edward Said made such pronouncements professionally precarious. "My own works have been discarded as works of emptiness, but it is not to be taken for the nihilism of the West. The spiritual foundation would seem quite different" (41). When a Zen disciple sits silent, motionless, with his eyes closed, for long hours, he enters an impassive state free from thoughts, ideas, or words. "He departs from the self and enters the realm of nothingness. This is not the nothingness or the emptiness of the West," Kawabata repeated, further delineating a simple Oriental–Occidental dichotomy. "It is rather the reverse, a universe of the spirit in which everything communicates freely with everything, transcending bounds, limitless" (56).

To lend coherence to Salinger's silence, then, it is convenient to attribute to him a point of view that similarly differentiates cleanly between East and West, and which favors the East. This is easily justified, considering the obsessions of his characters. Seymour, we are told, "was drawn, first, to Chinese poetry, and then, as deeply, to Japanese poetry, and to both in ways that he was drawn to no other poetry in the world" (*Raise High* 117). Buddy is similarly enthralled: "I haven't the gall to try to say what makes the Chinese or Japanese poet the marvel and the joy he is" (*Raise High* 119). This exclusive pairing of Japanese and Chinese literature assumes a natural kinship that does not in fact exist. But a kinship can be synthesized if one views both cultures as equally non-Western, assumes that artists in both have been influenced by a stew of mystical religious movements similar to that which the Glass siblings have studied, and attributes to both traditions a special sense of enlightenment rooted in a silence that is outside the realm of Western experience. Scholars have assumed that, in Eastern religions and mystical variants of Christianity, Salinger found answers to his quest for balancing spiritual and secular pursuits as well as life and art. His withdrawal from the publishing world can be made to fit this view. "Ultimately his 'silence' becomes the culminating gesture when his life becomes the message," Pattaniak explained, "a testament of the values his art hitherto professed" (115–16).

But, in fact, his art hitherto professed values that suggested the gifted artist must *not* disappear into a culminating gesture of silence. Rather, the artist owes it to the public to create and share that creation with a mass audience, Salinger's fiction implied. This is the fundamental complication inherent in any analysis of Salinger's post-1965 career in light of themes presented in his published work, particularly "Zooey."

In the 1953 story "De Daumier-Smith's Blue Period," Salinger offered a narrative in which a supremely gifted artist, Sister Irma, is nearly drawn into the corrupt world of public adulation by the narrator, an art instructor employed at a correspondence school. But administrators at the convent where Sister Irma works as an elementary school art teacher cut off contact between pupil and instructor, perhaps because the narrator's praise of her art is excessive (and, therefore, inappropriately personal and potentially amorous); perhaps because the administrators fear Irma's talents, if developed, might lure her away from her path of spiritual enlightenment; or perhaps because they fear her talents, if developed, might afford her professional alternatives and cost them their drawing instructor. Their motives are unclear. One is tempted to extract from the story a lesson about Salinger's disavowal of the corrupting forces of fame, but the extent to which this story can be said to parallel Salinger's own biography is limited. Irma is an innocent, not a famous artist who abandons a thriving career. She does not disavow fame; rather, others make that gesture on her behalf. And, presumably, she does not slip into reclusion. Rather, she continues to instruct her "kittys"—the beloved pupils at her school—as she always has (*Nine Stories* 148). In her peculiar case, forfeiting a successful artistic career prolongs the intimate and meaningful relationship she enjoys with humanity.

But the case of Franny Glass is very different. In *Franny and Zooey*, Franny is determined to cut herself off, first from the theater audience, but also more broadly from the mass of people whom she finds detestable for their mundane aspirations and egotistical pursuits. Most urgent is her fear that she, too, will be seduced by the glitter of conventional success. "I'm not afraid to compete," she tells her boyfriend, Lane. "It's just the opposite. Don't you see that? I'm afraid I *will* compete—that's what scares me" (*Franny* 30).

"Zooey" is the final chapter of what Eberhard Alsen termed Salinger's "composite novel" about the Glass family, which comprises three short stories and five novellas, all but one originally published in the *New Yorker*. (They are, in order of publication: "A Perfect Day for Bananafish," "Uncle Wiggily in Connecticut," "Down at the Dinghy," "Franny," "Raise High the Roof Beam, Carpenters," "Zooey," "Seymour—An Introduction," and "Hapworth 16, 1924.") Though "Seymour—An Introduction" and "Hapworth 16, 1924" appeared later, "Zooey" provides the thematic climax to the sequence. It delivers the ultimate and most fully formed statement readers can unhesitatingly attribute to the author legend constructed in Salinger's published works. As Alsen reasoned, "It is the only Glass story that contains explicit criticism of Seymour's religious ideas, but it also explains that the core of his later teachings is valid, even though Seymour was unable to practice what he preached and even though he killed himself in despair" (220). Indeed, by the end of the novella, Zooey uses Seymour's battle-tested ideas to lift Franny out of her religious crisis and place her on the path to a more charitable acceptance of her university colleagues and a more generous and open relationship with theater patrons.

What is so despairing in these works of fiction is the completeness of Franny's abhorrence, not only of successful artists, but of all persons thriving in the conventional world: her pretentious English-major boyfriend, Lane; his friends, "who look like everybody else, and talk and dress and act like everybody else" (*Franny* 24); the poets on her university faculty, who "write poems that get published and anthologized all over the place" but who are not real poets (18); her talented but somehow inadequate fellow actors. "It's *everybody*," she confesses to Lane (26). "I'm sick of everybody that wants to *get* somewhere, do something distinguished and all, be somebody interesting. It's disgusting—it is, it *is*. I don't care what anybody says" (29–30). And, apparently, one cannot escape from the bind of conventional expectations: "[I]f you go bohemian or something crazy like that, you're conforming just as much as everybody else," she laments, "only in a different way" (26). Her "solution," if it can be called that, is to drop out of theater, skip her college classes, and finally curl up on her parents' couch, attempting to put herself into a religious trance by endlessly repeating "the Jesus Prayer." That is to say, she chooses to withdraw from society, end her artistic relationship with the public, and lose herself in a mystical religious experience—precisely what Salinger is widely judged to have done.

Into the fray steps Zooey, called home by their mother to help Franny out of her incapacitated state. He tells her that, as a successful television actor himself, he can relate to her frustration: working on bad movie scripts has given him an ulcer. And participating in better-than-average projects is actually worse, as it only gives rise to widespread backslapping and "an orgy of mutual appreciation" over the courage and integrity involved (135). But, he insists, an artist must persist at his craft, regardless of the egos it encourages, even one's own. To do otherwise is merely to enter into a "little snotty crusade" against everybody (161) and usurp from our betters—Buddha, Christ—the prerogative to judge which behavior is or is not deplorably egotistical. "As a matter of simple logic," he adds, "there's no difference at all, that *I* can see, between the man who's greedy for material treasure—or even intellectual treasure—and the man who's greedy for spiritual treasure," clearly implying that, like the double bind of bohemian nonconformity, the spiritual pursuits of a reclusive nonartist offer no escape from the trap of egotism (148).

To bring his point home, Zooey repeats the instructions their eldest brother, Seymour, now deceased, gave them both when they were panelists on a children's radio quiz show. Seymour once insisted that Zooey had to shine his shoes before leaving for the studios, which made Zooey furious.

> The studio audience were all morons, the announcer was a moron, the sponsors were morons, and I just damn well wasn't going to shine my shoes for them, I told Seymour.... He said to shine them for the Fat Lady. I didn't know what the hell he was talking about, but he had a very Seymour look on his face, and so I did it. He never did tell me who the Fat Lady was, but I shined my shoes for the Fat Lady every time I ever went on the air again. (200)

Franny, as Zooey no doubt guessed, had received the same imperative from their brother to convince her to perform to her full potential, since "the Fat Lady," of course, is convenient shorthand for everyone in the audience, or in their lives. "That includes your Professor Tupper, buddy," Zooey tells Franny, referring to one of her annoying university instructors. "And all his goddam cousins by the dozen" (201). Moreover, he tells her, Seymour's Fat Lady is actually Christ, and as such every artist owes her (him) their finest effort. This realization is apparently what prompted Seymour himself to serve as a panelist on the show years earlier, painful though it must have been for the boy genius. In "Raise High the Roof Beam, Carpenters," the matron of honor deplores the exhibitionism of the absent groom's childhood, but Buddy corrects her, insisting Seymour was never an exhibitionist. "He went down to the broadcast every Wednesday night as though he were going to his own funeral," he reports. "He didn't even talk to you, for God's sake, the whole way down on the bus or subway" (59–60). But he went.

Such is the clear imperative Zooey gives Franny: she must still perform—she owes it to the Fat Lady, to the public, to Christ, to the God who dispenses talent. And, by the indications of the final paragraph of "Zooey," she will do precisely that. Having received the lecture from her brother, the heretofore insomniac and frazzled Franny takes off her footwear and slips peacefully into bed: "For some minutes, before she fell into a deep, dreamless sleep, she just lay quiet, smiling at the ceiling" (202).

The ending of "Zooey" was criticized for its simplistic resolution to Franny's crisis and its condescension toward the very Fat Lady it means to valorize. "It is rather like the end of a Russian movie," wrote Alfred Chester in 1963; "the heartbroken girl unexpectedly hears a speech by a commissar and is made miraculously whole" (472). Even David Samuels in a retrospective appreciation of *Franny and Zooey* conceded, "There are probably higher peaks of wisdom to climb" than the Fat-Lady-is-Christ idea (133). But this was how Salinger chose to resolve the thematic concerns of the entire Glass-family cycle, as it stands so far. Clearly, that resolution is at odds with the author's withdrawal from his audience.

"An artist's only concern is to shoot for some kind of perfection, and *on his own terms*, not anyone else's," Zooey assures Franny (199, emphasis in original). Yet Salinger seems to have proceeded after 1965 on terms other than his own, as spelled out in his fiction. Of course, new Salinger works may appear late in the author's life or posthumously, revising the artist's terms. But until they do, Salinger's silence stands in opposition to the message of his published fiction. The author himself has violated the spirit of his own works.

An alternative approach to analyzing Salinger would be to consider not the *content* but the *form* of the author's published works, particularly his later novellas, and recognize the logical relationship that their form has to the author's subsequent silence. Illuminating this form-centered analysis are two early essays by Susan Sontag. In 1967, in "The Aesthetics of Silence," Sontag described the aggressive attempts of modernist authors to direct attention away from the content of their works and to alienate their readership by adopting a difficult, disruptive writing style, the frustrating effect of which approximated the stony unresponsiveness of willful silence. Three years earlier, in the essay "Against Interpretation," Sontag insisted on the necessity of literary critics' discarding standard Platonic methods of hermeneutics in art—based currently on the influential doctrines of Marx and Freud—and replacing them with a method she termed "an erotics of art" (14), which would no longer bracket observable phenomena, including art objects, as *manifest content* that must be probed and ultimately discarded in order to arrive at the "true meaning" of events, books, paintings (7). Literary interpretation, she noted dismissively, was not merely "the revenge of intellect upon art" (7) or "the compliment that mediocrity pays to genius" (8–9); in most modern instances, she declared, it amounted to "the philistine refusal to leave the work of art alone" (8).

It would normally behoove a literary scholar to defend his right to interpretation, but in this case I sympathize with Sontag's point, since Salinger's silence, having been categorized as an art object, has ever since been picked at, interrogated, tamed, and otherwise *interpreted* in ways that are clearly opportunistic and even foolish. Readers and critics cannot leave it alone. "Our task is not to find the maximum content in a work of art," Sontag instructed, "much less to squeeze more content out of the work than is already there" (14). Rather, more attention must be paid to form, she wrote; equally valuable would be acts of criticism that supply "a really accurate, sharp, loving description of the appearance of a work of art" (13).

Truly accurate criticism in the case of Salinger's silence would be quite brief. Form? It has none. Description? It does not exist and, therefore, is impossible to describe. But because most criticism is steeped in interpretation, even of nonexistent works, critical texts on Salinger's "late period" often prove to be quite lengthy and involved. Without mentioning Salinger by name, Sontag suggested that artists often respond to such elaborate interpretive gestures through deliberate means of subversion. "In fact, a great deal of today's art may be understood as motivated by a flight from interpretation," she claimed. To avoid interpretation, art becomes difficult, abstract, parodistic, decorative. "Or it may become non-art" (10).

The ultimate non-art, silence, was the focus of Sontag's concern in "The Aesthetics of Silence," in which she cited a perennial discontent with language that she claimed arises in every major civilization "whenever thought reaches a certain high, *excruciating* order of complexity and spiritual seriousness" (*Styles* 21, emphasis in original). She cited early signs of discontent in modern Western civilization among the Romantic poets, but saw the high modernists as practitioners of a more fully developed disdain for language. In their great works, she detected a craving for knowledge beyond words, the substitution of chance for intention, a penchant for antiart, and an active pursuit of silence through the only means necessary, words. The exemplary modern artist rarely carries the pursuit to the final simplification of literal silence: "More typically, he continues speaking, but in a manner that his audience can't hear" (7). That is, he produces a nearly unintelligible book like *Finnegans Wake*, which goes unread. He constructs an elaborate, wordy void.

According to Sontag, the pursuit of silence is an arrogant gesture, both because in practice it results in abrupt, disjointed, arbitrary works that alienate the common reader, and because it implies superiority of thought. To be consumed by a craving for silence—for "the cloud of unknowing" beyond knowledge and conventional speech—suggests that "the artist has had the wit to ask more questions than other people, and that he possesses stronger nerves and higher standards of excellence." This arrogant gesture can be executed successfully only by a select few, Sontag claimed, for it requires an established reputation. "An exemplary decision of this sort can be made only after the artist has demonstrated that he possesses genius and [has] exercised that genius authoritatively" (7).

Salinger clearly belonged to this elite group before he ceased to publish. "Few other authors, major or minor, have had such immediate response from critics, who have almost caressingly touched upon special qualities in Salinger," asserted Carl F. Strauch in 1963 (39). "No serious history of post–World War II American fiction can be written without awarding him a place in the first rank, and even, perhaps, the preeminent position," wrote James E. Miller Jr. two years later (45). Even hostile critics have acknowledged the author's preeminence. In her unfavorable 1961 review of *Franny and Zooey*, Joan Didion wrote, "Among the reasonably literate young and young at heart, he is surely the most read and reread writer in America today, exerting a power over his readers which is in some ways extra-literary" (233). Didion's assertion clouds the fact that the "young at heart" comprised nearly the entire scholarly community. "Who is to inherit the mantle of Papa Hemingway?" Mary McCarthy asked in her sour dismissal of *Franny and Zooey*. "Who if not J. D. Salinger?" (35). And yet, as Walter Clemons subsequently observed, "Salinger no sooner won an ardent following than he began to abuse its loyalty" (73). Or as Elizabeth N. Kurian phrased it in her respectful monograph on the existential dilemma in Salinger's fiction, "His later stories are so asymmetrical, tolerant of chance and digression, that they warrant the name of antiform" (145).

Like James Joyce, Gertrude Stein, Samuel Beckett, and William S. Burroughs—Sontag's examples of modernist authors pursuing silence—Salinger employed circular, repetitive speech in his works. David Castronovo has suggested that Salinger's very first book, *The Catcher in the Rye*, was "anti-literary in a new way: its pages are filled with babbling rather than talk that builds to a climax" (180). But most commentators detect a full embrace of digression in "Seymour—An Introduction" (1959), with "Franny" and "Raise High the Roof Beam, Carpenters" (both 1955) marked as transitional stories not nearly as compact or concise as the works composing *Nine Stories*, and "Zooey" (1957) showing further progress toward the silence of indecipherability.

In 1963, Ihab Hassan compared "Zooey" to "Raise High the Roof Beams, Carpenters" and found it longer and more diffuse, its language "brilliantly shattered into letters, invocations of the audience, memoirs, footnotes, asides, quotations on beaverboard, telephone conversations, and, of course, endless dialogue" (10). Not merely its language but also its form was a departure: in their 1958 consideration of Salinger's fiction, Frederick L. Gwynn and Joseph L. Blotner complained that "Zooey" comprised eight undesignated sections, only two or three of which are integral to the plot, and of those none is in "happy proportion to one another or to the whole" (48). "Zooey," then, took a giant step away from what Hassan called "a critic's idea of a well-made fiction" and "a reader's ideal of a racy story" (5). From this point on, Salinger's work became unmistakably experimental, warranting the label antiform and characterized by what Bruce Bawer deemed a "nearly pathological logorrhea," the effect of which was "to keep the rest of us out of the lives of this family that he has created for himself by erecting an all but insurmountable lexical fence around them" (177).

And yet, following an initially ambivalent critical response to "Zooey" in 1957, *Franny and Zooey* was a spectacular popular success when published in book form in 1961. The Salinger Myth proliferated as a result, and the author's position among the first rank of American postwar authors was strengthened. "With the passage of time and the intervention of newer, more difficult works," Sontag explained of such aggressive moves into unintelligibility and inaudibility, "the artist's transgression becomes ingratiating, eventually legitimate" (*Styles* 7). Thus a puzzling work like *Ulysses*, two decades on, becomes a coherent masterpiece compared to *Finnegans Wake*. "The ugly and discordant and senseless become 'beautiful,'" Sontag asserted (8). In fact, the history of art, viewed from this perspective, is nothing but a sequence of successful transgressions, she claimed.

Thus the stakes were inevitably raised, and works subsequent to "Zooey" had to be much more aggressively hostile to the reader if Salinger was to disappear into silence, even while the earlier trail of off-putting fiction gained legitimacy as a result. "Seymour—An Introduction" (1959) appeared to be just such a work; its narrator even admitted tearing up some fifty previous stories "simply because they had that old Chekhov-baiting noise Somerset Maugham calls a Beginning, a Middle, and an End" (212). Whereas "Zooey" had been described by Maxwell Geismar as "an interminable, an appallingly bad story" ("Wise" 96) and dismissed by Gwynn and Blotner as the "dullest 'short story' ever to appear in the *New Yorker*" (48), "Seymour—An Introduction" elicited much harsher condemnation. "Hopelessly prolix," wrote Irving Howe (*Celebrations* 95); "static" and "anti-social" was John P. McIntyre's verdict (25); "turgid," "boring," and "preposterous" pronounced Stanley Edgar Hyman (126); George Steiner called it "a piece of shapeless self-indulgence" ("Salinger" 116).

The following quote from the novella's opening pages gives ample sense of the narrator's modus operandi. In this case, it is not misleading that the quote begins midparagraph and midthought, since throughout the piece paragraphs extend for pages, and lines of thought are routinely jumbled. Buddy Glass is addressing the reader:

> In this *entre-nous* spirit, then, old confidant, before we join the others, the grounded everywhere, including, I'm sure, the middle-aged hot-rodders who insist on zooming us to the moon, the Dharma Bums, the makers of cigarette filters for thinking men, the Beat and Sloppy and the Petulant, the chosen cultists, all the lofty experts who know so well what we should or shouldn't do with our poor little sex organs, all the bearded, proud, unlettered young men and unskilled guitarists and Zen-killers and incorporated aesthetic Teddy boys who look down their thoroughly unenlightened noses at this splendid planet where (please don't shut me up) Kilroy, Christ, and Shakespeare all stopped—before we join these others, I privately say to you, old friend (unto you, really, I'm afraid), please accept from me this unpretentious bouquet of very early-blooming parentheses: (((()))). (97–98)

Six years later, in "Hapworth 16, 1924," Salinger resumed writing in this digressive manner, adding to the unusual effect by attributing the language to the epistolary pen of a seven-year-old child. ("I am relishing this leisurely communication!" young Seymour writes [33].) The piece was, in the words of Bernice and Sanford Goldstein, "universally despaired" ("Ego" 159). Indeed, the general critical dismissal of the novella was at least as harsh as that of "Seymour—An Introduction." Deeming the work "virtually unreadable" and "possibly the least structured and most tedious piece of fiction ever produced by an important writer," John Wenke lamented that "'Hapworth' seems *designed* to bore, to tax patience, as if Salinger might be trying to torment his readers away from ever wanting the next new thing from him" (67, 108, emphasis in original). Terry Teachout deemed it "dreadful" ("Salinger" 64); Max F. Schulz found it even "more inchoate in structure" than "Seymour" (129). Most commentators since have dismissed it in terms similar to Wenke's: Paul Alexander called it "barely publishable" (230); Kerry McSweeney chose the adjectives "interminable" and "unreadable" ("Salinger" 61); and Bruce Bawer wrote it was "bizarre" and "virtually unreadable" (180).

By Sontag's estimation, then, Salinger succeeded. Without actually lapsing into literal silence—not yet—he made each successive work categorically less accessible and nearly as uncommunicative as silence owing to its turgid language and arbitrary structure. Buddy Glass could have gone on and on beyond the stories' conclusions, Wenke observed, or he could have ended his narratives thirty or fifty pages earlier than he did (105). It made no difference for the purposes of conventional storytelling. And the narrator was as aware of the problem as anyone. "I'm going on too long about this, I know," Buddy concedes about his disquisition on Seymour's sporting prowess, "but I really can't stop now" (*Raise High* 198).

And yet, as Sontag also predicted, over time some in the literary community acclimated, even warmed, to the final Glass-family works. In a 2001 *New York Review of Books* article, Janet Malcolm wrote, "Today 'Zooey' does not seem too long, and is arguably Salinger's masterpiece. . . . It remains brilliant and is in no essential sense dated. It is the contemporary criticism that has dated" (16). The "extraordinary rage" generated by critics against the Glasses, Malcolm concluded, merely points us toward the author's stylistic innovations.

In hindsight, these works are now deemed reader friendly in comparison to actual silence. James Lundquist in his 1979 monograph *J. D. Salinger* recategorized the late novellas, not as turgid and diffuse, but as "complex," "experimental," and "increasingly post-modern" (2). "Salinger does not impose any arbitrary pattern on his work, because he believes the work will grow its own shape and meaning if the writer follows his inspiration," reasoned Elizabeth N. Kurian (145–46). Bernice and Sanford Goldstein repositioned "Seymour—An Introduction" as "one of Salinger's most ambitious stories" and asserted that the prose style of "Hapworth 16, 1924" was "thoroughly intentional" for the purpose of presenting young Seymour's struggle to deepen his level of spiritual awareness ("Seymour" 249; "Ego" 166–67). And Eberhard Alsen, examining the Glass stories together as a single text, found their design coherent and organic. "Despite its fragmentary plot and despite the radical differences between the form of the early and the later stories," Alsen wrote, "Buddy's composite novel has a special kind of unity" (235).

Alsen's attribution of unity, however, carried unintentional irony. He asserted that, Buddy Glass's own demurrals notwithstanding, "Seymour" has a coherent structure. "Spacing and typography reveal a division into six major sections, Alsen observed:

   I Buddy's credo
  II Seymour as God-lover

III Seymour as artist-seer
IV Seymour as entertainer
 V Seymour as Buddy's mentor
VI Physical description of Seymour (64)

The final section is further divided into eight subsections, Alsen noted with apparent seriousness:

1. Seymour's hair jumping in the barbershop
2. Seymour's hair and teeth
3. Seymour's height, smile, and ears
4. Seymour's eyes, nose, and chin
5. Seymour's hands, voice, and skin
6. Seymour's clothes
7. Seymour as athlete and gamesman
8. Seymour as Buddy's Davega bicycle (65)

While this may technically qualify as a structural design for a story, it is not a design that can generate a satisfying narrative. As John Wenke observed, "Buddy can render an *attempt* to present a face—he catalogs Seymour's hair, smile, ears, eyes, nose, and skin—but no one face emerges. The attempt must fail" (105, emphasis in original). Or as David Seed concluded, the difficulties and ultimate failures of narrative *become* the subject of "Seymour—An Introduction" (157). Such subject matter may give the story its metafictional bona fides, but when manifested in the narrative itself the subject of unsuccessful or inept storytelling does not captivate a readership. Rather, the reader is compelled to head for the exit, as instructed, or trudge through, observing firsthand the qualities of failed narrative. In the first case, the story lapses into silence—it goes unread; in the second, the author is challenged to top himself next time with a more outrageous attempt to dispel his readership. The most outrageous attempt possible, of course, is literal silence.

   "'Seymour—An Introduction' represents a fictional extreme beyond which Salinger cannot go," claimed David Seed (158). Susan Sontag wrote, "Since the artist can't embrace silence literally and remain an artist, what the rhetoric of silence indicates is a determination to pursue his activity more deviously than before" (*Styles* 12). My contention is that both Seed and Sontag were wrong. Salinger *could* literally embrace silence and remain an artist. He went beyond the extreme of "Seymour" to nonpublication and reclusion, yet many in the literary community persisted in reading and interpreting the text he "produced" and accused him of crass manipulation. "Don't you think it's a little bit pretentious to make such a big deal out of not publishing any more?" wrote the unsolicited e-mailer Dan Paton to the author in *Letters to J. D. Salinger*, neglecting to clarify what exactly he meant by the "big deal" Salinger was making. "You can't make yourself unfamous," he taunted. "Cough it up. Either publish everything you've got left in you or hurry up and die" (Kubica and Hochman 219).

It is a harsh sentiment, but one widely shared. "[T]he piece of prose his admirers anticipate most eagerly is his obituary," Craig Stolz posited about Salinger (13), who reportedly continues to work on new fiction, in solitude, but who has not signaled what his ultimate intent is for the manuscripts. Recent tell-all memoirs published by both Joyce Maynard and the author's daughter, Margaret Salinger, were hostile toward the author on many topics, but on this they were in agreement with him: Salinger continues to write. But does he intend to publish, even posthumously? In 1973, Lucey Fosburgh asked Salinger if he expected to publish new work soon.

> There was a pause.
> "I really don't know how soon," he said. There was another pause, and then Mr. Salinger began to talk rapidly about how much he was writing, long hours, every day, and he said he was under contract to no one for another book.
> "I don't necessarily intend to publish posthumously," he said, "but I do like to write for myself." (69)

It is an ambiguous phrasing. He may intend to publish, but not necessarily posthumously; or he may not necessarily intend to publish at all, even posthumously. In any case, Salinger's silence in its current incarnation will end, with his death, timely publication, or death followed by publication. And with that will almost certainly come a shift in the interpretation of his decades-long silence, regardless of the author's best efforts. "Make sure you burn it all," warned novelist Stewart O'Nan in *Letters to J. D. Salinger*. "Maybe the house, too. That might sound nuts, but trust me" (Kubica and Hochman 50). Prior experience suggests such drastic efforts would prove futile. Whatever gap Salinger leaves behind, whatever absence of primary or secondary texts remains, it will necessarily be filled by those in the literary community for whom the term "silent author" is no mere oxymoron but a strict impossibility.

Chronology

1919	Jerome David Salinger was born in Manhattan on January 1, the second child of Sol, a prosperous Jewish importer, and Marie Jillich, of Scots-Irish descent, who changed her name to Miriam when she married Sol. His only sibling, a sister, Doris, had been born eight years before him.
1930	During the summer, Salinger attends Camp Wigwam in Harrison, Maine, where he is voted "most popular actor" for 1930.
1932	Salinger enrolls in the McBurney School, a private school on West 64 Street, where he reports for the school newspaper and is captain of the fencing team, but due to a poor academic record, he does not complete his studies here.
1934	In September, Salinger enters Valley Forge Military Academy in Wayne, Pennsylvania, where he serves as literary editor of the school newspaper and yearbook, *Crossed Sabres*.
1936	In June, Salinger graduates from Valley Forge Military Academy, where he has maintained a satisfactory academic record.
1937	Salinger enrolls at New York University but quits within the year.

1937–1938   In the fall, Salinger visits Vienna and Poland with his father, reputedly to learn the family importing business. During this time in Europe, Salinger writes several stories and submits them to various magazines for publication. He returns to the United States in spring 1938.

1938   In the fall, Salinger briefly attends Ursinus College in Collegeville, Pennsylvania, where he writes a column, "The Skipped Diploma," which includes movie reviews, for the college newspaper *Ursinus Weekly*. After nine weeks at Ursinus, however, Salinger drops out and returns to New York.

1939   In the spring, Salinger enrolls in a course in short-story writing at Columbia University taught by Whit Burnett, then editor of *Story* magazine. Though reticent at first, Salinger turns in three short stories and makes a profound impression on Burnett.

1940   Salinger's first published story, "The Young Folks," appears in *Story* magazine, for which he is paid twenty-five dollars. "Go See Eddie" is published in the *University of Kansas City Review* following its rejection by *Esquire*.

1941   "The Hang of It" is published in *Collier's*; "The Heart of a Broken Story" is published in *Esquire*. In November, Salinger sells his first story about Holden Caulfield to *The New Yorker*, although publication is delayed until 1946 due to the United States' entry into World War II. Salinger is classified 1-B (fit only for limited duty) by the Selective Service.

1942   "The Long Debut of Lois Taggett" is published in *Story*; "Personal Notes of an Infantryman" is published in *Collier's*. Salinger is drafted into the U.S. Army and attends Officers, First Sergeants, and Instructors School of the Signal Corps. During this year, Salinger corresponds with Oona O'Neill, the daughter of playwright Eugene O'Neill, who will later become Charlie Chaplin's wife.

1943   While stationed in Nashville, Tennessee, Salinger publishes "The Varioni Brothers" in the *Saturday Evening Post*. Later in the year, Salinger is transferred to the Army Counter-Intelligence Corps and receives training at Tiverton in Devonshire, England.

1944   Salinger publishes "Last Day of the Last Furlough," "Both Parties Concerned," and "Soft Boiled Sergeant" in the *Saturday Evening Post* and "Once a Week Won't Kill You" in *Story*. He sends Whit Burnett $250 to encourage young writers to compete in a contest. On June 6 Salinger participates in the Normandy invasion and comes ashore at Utah Beach with the Fourth Infantry Division. He arrives in Paris on August 25 following a treacherous march. In September, he visits Ernest Hemingway, who is working as a war correspondent. Hemingway expresses his appreciation for "Last Day of the Last Furlough."

1945   Following the end of the war, Salinger is discharged from the Army. In July, he is hospitalized in Germany for what is described as battle fatigue or a minor breakdown. Margaret Salinger states that he wrote a letter to Hemingway, making light of his war experiences but emphatically stating that he absolutely would not submit to a psychiatric evaluation. Salinger is married, briefly, to a French woman named Sylvia, a doctor whom he had previously arrested and interrogated. "Elaine" is published in *Story*; "A Boy in France" in the *Saturday Evening Post*; "This Sandwich Has No Mayonnaise" in *Esquire*; "The Stranger" and "I'm Crazy" (the first published story to include material that would later appear in *The Catcher in the Rye*) in *Collier's*.

1946   Salinger and Sylvia are divorced. Back in New York in May, Salinger starts enjoying the nightlife of Greenwich Village in the company of aspiring writers and actors and begins to study Zen Buddhism, which would later become a central part of his life. "Slight Rebellion Off Madison," also containing material that will later be incorporated into *The Catcher in the Rye*, is published in *The New Yorker*. Salinger's novella about Holden Caulfield is accepted for publication, but Salinger decides to withdraw it.

1947   "A Young Girl in 1941 with No Waist at All" is published in *Mademoiselle* and "The Inverted Forest" in *Cosmopolitan*.

1948   "A Fine Day for Bananafish" (the story's original title), "Uncle Wiggily in Connecticut," and "Just Before the War with the Eskimos" are published in *The New Yorker*; "Blue Melody" is published in *Cosmpolitan*; and "A Girl I Knew" is published in *Good Housekeeping* (later chosen for *Best American Short Stories of 1949*). Salinger moves to Westport, Connecticut.

1949	"The Laughing Man" is published in *The New Yorker* and "Down at the Dinghy" is published in *Harper's*.
1950	*The New Yorker* publishes Salinger's "For Esmé—with Love and Squalor." By now, Salinger has acquired a reputation as a writer of short fiction. He receives an offer from Harcourt Brace to publish *The Catcher in the Rye* but withdraws his manuscript when he encounters problems with the editorial staff. During the latter months of the year, Salinger becomes interested in alternative religions, specifically the teachings of Ramakrishna's Advaita Vedanta Hinduism, in New York City, a school of thought that stresses nonduality.
1951	On July 16 *The Catcher in the Rye* is published by Little, Brown. The novel wins critical and popular acclaim and is on *The New York Times* best-seller list for seven months. Salinger wishes to maintain his privacy, but the success of his book forces him reluctantly into the limelight. "Pretty Mouth and Green My Eyes" is published in *The New Yorker*.
1952	"De Daumier-Smith's Blue Period" is published in *World Review* (London). Salinger is one of three receiving Distinguished Alumni of the Year awards at Valley Forge Military Academy.
1953	To escape publicity, Salinger moves to Cornish, New Hampshire, on New Year's Day, on his thirty-fourth birthday, and meets Claire Douglas, whom he will later marry. In April, *Nine Stories* is published by Little, Brown, and "Teddy" appears in *The New Yorker*.
1954	Salinger asks Claire to drop out of Radcliffe College and live with him in Cornish. When Claire refuses to do this, Salinger temporarily cuts off communication with her. Salinger eventually reappears in her life during the summer, and by the fall Claire moves in with him. As she was still completing her coursework at Radcliffe, Claire and J.D. spend Tuesday through Thursday of each week in Cambridge, Massachusetts, where, out of propriety, Salinger takes a room at the Commodore Hotel, while Claire shares an apartment with five other divorced women. Salinger is very unhappy with this arrangement and the interruption of his work. Claire eventually drops out of college, just four months before graduation.

1955	On February 17, Salinger marries Claire Douglas, but their marriage is not a happy one. Though they see friends in New York and Boston, the couple become thoroughly isolated in New Hampshire once Claire becomes pregnant with their first child, Margaret Ann. Claire had even gone so far as to burn the papers she wrote in college, including some fictional pieces. Salinger works sixteen hours a day, searching for a philosophy of life to live by, and begins eating only organically grown food. Their daughter is born on December 10. "Franny" (January 29) and "Raise High the Roof Beam, Carpenters" (November 19) are published in *The New Yorker*.
1957	On May 4, "Zooey" is published in *The New Yorker*.
1959	On June 6, "Seymour: An Introduction" is published in *The New Yorker*.
1960	A son, Matthew, is born on February 13.
1961	*Franny and Zooey* is published in book form by Little, Brown on September 14; it is an immediate success.
1963	"Raise High the Roof Beam, Carpenters" and "Seymour: An Introduction" are published in book form on January 28.
1965	Salinger's last published work of fiction, "Hapworth 16, 1924," an epistolary novella told in the voice of seven-year-old Seymour Glass writing home from summer camp, appears in *The New Yorker* on June 19, 1965.
1967	In November, Claire and Salinger are divorced.
1974	An unauthorized edition, titled *Complete Uncollected Short Stories of J.D. Salinger*, is published in two volumes. In an interview with the *New York Times*, Salinger publicly declares this a violation of his privacy.
1987	Salinger successfully sues Ian Hamilton and Random House to stop publication of his unauthorized biography.
1988	Salinger's last published short story, "Hapworth 16, 1924," is released in book form. Ian Hamilton publishes *In Search of J.D. Salinger*, which omits all references to Salinger's letters.

Contributors

HAROLD BLOOM is Sterling Professor of the Humanities at Yale University. He is the author of 30 books, including *Shelley's Mythmaking, The Visionary Company, Blake's Apocalypse, Yeats, A Map of Misreading, Kabbalah and Criticism, Agon: Toward a Theory of Revisionism, The American Religion, The Western Canon,* and *Omens of Millennium: The Gnosis of Angels, Dreams, and Resurrection. The Anxiety of Influence* sets forth Professor Bloom's provocative theory of the literary relationships between the great writers and their predecessors. His most recent books include *Shakespeare: The Invention of the Human,* a 1998 National Book Award finalist, *How to Read and Why, Genius: A Mosaic of One Hundred Exemplary Creative Minds, Hamlet: Poem Unlimited, Where Shall Wisdom Be Found?,* and *Jesus and Yahweh: The Names Divine.* In 1999, Professor Bloom received the prestigious American Academy of Arts and Letters Gold Medal for Criticism. He has also received the International Prize of Catalonia, the Alfonso Reyes Prize of Mexico, and the Hans Christian Andersen Bicentennial Prize of Denmark.

JAMES BRYAN has published several essays on Salinger's short fiction, as well as essays on William Dean Howells, Ernest Hemingway, and Sherwood Anderson.

DAVID GALLOWAY is the author of "Holocaust as Metaphor: William Styron and *Sophie's Choice*" (1981), *Edward Lewis Wallant* (1979), and "William Melvin Kelley: 'The Poker Party'" (1977).

ALAN NADEL has published essays and reviews in *Georgia Review,*
Modern Fiction Studies, New England Review, and *College Literature.* He
is the author of *Invisible Criticism: Ralph Ellison and the American Canon*
(1991), *May All Your Fences Have Gates: Essays on the Drama of August Wilson*
(1993), and *Containment Culture: American Narratives, Postmodernism, and
the Atomic Age* (1995).

DAVID SEED has been a professor of American literature at the University
of Liverpool. He is the author of *Brainwashing: The Fictions of Mind Control:
A Study of Novels and Films Since World War II* (2004), *American Science
Fiction and the Cold War: Literature and Film* (1999), *James Joyce's A Portrait
of the Artist as a Young Man* (1992) and the editor of *A Companion to Science
Fiction* (2005).

RUTH PRIGOZY has been professor of English and film studies at Hofstra
University. She is executive director of the F. Scott Fitzgerald Society, which
she cofounded in 1990. She has published widely on F. Scott Fitzgerald
as well as on Ernest Hemingway, J.D. Salinger, the Hollywood Ten, film
directors Billy Wilder and D.W. Griffith, and director Vittorio de Sica. She
is the author of *F. Scott Fitzgerald* (2002) and *The Life of Dick Haymes: No
More Little White Lies* (2006) and editor of *The Cambridge Companion to F.
Scott Fitzgerald* (2002).

PAUL ALEXANDER is the author of *Boulevard of Broken Dreams: The*
ANTHONY KAUFMAN is professor emeritus of English at the University
of Illinois. He is the recipient of the Lucyle Hook Guest Lectureship at
Barnard College (2006) where he has lectured on theories of comedy in the
plays of Oscar Wilde, Alan Ayckbourn, Joe Orton, and Tom Stoppard. He
is also the editor of *Steven Soderbergh: Interviews* (2002).

ROBERT COLES is a child psychiatrist and has been a professor of
psychiatry and medical humanities at Harvard University. He is the author
of numerous books, including *The Secular Mind* (1997), *Anna Freud: The
Dream of Psychoanalysis* (1991), *Irony in the Mind's Life: Essays on Novels by
James Agee, Elizabeth Bowen, and George Eliot* (1974), and *Children of Crisis:
A Study of Courage and Fear* (1967).

PAMELA HUNT STEINLE has been graduate director and professor
of American studies at California State University, Fullerton She is the
author of "The Art of Viewing Off-Center: Television and the Intellectual
Enterprise" (1998) and has served on the national advisory board of the *Iowa
Journal of Cultural Studies.*

EBERHARD ALSEN has been professor of English at the State University of New York, Cortland. He is the author of "Racism and the Film Version of Eugene O'Neill's *The Emperor*" (2006), "Richard Wright (1908–1960)" (2000), and *Romantic Postmodernism in American Fiction* (1996) and is the editor of *The New Romanticism: A Collection of Critical Essays* (2000).

CARL FREEDMAN has been an associate professor of English at Louisiana State University. He is the author of *Critical Theory and Science Fiction* (2000) and *The Incomplete Projects: Marxism, Modernity, and the Politics of Culture* (2002).

YASUHIRO TAKEUCHI has been an associate professor in the department of European and American culture and information studies. He is the author of "Resistance and Japanese Literature" (1972), "The National Liberation Struggle as Reflected in Japanese Literature" (1970), and "The Burning Carousel and the Carnivalesque: Subversion and Transcendence at the Close of *The Catcher in the Rye*" (2002).

MYLES WEBER has been assistant professor of English at Ashland University where he teaches playwriting and modern drama. He is the author of *Middlebrow Annoyances: American Drama in the 21st Century* (2003), and his essays have appeared in such journals as *New England Review*, *Kenyon Review*, *Georgia Review*, *Sewanee Review*, and *Salmagundi*.

Bibliography

Alsen, Eberhard. *Salinger's Glass Stories as a Composite Novel.* Troy, NY: Whitson, 1983.

———. "New Light on the Nervous Breakdowns of Salinger's Sergeant X and Seymour Glass." *CLA Journal* 45, vol. 3 (March 2002): 379–387.

———. "The Role of Vedanta Hinduism in Salinger's Seymour Novel." *Renascence* 33, vol. 2 (Winter 1981): 99–116.

Antico, John. "The Parody of J.D. Salinger: Esmé and the Fat Lady Exposed." *Modern Fiction Studies* 12 (Fall 1966): 325–340.

Baskett, Sam S. "The Splendid/Squalid World of J.D. Salinger." *Wisconsin Studies in Contemporary Literature* 4, vol. 1 (Winter 1963): 48–61.

Baumbach, Jonathan. "The Saint as a Young Man: A Reappraisal of *The Catcher in the Rye.*" *Modern Language Quarterly* 25 (December 1964): 461–472.

Beebe, Maurice, and Jennifer Sperry. "Criticism of J.D. Salinger: A Selected Checklist." *Modern Fiction Studies* 12, no. 3 (Autumn 1966): 377–390.

Bloom, Harold, ed. *Bloom's Guide to The Catcher in the Rye.* New York: Chelsea House, 2007.

———. *Holden Caulfield: Bloom's Major Literary Characters.* New York: Chelsea House, 2005.

Boe, Alfred F. "Street Games in J.D. Salinger and Gerald Green." *Modern Fiction Studies* 33, vol. 1 (Spring 1987): 65–72.

Branch, Edgar. "Mark Twain and J.D. Salinger: A Study in Literary Continuity. *American Quarterly* 9 (Summer 1957): 144–158.

Costello, Donald P. "The Language of *The Catcher in the Rye*." *American Speech* 34 (October 1959): 172–181.

Cotter, James Finn. "A Source for Seymour's Suicide: Rilke's Voices and Salinger's *Nine Stories*." *Papers on Language and Literature* 25, vol. 1 (Winter 1989): 83–98.

———. "Religious Symbols in Salinger's Shorter Fiction." *Studies in Short Fiction* 15 (1978): 121–132.

Davison, Richard Allan. "Salinger Criticism and 'The Laughing Man': A Case of Arrested Development." *Studies in Short Fiction* 18, vol. 1 (Winter 1981): 1–15.

Edwards, Duane. "Holden Caulfield: 'Don't Ever Tell Anybody Anything.'" *ELH* 44, vol. 3 (Fall 1977): 554–565.

French, Warren. *J.D. Salinger, Revisited*. Boston: Twayne, 1988.

———. "The Age of Salinger" in Warren French, ed., *The Fifties: Fiction, Poetry, Drama*. (DeLand, FL: Everett/Edwards, 1970): 1–39.

Furst, Lillian R. "Dostoyevsky's *Notes from Underground* and Salinger's *The Catcher in the Rye*." *Canadian Review of Comparative Literature* 5 (1978): 72–85.

Grunwald, Henry Anatole, ed. *Salinger: A Critical and Personal Portrait*. New York: Harper, 1962.

Gwynn, Frederick L., and Joseph L. Blotner. *The Fiction of J.D. Salinger*. Pittsburgh: University of Pittsburgh Press, 1958.

Hamilton, Ian. *In Search of J.D. Salinger*. New York: Random House, 1988.

Hamilton, Kenneth. "J.D. Salinger's Happy Family." *Queens Quarterly* 71 (1964): 176–187.

———. *J.D. Salinger: A Critical Essay*. Grand Rapids, MI: Eerdmans, 1967.

Hassan, Ihab. "Rare Quixotic Gesture: The Fiction of J.D. Salinger." *The Western Review* 21 (Summer 1957): 261–280.

———. "J.D. Salinger: Rare Quixotic Gesture." *Radical Innocence: Studies in the Contemporary American Novel*. Princeton, NJ: Princeton University Press, 1961, 259–289.

Heiserman, Arthur and James E. Miller, Jr. "J.D. Salinger: Some Crazy Cliff." *Western Humanities Review* 10 (Spring 1956): 129–137.

"J.D. Salinger 'Special Number.'" *Modern Fiction Studies* 12, no. 3 (Autumn 1969).

Kazin, Alfred. *Bright Book of Life*. Boston: Little, Brown & Co., 1973.

Kirschner, Paul. "Salinger and Scott Fitzgerald: Complementary American Voices." *Dutch Quarterly Review of Anglo-American Letters* 17, vol. 1 (1987): 53–73.

Korte, Barbara. "Narrative Perspective in the Works of J.D. Salinger." *Literatur in Wissenschaft und Unterricht* 20, vol. 2 (1987): 343–351.

Levine, Paul. "J.D. Salinger: The Development of the Misfit Hero." *Twentieth Century Literature* 4, vol. 3 (October 1958): 92–99.

Lott, Sandra and Steven Latham. "'The World Was All before Them': Coming of Age in Ngugi wa Thiong'o's *Weep Not, Child* and J.D. Salinger's *Catcher in the Rye*." In *Global Perspectives on Teaching Literature, Shared Visions and Distinctive Visions*. Urban, IL: National Council of Teachers of English (1993): 135–151.

Lundquist, James. *J.D. Salinger*. New York: Ungar, 1979.

McSweeney, Kerry. "Salinger Revisited." *Critical Quarterly* 20, no. 1 (Spring 1978): 61–68.

Medovoi, Leerom. "Democracy, Capitalism, and American Literature: The Cold War Construction of J.D. Salinger's Paperback Hero." In *The Other Fifties: Interrogating Midcentury American Icons*, edited by Joel Foreman. Urbana: University of Illinois Press (1997): 255–287.

Miller, Edwin Haviland. "In Memoriam: Allie Caulfield in the *Catcher in the Rye*." *Mosaic* 15, vol. 1 (Winter 1982): 129–140.

Miller, James E. *J.D. Salinger*. University of Minnesota Pamphlets on American Writers, No. 51. University of Minnesota Press, 1965.

Mitchell, Susan K. "To Tell You the Truth." *CLA Journal* 36, no. 2 (December 1992): 145–156.

O'Connor, Dennis L. "J.D. Salinger's Religious Pluralism: The Example of *Raise High The Roof Beam, Carpenters*." *The Southern Review* 20, vol. 2 (Spring 1984): 316–332.

Ohmann, Carol, and Richard Ohmann. "Reviewers, Critics, and *The Catcher in the Rye*. *Critical Inquiry* 3 (Autumn 1976): 15–37.

Pinsker, Sanford. "*The Catcher in the Rye* and All: Is the Age of the Formative Book Over? *Georgia Review* 40 (1986): 953–967.

———. *The Catcher in the Rye: Innocence Under Pressure*. New York: Twayne Publishers, 1993.

Purcell, William F. "World War II and the Early Fiction of J.D. Salinger." *Studies in American Literature* 28 (1991): 77–93.

Rosen, Gerald. "A Retrospective Look at *The Catcher in the Rye*." *American Quarterly* 29 (Winter 1977): 547–562.

Salzman, Jack. *New Essays on The Catcher in the Rye*. Cambridge and New York: Cambridge University Press, 1991.

Seng, Peter J. "The Fallen Idol: The Immature World of Holden Caulfield." *College English* (December 1961): 203–209.

Smith, Dominic "Salinger's Nine Stories: Fifty Years Later." *Antioch Review* 61, no. 4 (Fall 2003): 639–649.

"Special Number: Salinger." *Wisconsin Studies in Contemporary Literature* 4 no. 1 (Winter 1963).

Stoltz, Craig. "J.D. Salinger's Tribute to Whit Burnett." *Twentieth Century Literature* 27, vol. 4 (Winter 1981): 325–331.

Strauch, Carl F. "Kings in the Back Row: Meaning Through Structure—A Reading of Salinger's *The Catcher in the Rye.*" *Wisconsin Studies in Contemporary Fiction* 2 (Winter 1961): 5–30.

Sublette, Jack R. *J.D. Salinger: An Annotated Bibliography: 1938–1981.* New York: Garland, 1984.

Takeuchi, Yasuhiro. "The Burning Carousel and the Carnivalesque: Subversion and Transcendence at the Close of The Catcher in the Rye." *Studies in the Novel* 34, vol. 3 (Fall 2002): 320–336.

Vanderbilt, Kermit. "Symbolic Resolution in *The Catcher in the Rye*: The Cap, the Carousel, and the American West." *Western Humanities Review* 17 (Summer 1963): 271–277.

Weesner, Ted, Jr.: "J.D. Salinger's The Catcher in the Rye." In *American Writers Classics 1*, edited by Jay Parini. New York: Thomson Gale (2003): 35–52.

Weinberg, Helen. "J.D. Salinger's Holden and Seymour and the Spiritual Activist Hero." *The New Novel in America: The Kafkan Mode in Contemporary Fiction.* Ithaca, NY: Cornell University Press, 1970.

Wenke, John. "Sergeant X, Esmé, and the Meaning of Words." *Studies in Short Fiction* 17 (1980): 39–47.

Whitfield, Stephen J. "Cherished and Cursed: Toward a Social History of *The Catcher in the Rye.*" *New England Quarterly* 70, vol. 4 (December 1997): 567–600.

Acknowledgments

James Bryan, reprinted by permission of the Modern Language Association of America from "The Psychological Structure of The Catcher In The Rye" by James Bryan, from PMLA: Publications of the Modem Language Association, vol. 89, no. 5, 1974: pp. 1065–74.

David Galloway, from *The Absurd Hero in American Fiction,* second revised edition, Copyright © 1966 by David D. Galloway; Copyright © 1970 by David D. Galloway; Copyright © 1981 by David D. Galloway. By permission of the University of Texas Press.

Alan Nadel, "Rhetoric, Sanity, and the Cold War: The Significance of Holden Caulfield's Testimony" by Alan Nadel. This work originally appeared in *The Centennial Review,* vol. XXXII, no. 4, Fall 1988, published by Michigan State University Press. Reprinted with permission.

David Seed, "Keeping it in the Family: The Novellas of J.D. Salinger." From *The Modern American Novella,* edited by A. Robert Lee, 1989, Vision Press Ltd. and St. Martin's Press, Inc., reproduced by permission of Palgrave Macmillan and David Seed.

Ruth Prigozy, "Nine Stories: J.D. Salinger's Linked Mysteries." From *Modern American Short Story Sequences,* edited by J. Gerald Kennedy: pp. 114–132. © Cambridge University Press 1995. Reprinted with the permission of Cambridge University Press.

Anthony Kaufman, "'Along this road goes no one': Salinger's 'Teddy' and the Failure of Love." From *Studies in Short Fiction*, Spring 1998, vol. 35, no. 2: pp. 129–140. © 1998 by Newberry College.

Robert Coles, "Anna Freud and J.D. Salinger's Holden Caulfield." From the *Virginia Quarterly Review*, Spring 2000, Vol. 76, N. 2: pp. 214-224. Copyright 2000, by the *Virginia Quarterly Review*, The University of Virginia.

Pamela Hunt Steinle, from *In Cold Fear:The Catcher in the Rye Censorship Controversies and Postwar American Character*, pp. 15–28, 190–192. Copyright © 2000 by The Ohio State University.

Eberhard Alsen, *A Reader's Guide to J.D. Salinger.* Copyright © 2002 by Eberhard Alsen. Reproduced with permission of Greenwood Publishing Group, Inc., Westport, CT.

Carl Freedman, "Memories of Holden Caulfield—and of Miss Greenwood." From *The Southern Review*, Spring 2003, vol. 39, no. 2: pp. 401–417. Copyright 2003 by Louisiana State University. Reprinted with permission of the author.

Yasuhiro Takeuchi, "The Zen Archery of Holden Caulfield." From *English Language Notes*, XLII, September 2004, pp. 55–63. © Copyright 2004, Regents of the University of Colorado. Reproduced with permission.

Myles Weber, excerpt from *Consuming Silences: How we read authors who DON'T publish*: pp. 88–116. © 2005 by the University of Georgia Press. Reprinted with permission

Index